The Novelist at the Crossroads
and other essays on fiction and criticism

By the same author

Language of Fiction

THE NOVELIST AT
THE CROSSROADS

and Other Essays on
Fiction and Criticism

DAVID LODGE

Cornell University Press

ITHACA, NEW YORK

"A Clean, Well-Lighted Place" (Copyright 1933 Charles Scribner's Sons; re-
newal copyright © 1961 Ernest Hemingway) is reprinted by permission of
Charles Scribner's Sons from *Winner Take Nothing* by Ernest Hemingway.
Samuel Beckett's "Ping" is reprinted by permission of Grove Press, Inc.

First published 1971 by Cornell University Press
Second printing 1972

International Standard Book Number 0-8014-0674-9
Library of Congress Catalog Card Number 77-163130

PRINTED IN THE UNITED STATES OF AMERICA
BY VALLEY OFFSET, INC.

For Martin and Carol

Contents

Preface and Acknowledgments

The title-essay of this collection is concerned with the amazingly wide spectrum of modes and genres—none of which can be considered dominant—displayed by contemporary fiction. Much the same situation, it seems to me, now obtains in literary criticism; and if I had chosen a general title for this book it might have been 'The Critic at the Crossroads'. The radical and exclusive choices made by some contemporary novelists, or the anguished doubt and hesitation of others, do not, however, necessarily apply to the critic, for whom a plurality of methods, styles and approaches seems far more natural.

Criticism, after all, is a far more elaborately conditioned activity than creative writing. Consider the variety of motives and circumstances in which it is undertaken. One is invited to review books, or to give a lecture, and a subject not of one's own choosing begins to reveal fascinating possibilities. One has an insight into a text, or one disagrees with someone else's interpretation, and one feels a human need to communicate these things. One is puzzled by a text and tries to tease out the solution. One feels that this author is neglected and that author overpraised, and one seeks to redress the balance. Sometimes one writes at length on a limited subject, and sometimes in compressed form on a very large subject. On this occasion one tries to be definitive, on that occasion suggestive, and on another merely informative.

All the essays in this collection have been conditioned by one or another of these motives and circumstances, and therefore display considerable variation in form as well as matter. The main reservation I have about my own first book of criticism, *Language of Fiction* (1966) is that it appears to place more restrictions upon the ends and means of criticism than I myself (let alone other critics) accept in practice. One of the essays in this volume, 'Towards a Poetics of Fiction: An Approach through Language', shows that I still hold unrepentantly to the primacy of language in literary matters, and several of the other essays are directly continuous with *Language of Fiction* in their approach. But in 'Towards a Poetics of Fiction' I make a point that was perhaps obscured in the book, that 'all good criticism is a response to language— that it is good insofar as it is a sensitive response—whether or not there is any explicit reference to language in the way of quotation and analysis.'

1*

Clearly, there are many perfectly legitimate kinds of criticism—literary history, studies of literary genres, of literature and ideas, of literary situations, of literary theory, and so on—where the object of the exercise necessarily limits or even excludes close verbal analysis. To adopt an analogy used by Northrop Frye, one may stand with one's nose to a painting to admire its detailed brushwork, or at the other side of the gallery to appreciate its arrangement of shapes and colours. Both are legitimate ways of looking at the picture, and whether one stands close up or far away (or somewhere in between) depends entirely on what one is interested in at the time. Over the past few years, as will be evident from these essays, I have been much stimulated by two books whose authors stand well back from a great mass of material and boldly attempt to discern in it some kind of intelligible order: *The Nature of Narrative* by Robert Scholes and Robert Kellogg, and *The Sense of an Ending* by Frank Kermode. The vulnerability of these books on points of detail is a direct function of their schematic usefulness; and, if pressed, I should have to defend my title-essay, and some of the others, on the same grounds.

The critical pluralism I am defining and defending here is very much connected in my mind with the interpenetration of academic criticism, creative writing and literary journalism, which is such a marked feature of the present literary situation. I make some general comments on this development in the last of the essays collected in this volume, but it is also something in which I am personally involved. How the writing of fiction can be combined with reviewing fiction and with teaching, analysing and theorizing about fiction in an academic context is, I find, to many people an occasion of puzzlement, scepticism and even scandal. I have therefore included in the section on 'Fiction and Criticism' a confessional piece of self-analysis which may have some interest in this connection.

With the exception of this item, all the essays in this volume have appeared in print before, sometimes in a slightly different form, or under different titles. 'The Novelist at the Crossroads' (1969), 'Waiting for the End' (1968), 'The Uses and Abuses of Omniscience' (1970) and 'Objections to William Burroughs' (1966) first appeared in the *Critical Quarterly*; 'Samuel Beckett: Some *Ping* Understood' (1968), 'Assessing H. G. Wells' (1967) and 'Utopia And Criticism' (1969) in *Encounter*; 'Towards a Poetics of Fiction' (1968) in *Novel: a forum on fiction*; 'Post-pill Paradise Lost' (1970) in *New Blackfriars*; 'The Chesterbelloc and the Jews' (1970) in *The Critic*; 'Hemingway's Clean, Well-lighted, Puzzling Place' (1970) in *Essays in Criticism*. 'Graham

Greene' was no. 17 in the series, *Columbia Essays on Modern Writers*, published by Columbia University Press (1966), and 'Crosscurrents in Modern English Criticism' first appeared in the Sphere Books *History of Literature in the English Language* (1970), Volume VII, ed. Bernard Bergonzi. I am grateful to the publishers and editors concerned for permission to reprint these essays, and, in many cases, for the original stimulus to write them. My story, 'The Man Who Wouldn't Get Up', was first published by the *Weekend Telegraph*.

Part I

1 The Novelist at the Crossroads

Marvin asks Sam if he has given up his novel, and Sam says, 'Temporarily.' He cannot find a form, he explains. He does not want to write a realistic novel, because reality is no longer realistic.

Norman Mailer: *The Man Who Studied Yoga*

Robert Scholes's recent book *The Fabulators* (O.U.P., 1967) has given a new impetus to the old guessing game of 'Whither the Novel?' At least, it has prompted me to try to organize my own tentative thoughts on the subject. To do this, however, and to understand *The Fabulators*, it is necessary to go back, first, to an earlier book of Mr Scholes, *The Nature of Narrative* (1966), written in collaboration with Robert Kellogg. There, the authors proposed that there are two main, antithetical modes of narrative: the *empirical*, whose primary allegiance is to the real, and the *fictional*, whose primary allegiance is to the ideal. Empirical narrative subdivides into history, which is true to fact, and what the authors call mimesis (i.e. realistic imitation), which is true to experience. Fictional narrative subdivides into romance, which cultivates beauty, and aims to delight, and allegory, which cultivates goodness and aims to instruct. This genre theory is combined with a large-scale historical scheme, according to which the primitive oral epic was a synthesis of empirical and fictional modes that under various cultural pressures (chiefly the transition from oral to written forms of communication) broke up into its component parts; and this fragmentation occurred twice—once in late classical literature, and again in the European vernacular literatures, where the different modes were developed independently, or in partial combinations. In the late Middle Ages and the Renaissance there is a perceptible movement in narrative literature towards a new synthesis of empirical and fictional modes which finally produces, in the eighteenth century, the novel. In the experiments of modern narrative writers, however, and in the advent of new media such as motion pictures, Scholes and Kellogg saw evidence that the synthesis is about to dissolve once more.

Now, while this ambitious scheme is obviously vulnerable to scholarly sniping on points of detail, it is, I think, a suggestive and useful one when we try to take an overview of the nature and development of the novel. It gives some substance, for instance, to our vague intuition that the novel stands to modern, post-Renaissance civilization as the epic did to ancient civilization. Perhaps more important, by suggesting that the novel is a new synthesis of pre-existing narrative traditions, rather than a continuation of one of them or an entirely unprecedented phenomenon, it accounts for the great variety and inclusiveness of the novel form: its capacity for being pushed, by different authors, in the directions of history (including autobiography), allegory or romance while still remaining somehow 'the novel'. It will be noticed that I do not invoke, here, the fourth of Scholes's and Kellogg's categories—what they call 'mimesis', and what I should prefer to call 'realism'. To talk of the novel 'being pushed in the direction of realism while still remaining somehow a novel' does not make immediate sense because it is difficult to conceive of there being a conflict of interests between the novel and realism—whether one uses that elastic term primarily in a formal sense (as I do), to denote a particular mode of presentation which, roughly speaking, treats fictional events as if they were a kind of history, or in a more qualitative sense, to denote a literary aesthetic of truth-telling. For most of the novel's life-span, one of these notions of realism has tended to imply the other. If realism of presentation was not actually invented by the eighteenth-century novelists and their nineteenth-century successors, it was certainly developed and exploited by them on a scale unprecedented in earlier literature; and when all the necessary exceptions and qualifications have been made, it is generally true that the major novelists of this period justified the form, and their own particular contributions to it, by appealing to some kind of 'realist' aesthetic.

Thus, if Scholes and Kellogg are right to see the novel as a new synthesis of pre-existing narrative modes, the dominant mode, the synthesizing element, is realism. It is realism which holds history, romance and allegory together in precarious synthesis, making a bridge between the world of discrete facts (history) and the patterned, economized world of art and imagination (allegory and romance). The novel supremely among literary forms has satisfied our hunger for the meaningful ordering of experience *without* denying our empirical observation of its randomness and particularity. It is therefore based on a kind of compromise, but one which has permitted many varieties of emphasis, on one side or the other, from Richardson and Fielding onwards, and which has survived numerous attempts to break it up. The Gothic novel was one such attempt: a revolt against realism, sponsored for the most part by second-class minds, it was by the major novelists of the nineteenth century either ridiculed out of countenance (e.g. Jane Austen) or tamed, domesticated, and assimilated into a more realistic account of experience (e.g. the Brontës). To be sure, the compromise (or synthesis) was always more stable in Europe than in America. But even in Hawthorne and Melville, writers strongly attracted to history, allegory and romance, realism exerts a strong if intermittent influence; while in *Huckleberry Finn*, the book from which Hemingway traced all significant modern American literature, we have a classic novelistic achievement: mythic and thematic interests controlled and expressed through the realistic rendering of particular experience.

If the above argument is granted, it follows that the disintegration of the novel-synthesis should be associated with a radical undermining of realism as a literary mode; and that is precisely what is claimed in *The Nature of Narrative*. Literary realism we may say, depicts the individual experience of a common phenomenal world,* and Scholes and Kellogg point out that both parts of this undertaking are under pressure in modern culture. As, influenced by developments in human knowledge, particularly in the field of psychology, the writer pursues the reality of individual experience deeper and deeper into the subconscious or unconscious, the common perceptual world recedes and the concept of the unique person dissolves: the writer finds himself in a region of myths, dreams, symbols and archetypes that demand 'fictional' rather than 'empirical' modes for their expression. 'The mimetic impulse towards the characterisation of the inner life dissolves inevitably into mythic and expressionistic patterns upon reaching the citadel of the psyche.'† On the other hand, if the writer persists in seeking to do justice to the common phenomenal world he finds himself, today, in competition with new media, such as tape and motion pictures, which can claim to do this more effectively.

This latter point is taken up and developed by Mr Scholes in *The Fabulators*, which is a more topical and polemical sequel to *The Nature of Narrative:*

* This seems to be common ground to both formal definitions of realism (e.g. Ian Watt in *The Rise of the Novel*) and qualitative definitions (e.g. Raymond Williams in *The Long Revolution*, Chap. 7).

† This is not of course an exclusively post-Freudian discovery, as the examples of Poe or Lewis Carroll show; nor is it incompatible with realism, witness Richardson's *Clarissa*. But the special relevance of the observation to modern literature is well illustrated by Joyce's development from *Dubliners* to *Finnegans Wake*.

the cinema gives the *coup de grace* to a dying realism in written fiction.
Realism purports—has always purported—to subordinate the words
themselves to their referents, to the things words point to.
Realism exalts life and diminishes art, exalts things and diminishes
words. But when it comes to representing *things*, one picture is
worth a thousand words, and one motion picture is worth a million.
In face of competition from cinema, fiction must abandon its attempt
to 'represent reality' and rely more on the power of words to
stimulate the imagination.

Mr Scholes's book consists largely of appreciative studies in a number
of contemporary narrative writers who have, in his view, already
recognized the obsolescence of realism and hence of the traditional
novel, and are exploring, with modern sophistication, the purely
'fictional' modes of allegory and romance. To describe this kind of
narrative he has revived the archaic word 'fabulation'. It is, as will be
evident, a development he welcomes. 'The novel may be dying', he
says, 'but we need not fear for the future.'

Lawrence Durrell, Iris Murdoch, John Hawkes, Terry Southern,
Kurt Vonnegut and John Barth are the writers principally discussed.
Durrell's *Alexandria Quartet* is seen as a sophisticated exploitation of the
labyrinthine intrigues and reversals of (appropriately) Alexandrian
romance. Murdoch's *The Unicorn* is interpreted as an elaborate and
multi-faceted allegory, worked out in terms of Gothic fiction, about
the conflict of secular and religious attitudes. Hawkes, and the 'Black
Humorists' Southern and Vonnegut, are seen as practising a surrealistic form of picaresque. Barth's *Giles Goat-boy*, with its rich and
exuberant mixture of mythic, romantic and allegorical modes, is the
perfect exemplification of Scholes's theory, and his prize exhibit.*

---

* To readers not acquainted with this remarkable work, I offer a brief description,
which may give more definition to the concept of 'fabulation'. In *Giles Goat-boy*
the world is conceived as a huge university which, after two Campus Riots, is
divided between an East Campus and a West Campus, at present divided by a
Quiet Riot. The two rival campuses are separated by their respective Power Lines
that feed two giant computers known as EASCAC and WESCAC, which control the
lives of the students on each campus and have the capacity to annihilate each other
by 'EAT-waves'. Into this allegorical rendering of the modern world, Barth introduces a story with mythical and romantic dimensions—the story, told by himself,
of the hero, Giles Goat-boy. Like all traditional heroes, his origins are mysterious;
but it appears that he was conceived through the impregnation of a virgin by
WESCAC, programmed to produce GILES (Grand-tutorial Ideal, Laboratory
Eugenical Specimen), but as a result of an intrigue was adopted by Max Spielman,
a Moishan (Jewish) liberal intellectual scientist who repented of his part in the

'The only legitimate way to approach "intention" in a literary work', Mr Scholes observes, 'is through a highly discriminated sense of genre.' In this respect his explications are useful and perceptive, but as evaluations they are somewhat undiscriminating. Reading *The Unicorn* for the first time under Mr Scholes's guidance, I felt I understood what Miss Murdoch was up to more clearly than in previous readings of her novels; but whether the 'ideas' in that book, or its involved and melo-dramatic plot, or the process of abstracting the former from the latter, yield any great pleasure or instruction seemed to me still open to question. It is a question that Mr Scholes scarcely faces: for him the intention to reject realism in favour of fabulation is itself a guarantee of value.

In considering this point of view it behoves the English reader to proceed carefully, and with a certain self-awareness. There is a good deal of evidence that the English literary mind is peculiarly com-mitted to realism, and resistant to non-realistic literary modes to an extent that might be described as prejudice. It is something of a commonplace of recent literary history, for instance, that the 'modern' experimental novel, represented diversely by Joyce, Virginia Woolf and D. H. Lawrence, which threatened to break up the stable synthesis of the realistic novel, was repudiated by two subsequent generations of English novelists. And, reviewing the history of the English novel in the twentieth century it is difficult to avoid associating the restoration of traditional literary realism with a perceptible decline in artistic

---

EATing of the Ameratsus (Japanese) in Campus Riot II and retired to a goat farm, where he reared the hero as one of his herd. Giles, picturesquely, never entirely sheds the effect of this early caprine environment; but, apprised of his human nature and hints concerning his origins, he conceives the idea that he is destined to be a Grand Tutor (Saviour) who will bring peace to the whole Campus by disarming WESCAC and teaching students how to 'pass' and avoid being 'flunked'. Accordingly he sets out for New Tammany, the richest and most powerful college on the West Campus, and his own birthplace, presided over by Chancellor 'Lucky' Rexford (who bears a striking resemblance to President Kennedy). As well as Rexford and a number of other thinly disguised historical personages, Giles becomes involved with some other more ambiguous characters, particularly Anastasia, an 'eternal woman' figure, infinitely compliant yet strangely innocent; her husband, Maurice Stoker, a demonic anarchist, who is in charge of New Tammany's powerhouse, and a mysterious rival to Giles, Harold Bray, who claims to be the true Grand Tutor but proves to be the 'Dean o' Flunks' himself. True to the traditional pattern, the hero's mission commits him to passing many tests and performing many tasks. More than once he appears to exchange the role of saviour for that (appropriately enough) of scapegoat. Or are these two roles different anyway?—that is the sort of question the book constantly poses.

achievement. There is a certain uncomfortable truth in Mr Rubin Rabinovitz's comments at the end of his recent book, *The Reaction Against Experiment in the English Novel 1950–1960* (Columbia U.P., 1968):

> The critical mood in England has produced a climate in which traditional novels can flourish and anything out of the ordinary is given the denigratory label 'experiment' and neglected. . . . The greatest fear of the English contemporary novelist is to commit a *faux pas*; every step is taken within prescribed limits, and the result is intelligent, technically competent, but ultimately mediocre. . . . The successful novelist in England becomes, too quickly, a part of the literary establishment. . . . All too often he uses his position as a critic to endorse the type of fiction he himself is writing and he attacks those whose approach is different.

Though Mr Rabinovitz has little to offer that is either new or interesting, by way of critical comment on the English novel of the 'fifties, he has burrowed deep into the journalistic archives of the period and produced some interesting documentation. It is instructive, for instance, to learn (or be reminded) that *Lord of the Flies* (1954) was reviewed by Walter Allen in the *New Statesman* in these terms:

> *Lord of the Flies* is like the fragment of a nightmare, for all that it is lightly told. It commands a reluctant assent: yes, doubtless it could be like that, with the regression from choir school to Mau Mau only a step. The difficulty begins when one smells allegory. 'There's not a child so small and weak But has his little cross to take.' These children's crosses, it seemed to me, were altogether too unnaturally heavy for it to be possible to draw conclusions from Mr Golding's novel, and if that is so, it is, however, skilfully told, only a rather unpleasant and too-easily affecting story.

The unexamined assumptions behind this critique, that allegory is necessarily a literary vice, because it makes the action of the book 'unnatural', undermining the essential criterion of 'it could be like that', without the satisfaction of which all 'skill' is vain—these essentially realist assumptions are entirely typical of the post-war English literary temper. It now seems fairly obvious that this was an inappropriate response to *Lord of the Flies* (at least Mr Allen has acknowledged as much by his praise of the book in *Tradition and Dream* [1964]), but the instance is a cautionary one. Most of Golding's subsequent novels have provoked similar objections, at least initially.

Turning to the writers Scholes holds up for admiration we find two English novelists (Murdoch and Durrell) who have generally enjoyed a higher reputation abroad than at home, and whose later work has been received with less and less favour in England; and four American writers who have made comparatively little impact on English readers. Vonnegut is not widely read in England, and although Southern is well known for the scandalous *Candy*, this scarcely amounts to a literary reputation. Hawkes's novels failed disastrously in England until the determined efforts of a few admirers, notably Christopher Ricks, recently obtained for them a respectful but grudging attention. Barth's *Giles Goat-boy*, rapturously received in America, was put down by most English reviewers.

The picture we get by putting Rabinovitz's and Scholes's books together—of an incorrigibly insular England defending an obsolete realism against the life-giving invasions of fabulation—is, however, an oversimplification. For one thing, the consensus of English literary opinion as described by Mr Rabinovitz has been greatly shaken up since 1960; for another, fabulation is not the only alternative to traditional realism that is being explored by contemporary narrative writers.

I shall take the latter point first. Mr Scholes may be right to see the novel as closer to disintegration today than it has ever been in its always hectic and unstable history, but his diagnosis of its condition in *The Fabulators* is one-sided. Since, in his view, the synthesis of empirical and fictional modes is no longer worth the trouble of maintaining, he recommends that narrative should exploit the fictional modes, for which he has a personal predilection, more or less exclusively. Logic suggests, however, that it would be equally possible to move in the opposite direction—towards empirical narrative, and away from fiction. This in fact is what we find happening.

The term 'non-fiction novel' was first coined, I believe, by Truman Capote to describe his book *In Cold Blood*, an account of a brutal multiple murder committed in Kansas in 1959. Every detail of this book is 'true', discovered by painstaking research—Capote spent many hours with the murderers in prison, for instance, getting to know their characters and backgrounds. Yet *In Cold Blood* also reads like a novel. It is written with a novelist's eye for the aesthetic possibilities of his *donnée*, for the evocative and symbolic properties of circumstantial detail, for shapeliness and ironic contrast in structure. The moral protests the book provoked in some quarters—the charge, for instance, that there was something callous and inhuman about so 'literary' a treatment of experience so painfully actual and immediate—is one indication of the way the book straddles the conventional boundary between fiction and reportage.

That Norman Mailer's *The Armies of the Night* (1968) straddles this boundary is very clearly advertised by its subtitle: 'History as a Novel— The Novel as History'. The first part ('History as a Novel') of this account of the anti-Vietnam War march on the Pentagon in 1967 is a detailed account of the author's own experience of the event, from his initial, reluctant agreement to participate, through the riotous eve-of-march gathering at the Ambassador Theatre in Washington, where Mailer drunkenly insisted on chairing the proceedings, scandalizing or embarrassing most of those present, to the early stages of the March, Mailer's self-sought arrest, imprisonment, trial and release. This section is, in Mailer's words, 'nothing but a personal history which while written as a novel was to the best of the author's memory scrupulous to facts'. It is distinguished from a straight autobiographical narrative primarily by the fact that Mailer writes about himself in the third person, thus achieving an ironic distance on his own complex personality which is one of the chief delights of the book:

> 'Let's sing them a song, boys', Mailer called out [on the bus taking arrested demonstrators to jail]. He could not help it—the mountebank in him felt as if he were playing Winston Churchill. Ten minutes ago he had been mired in long slow thoughts of four wives—now he had a stage again and felt not unheroic. 'Can it be?' he wondered to himself, 'that I have misspent twenty years as a novelist, and all along have been languishing as an actor?'

This self-irony enabled by the third-person narrative method also licenses Mailer to describe his fellow-participants, such as Dwight MacDonald and Robert Lowell, with a mischievous candour that might have seemed impertinent in a conventional autobiography, and to indulge in a good deal of prophetic cultural generalization about America which, like 'ideas' in a novel, we judge by their plausibility, rhetorical force and relevance to context rather than by the stricter criteria of logic and verifiability—for example:

> the American small town . . . had grown out of itself again and again, its cells traveled, worked for government, found security through wars in foreign lands, and the nightmares which passed on the winds in the old small towns now traveled on the nozzle of the tip of the flame thrower, no dreams now of barbarian lusts, slaughtered villages, battles of blood, no, nor any need for them—

technology had driven insanity out of the wind and out of the attic,
and out of all the lost primitive places: one had to find it now
wherever fever, force, and machines could come together, in Vegas,
at the race track, in pro football, race riots for the Negro, suburban
orgies—none of it was enough—one had to find it in Vietnam;
that was where the small town had gone to get its kicks.

It makes a significant difference to such passages if one transposes the
free indirect speech into the declarative present tense of the
conventional essay.

It is less easy to describe the narrative principles of the second part of
The Armies of the Night, partly because Mailer himself seems confused
about them. When, at the beginning of this section, 'The Novel as
History' he speaks of 'the novelist . . . passing his baton to the
Historian', he seems to mean that the narrative method of Part I, in
which events were seen from one, limited point of view, in the manner
of a Jamesian novel, will be exchanged for the method of the historian,
who assembles and collates data from various sources and presents a
coherent account of a complex sequence of events.

> The mass media which surrounded the March on the Pentagon
> created a forest of inaccuracy which would blind the efforts of a
> historian; our novel has provided us with the possibility, no, even
> the instrument to view our facts and conceivably study them in that
> light a labour of lens-grinding has produced.

I take this to mean that, both for the writer and for us the readers, the
research into the self that is carried out in Part I has exposed and purged
the inevitable bias of any human report. Thus the 'novel' has given the
'history' a unique kind of reliability. About half-way through Part II,
however, Mailer abandons this claim. When he gets to the point in his
narrative where the massed troops and demonstrators confront each
other across 'six inches of no-man's-land' he announces that Part II 'is
now disclosed as some sort of condensation of a collective novel—
which is to admit that an explanation of the mystery of the events at
the Pentagon cannot be developed by the methods of history—only
by the instincts of the novelist.' Mailer thus claims the freedom to
enhance his narrative with vivid invention—for instance, the briefing
he imagines the troops getting:

> 'Well men,' says the major, 'our mission is to guard the Pentagon
> from rioters and out-of-march scale prearranged-upon levels of
> defacement, meaning clear? Well, the point to keep in mind,

troopers, is those are going to be American citizens out there expressing their constitutional right to protest—that don't mean we're going to let them fart in our face—but the Constitution is a complex document with circular that is circulating sets of conditions —put it this way, I got my buddies being chewed up by V.C. right this minute maybe I don't care to express personal sentiments now, negative, keep two things in mind—those demos out there could be carrying bombs or bangelore torpedoes for all we know, and you're going out with no rounds in your carbines so thank God for the .45. And first remember one thing more—they start trouble with us, they'll wish they hadn't left New York unless you get killed in the stampede of us to get to them. Yessir, you keep a tight asshole and the fellow behind you can keep his nose clean.'

This, certainly, uses to advantage a novelist's gift for caricature by violating the rules of modern historical method (though the convention is a very familiar one in classical historiography).*

The Armies of the Night implies no disillusionment on the author's part with the novel as a literary form: on the contrary, it reaffirms the primacy of that form as a mode of exploring and interpreting experience. The non-fiction novel, however, is, like fabulation, often associated with such disillusionment. A case in point is the young English writer B. S. Johnson, whose break with the conventional novel was very explicitly made in *Albert Angelo* (1964). This, for about three-quarters of its length, is the story of a young architect who is unable to practise his profession, and is obliged to earn his living as a supply teacher in a number of tough London schools. He is a fairly familiar kind of English post-war hero, or anti-hero: young, frustrated, classless, mildly delinquent, disappointed in love. Though Johnson uses a number of experimental expressive techniques (simultaneous presentation of dialogue and thought in double columns, holes cut in the pages so that the reader can see what is coming), the narrative reads like realistic fiction. Then at the beginning of the fourth section, comes the shock:

---

* The novelist John Hersey, in contrast, in writing his documentary account of an episode in the Detroit race-riots of 1967, *The Algiers Motel Incident* (1968), felt obliged to renounce the privileges of the novelist: 'There was a need, above all, for total conviction. This meant that the events could not be described as if witnessed from above by an all-seeing eye opening on an all-knowing novelistic mind; the merest suspicion that anything had been altered, or made up, for art's sake, or for the sake of effect, would be absolutely disastrous. There could be no "creative reconstruction".'

—fuck all this lying look what im really trying to write about is
writing not all this stuff about architecture trying to say something
about writing about my writing im my hero though what a useless
appellation, my first character then im trying to say something
about me through him albert an architect when whats the point in
covering up covering up covering over pretending pretending i can
say anything through him that is anything i would be interested
in saying. . . .

In brief, Johnson goes on to expose and destroy the fictiveness of the
narrative he has elaborately created, telling us the 'true' facts behind
the story—for instance, the real name of the girl and the fact that while
in the novel the girl jilted Albert, in actuality Johnson jilted her. Of
course, one has to take the author's word that he *is* telling the truth in
this section; but even if one doubts this, the story of Albert has been
drastically stripped of what Henry James called 'authority'. It is an
extreme strategy for achieving an effect of sincerity and authenticity,
though coming so late in the work it is more of a gesture than an
achievement. Having blown up his fictional bridges behind him, the
author stands at the end of the book defiant and vulnerable on the bare
ground of fact. And there in his subsequent books, *Trawl* (1967) and
The Unfortunates (1969) he has remained, taking the fundamentalist
Platonic position that 'telling stories is telling lies', but at the same time
experimenting with form to bring writing into closer proximity with
living.

The Unfortunates, for instance, consists of twenty-seven unbound
sections, in a box. The first and last sections are marked as such, but the
rest are in random order, and the reader is invited to shuffle them
further if he so wishes. According to the blurb, this unconventional
format is designed to 'represent the random workings of the mind
without the forced consecutiveness of a book', but this is not in fact the
case. The random flow of sensation and association in the narrator's
mind is imitated by the movement of the words, clauses and sentences
within each section—a stream-of-consciousness technique in the manner
of Joyce. The randomness only affects the narrative presentation of this
consciousness in time. It makes explicit the almost infinite choice a writer
has in representing a particular sequence of events by refusing to commit itself to any one choice. Such is the nature of the human mind,
however, that, working with the key of the marked first section, we
mentally arrange the events of the book in their chronological order as
we read; and the puzzle or game element thus introduced into the

reading experience has the effect (ironically, in view of the author's declared intentions, but also advantageously in my opinion) of putting the painful, personal, 'real' experience of the book at an aesthetic distance, making it read more like fiction than autobiography.

For Johnson, one may gather readily from his books, the effort required to throw off the burden of the great tradition of the realistic novel has been considerable. For Frank Conroy, a young American writer whose first book *Stop-time* (1967) attracted considerable attention, it was evidently no effort at all. Where the young writer of an earlier generation would have worked his experience of growing up into a *Bildungsroman*, he simply wrote his autobiography (a form traditionally thought to be the privilege of maturity, if not fame)— but an autobiography with, in the words of Norman Mailer's significant tribute, 'the intimate and unprotected candour of a novel'. Here is a specimen—the author's memories of his father:

> I try to think of him as sane, and yet it must be admitted he did some odd things. Forced to attend a rest-home dance for its therapeutic value, he combed his hair with urine and otherwise played it out like the Southern gentleman he was. He had a tendency to take off his trousers and throw them out the window. (I harbour some secret admiration for this.) At a moment's notice he could blow a thousand dollars at Abercrombie and Fitch and disappear into the Northwest to become an outdoorsman. He spent an anxious few weeks convinced that I was fated to become a homosexual. I was six months old. And I remember visiting him at one of the rest-homes when I was eight. We walked across a sloping lawn and he told me a story, which even then I recognized as a lie, about a man who sat down on the open blade of a penknife embedded in a park bench. (Why, for God's sake would he tell a story like that to his eight-year-old son?)

'The history of the realistic novel', Harry Levin has observed in his book on Joyce, 'shows that fiction tends towards autobiography. The increasing demands for social and psychological detail that are made upon the novelist can only be satisfied out of his own experience. The forces which make him an outsider focus his observation upon himself.' Johnson and Conroy (and one might mention Henry Miller here as a precursor of this form of the non-fiction novel) take this principle to its logical conclusion. If the fictional reworking of personal experience inevitably falsifies it, and if the writer no longer feels the need or obligation to protect his own and others' privacy, the autobiographical *novel* is, in this perspective, redundant.

Scholes and Kellogg seem to endorse this point of view in *The Nature of Narrative*:

> If any distinction can be said to exist between the autobiography
> and the autobiographical novel it resides not in their respective
> fidelity to facts but rather in their respective originality in perceiving
> and telling the facts. It is in the knowing and the telling, and not in
> the facts, that the art is to be found (p. 156).

The last sentence is obviously true, but it obscures the point that the autobiographical novelist is free to alter, rearrange and add to 'the facts'; and that this freedom is exercised not merely to protect his privacy, but in the interest of literary values such as representative significance and formal coherence. In practice the reader is rarely in a position to judge with any confidence the 'fidelity to facts' of either the autobiography or the autobiographical novel, but he makes a different 'contract' with each kind of book, and brings different expectations to the reading experience. Works like *The Unfortunates* and *Stop-time* complicate and delay this process by combining the properties of both forms; but sooner or later one decides, I think, to read the former as a novel and the latter as an autobiography.

One can detect in B. S. Johnson's work the influence of Samuel Beckett and of some younger French practitioners of the *nouveau roman*. In French experiments with the non-fiction novel, however, the fiction that is purged from the novel is not so much a matter of invented characters and actions as a philosophical 'fiction', or fallacy, which the traditional novel encourages—namely, that the universe is susceptible of human interpretation. The purest statement of this point of view is to be found in the theoretical writings of Alain Robbe-Grillet. Essentially his argument is that traditional realism has distorted reality by imposing human meanings upon it. That is, in describing the world of things, we are not willing to admit that they are *just* things, with their own existence, indifferent to ours. We make things reassuring by attributing human meanings or 'significations' to them. In this way we create a false sense of solidarity between man and things.

> In the realm of literature this solidarity is expressed mainly
> through the systematic search for analogies or for analogical
> relationships. . . . Metaphor is never an innocent figure of speech
> . . . the choice of an analogical vocabulary, however simple,

always goes beyond giving an account of purely physical data . . .
setting up a constant rapport between the universe and the human
being who inhabits it. . . . It is the whole literary language that has
to change . . . the visual or descriptive adjective—the word that
contents itself with measuring, locating, limiting, defining—
indicates a difficult but most likely direction for the novel of the
future.[1]

Now, the language of analogy to which Robbe-Grillet objects is
exploited much more elaborately in non-realistic narrative (such
as allegory) than in the novel, which can claim to have honoured
the world of discrete 'things' more than any other previous form
of literature, by virtue of what Henry James called its 'solidity of
specification'. But Robbe-Grillet is right to see that the use of
descriptive particularity in realistic fiction assumes a meaningful
connection between the individual and the common phenomenal
world; and from his point of view the way in which traditional
realism *conceals* this connection while simultaneously exploiting it—
smuggling metaphorical significance into apparently innocent factual
descriptions of furniture, dress, weather, etc.—makes it all the more
subversive.

Of Robbe-Grillet's attempt to disinfect his own narratives of
analogical implication, Scholes says in *The Fabulators*:

> This cannot solve the problem, because all language is a human
> product and thus must humanize everything it touches. The
> writer must either acknowledge this and accept it as one of the
> terms of his work or turn to a wordless art like cinema—as M.
> Robbe-Grillet has so brilliantly done on occasion.

With the first part of this statement I entirely agree; but it is
precisely for this reason that I cannot accept Mr Scholes's contention
(quoted earlier) that literary realism 'subordinates words . . . to things'.
Being a verbal medium it cannot do so—it is constantly making
'things' over into 'words'. It may indeed create the *illusion* of subord-
inating words to things, and this may involve a certain restraint
in exploiting the literary resources of language. But the extreme
exercise of such restraint in Robbe-Grillet or (much more poignantly
and meaningfully) in Beckett, is not the norm of realistic fiction,
which has, historically, given many great writers quite as much
freedom as they needed to develop the expressive possibilities of their
medium. It is difficult to think of Jane Austen or George Eliot or

Flaubert or Henry James as being less creative users of words because of their commitment to realism.

I am not convinced, either, that the camera is, in human hands, any more neutral than language, or that it renders literary realism redundant. It is true that Robbe-Grillet himself invokes the film to define the 'new realism' he wants to impart to the novel; and other novelists have invoked the film medium in a similar spirit. The narrator of J. D. Salinger's *Zooey* describes the story as a 'sort of prose home-movie'. The main character of Doris Lessing's *The Golden Notebook*—that anguished account of a writer's effort to fix, identify and express reality—finds herself constantly alluding to the cinema to indicate the completely truthful, mimetic quality she is seeking in her writing; and her final, most satisfactory insight into her own experience comes in the form of a hallucination in which she seems to see her life as a film which she has directed herself. These are however rhetorical strategies—the visual medium is invoked to reinforce a verbal communication. For this purpose the film is made to stand for a highly mimetic art. Indeed, it is; but it is a commonplace that there is a language of the film which is as much a 'human product' as verbal language. It has its own rules, conventions and possibilities of choice, which have to be learned by both artist and audience, and which make possible an infinite variety of effects, none of them entirely neutral and objective. The contemporary cinema, in fact, exhibits as wide a spectrum of styles as the contemporary novel, all the way from 'non-fiction' underground movies of the Empire State Building or people's bottoms to 'fabulations' like Stanley Kubrick's *2001*, Godard's *Weekend* or *The Yellow Submarine*.

Much the same situation obtains in the contemporary theatre, where the 'well-made play' of scrupulously realistic illusion (the dramatic equivalent of the realistic novel and, in many ways, a by-product of the cultural dominance of the novel form) has been to a large extent displaced by experiments corresponding roughly to fabulation and the non-fiction novel in narrative. On the one hand we have drama that exploits the artificiality of theatrical presentation, inventing and often fantasizing freely (e.g. Brecht, Ionesco, N. F. Simpson), and on the other the 'theatre of fact' (Hochhuth, Weiss) or efforts like those of the American Living Theater Company, who seek to break down the formal conventions that separate audience from performers and to physically involve both in an uncontrolled and unpredictable 'happening'.

We seem, indeed, to be living through a period of unprecedented cultural pluralism which allows, in all the arts, an astonishing variety of styles to flourish simultaneously. Though they are in many cases radically opposed on aesthetic and epistemological grounds, no one style has managed to become dominant. In this situation, the critic has to be very fast on his feet. He is not, of course, obliged to like all the styles equally, but he must avoid the cardinal error of judging one style by criteria appropriate to another. He needs what Mr Scholes calls 'a highly discriminated sense of genre'. For the practising artist, however, the existence of a bewildering plurality of styles presents problems not so easily solved; and we should not be surprised that many contemporary writers manifest symptoms of extreme insecurity, nervous self-consciousness and even at times a kind of schizophrenia.

The situation of the novelist today may be compared to a man standing at a crossroads. The road on which he stands (I am thinking primarily of the English novelist) is the realistic novel, the compromise between fictional and empirical modes. In the 'fifties there was a strong feeling that this was the main road, the central tradition, of the English novel, coming down through the Victorians and Edwardians, temporarily diverted by modernist experimentalism, but subsequently restored (by Orwell, Isherwood, Greene, Waugh, Powell, Angus Wilson, C. P. Snow, Amis, Sillitoe, Wain, etc., etc.) to its true course. That wave of enthusiasm for the realistic novel in the 'fifties has, however, considerably abated. For one thing, the novelty of the social experience the fiction of that decade fed on—the break-up of a bourgeois-dominated class society—has faded. More important, the literary theorizing behind the 'Movement' was fatally thin. For example, C. P. Snow:

> Looking back, we can see what an odd affair the 'experimental' novel was. To begin with, the 'experiment' stayed remarkably constant for thirty years. Miss Dorothy Richardson was a great pioneer, so were Virginia Woolf and Joyce: but between *Pointed Roofs* in 1915 and its successors, largely American, in 1945, there was no significant development. In fact there could not be; because this method, the essence of which was to represent brute experience through the moments of sensation, effectively cut out precisely those aspects of the novel where a living tradition can be handed on. Reflection had to be sacrificed; so did moral awareness; so did the investigatory intelligence. That was altogether too big a price to pay and hence the 'experimental' novel . . . died from starvation, because its intake of human stuff was so low.[2]

Or Kingsley Amis:

> The idea about experiment being the life-blood of the English
> novel is one that dies hard. 'Experiment', in this context, boils
> down pretty regularly to 'obtruded oddity', whether in construc-
> tion—multiple viewpoints and such—or in style; it is not felt that
> adventurousness in subject matter or attitude or tone really
> counts. Shift from one scene to the next in mid-sentence, cut
> down on verbs or definite articles, and you are putting yourself
> right up in the forefront, at any rate in the eyes of those who
> were reared on Joyce and Virginia Woolf and take a jaundiced
> view of more recent developments.[3]

Simply as literary history, Snow's comment does not survive the most
cursory examination (no development between *A Portrait of the Artist*
and *Finnegans Wake?* Between *Pointed Roofs* and *The Sound and the
Fury?*). Amis's has a certain satiric force and cogency, and is aimed at a
more vulnerable target, but that kind of 'cultivated Philistinism'
refreshing in its time, could not be maintained indefinitely, even by
Amis, let alone anyone else.

Realistic novels continue to be written—it is easy to forget that most
novels published in England still fall within this category—but the
pressure of scepticism on the aesthetic and epistemological premises
of literary realism is now so intense that many novelists, instead of
marching confidently straight ahead, are at least considering the two
routes that branch off in opposite directions from the crossroads. One
of these routes leads to the non-fiction novel, and the other to what
Mr Scholes calls 'fabulation'.

To fill out the latter category we may add to the examples
discussed in *The Fabulators*: Günter Grass, William Burroughs, Thomas
Pynchon, Leonard Cohen (*Beautiful Losers*), Susan Sontag (*Death Kit*),
some of the novels of Anthony Burgess, and individual works by
novelists who have remained generally faithful to realism, such as
Bellow's *Henderson the Rain King*, Updike's *The Centaur*, Malamud's
The Natural, Angus Wilson's *The Old Men at the Zoo*, and Andrew
Sinclair's *Gog*. Such narratives suspend realistic illusion in some
significant degree in the interests of a freedom in plotting characteristic
of romance or in the interest of an explicitly allegorical manipulation
of meaning, or both. They also tend to draw inspiration from certain
popular forms of literature, or subliterature, in which the arousal and
gratification of very basic fictional appetites (such as wonder, wish
fulfilment, suspense) are only loosely controlled by the disciplines

of realism: especially science fiction, pornography and the thriller. Of these three, science fiction has the most respectable pedigree, going back to Utopian speculation, apocalyptic prophecy, and satirical fantasy like *Gulliver's Travels, Candide, Alice in Wonderland,* and *Erewhon.* It was this tradition that kept fabulation alive through the period of the realistic novel's dominance, and it continues to offer the most obvious vehicle for the novelist who wants to experiment with a more 'fictional' kind of narrative. Pornography and the thriller, being more debased forms, are approached more gingerly, but the fascination they hold for the contemporary literary imagination cannot be missed in such phenomena as the cult of James Bond (which was a highbrow cult before it was a mass cult). Kingsley Amis seems a representative figure here. His absorption with Fleming (see *The James Bond Dossier*), like his enthusiasm for science fiction (see *New Maps of Hell*), is difficult to reconcile with the stance he adopted in the 'fifties, both as novelist and critic, as a defender of a traditional kind of literary realism, except as a lust for fabulation, repressed by his literary 'censor', seeking outlet in certain licensed areas where traditional literary values are not expected to obtain. His publication of a James Bond novel, *Colonel Sun* (1968), under the pen-name Robert Markham, is surely a case of the realistic novelist taking a holiday from realism, finding a way to enjoy the forbidden fruit of romance without fully committing himself to the enterprise. (It is, I hope, unnecessary to labour the point that the James Bond novels are essentially romances, and that their superficial realism of presentation—the descriptive set-pieces, the brand-name dropping, the ostentatious display of technical knowledge of various kinds—does not convert the romantic stereotypes into anything individually realized, but merely gives them a gloss of contemporary sophistication and facilitates the reader's willing suspension of disbelief.) In fact *Colonel Sun* is considerably more realistic than most of the Fleming novels (Amis's Bond, for instance, survives by virtue of his wits and good luck rather than the gadgetry which, like the magical weapons of medieval romance, preserves Fleming's hero) and also duller. This is not surprising since the whole enterprise, undertaken, apparently, in a spirit of pious imitation, required Amis to keep in check his natural talent for parody and deflating comic realism. Anthony Burgess's *Tremor of Intent* (1966) is a much more entertaining highbrow contribution to the genre partly because of its parodic exaggerations of Bondian themes and motifs. This is a work of extraordinary virtuosity, in which Burgess sets himself to cap every effect exploited by Fleming and succeeds triumphantly:

the sex is sexier, the violence more visceral, the high-living more extravagant, the intrigues and reversals of the plot more stunning, and the style, naturally, infinitely more vivid and evocative. Yet in its overall effect the book wobbles uncertainly between parodying Bond by extravagant exaggeration and reaching after something genuinely felt and realized. Thus at one point in the story a precocious teenage boy has to shoot a man to save the hero and is violently sick immediately after: 'He went and stood, like a naughty boy, in the corner. His shoulders heaved as he tried to throw up the modern world.' This striking image sounds a note too serious for the narrative to bear, and only serves to remind us that it is not the modern world which this character is throwing up but a grotesque comic-strip version of it.

There is, I think, a similar ambiguity of motive, an insecurity of stance, an impression that regressive or perverse fantasies are being indulged under cover of pretensions to satirical caricature or displays of stylistic virtuosity, in so-called 'parodies' or 'spoofs' of pornography, such as *Candy* (1958), or Stephen Schneck's *The Nightclerk* (1965), or Gore Vidal's *Myra Breckinridge* (1968). Of these three novels, Vidal's is easily the most complex and accomplished, parodying and commenting acutely upon not only pornography but also the non-fiction novel of the French variety—

> Nothing is *like* anything else. Things are themselves entirely and do not need interpretation, only a minimal respect for their precise integrity. The mark on the wall is two feet three inches wide and four feet eight and a fraction inches high. Already I have failed to be completely accurate. I must write 'fraction' because I can't read the little numbers on the ruler without my glasses which I never wear

—and the kind of argument advanced by Mr Scholes, that the cinema has superseded the mimetic possibilities of literature:

> Tyler's close scrutiny of the films of the Forties makes him our age's central thinker, if only because *in the decade between 1935 and 1945, no irrelevant film was made in the United States.* During those years, the entire range of human (which is to say, American) legend was put on film, and any profound study of those extraordinary works is bound to make clear the human condition. For instance, to take an example at random, Johnny Weismuller, the zahftic Tarzan, still provides the last word on the subject of

2

soft man's relationship to hard environment . . . that glistening overweight body set against a limestone cliff at noon says the whole thing. Auden once wrote an entire poem praising limestone, unaware that anyone of a thousand frames from *Tarzan and the Amazons* had not only anticipated him but made irrelevant his efforts.

Myra Breckinridge is a brilliant, but somehow sterile and despairing work: as if Vidal, deeply contemptuous of the contemporary *avant garde* and the cultural climate, 'post-Gutenberg, pre-Apocalypse', that fosters it, has abandoned hope of positively resisting either, and cynically set himself to match their wildest excesses.

There are indeed good reasons for anticipating with something less than enthusiasm the disappearance of the novel and its replacement by the non-fiction novel or fabulation. Especially to anyone whose imagination has been nourished by the great realistic novelists of the past, both these side roads will seem to lead all too easily into desert or bog—self-defeating banality or self-indulgent excess. Yet, as I have already suggested, there are formidable discouragements to continuing serenely along the road of fictional realism. The novelist who has any kind of self-awareness must at least hesitate at the crossroads; and the solution many novelists have chosen in their dilemma is to *build their hesitation into the novel itself*. To the novel, the non-fiction novel, and the fabulation, we must add a fourth category: the novel which exploits more than one of these modes without fully committing itself to any, the novel-about-itself, the trick-novel, the game-novel, the puzzle-novel, the novel that leads the reader (who wishes, naïvely, only to be told what to believe) through a fair-ground of illusions and deceptions, distorting mirrors and trap-doors that open disconcertingly under his feet, leaving him ultimately not with any simple or reassuring message or meaning but with a paradox about the relation of art to life.

This kind of novel, which I shall call the 'problematic novel', clearly has affinities with both the non-fiction novel and fabulation, but it remains distinct precisely because it brings both into play. Mr Scholes's fabulators, for instance, play tricks on their readers, expose their fictive machinery, dally with aesthetic paradoxes, in order to shed the restricting conventions of realism, to give themselves freedom to invent and manipulate. In the kind of novel I am thinking of, however, the reality principle is never allowed to lapse entirely—indeed it is often invoked, in the spirit of the non-fiction novel, to expose the artificiality of conventional realistic illusion. Whereas the fabulator is impatient with 'reality', and the non-fiction novelist is impatient with fiction, the kind of novelist I am talking about retains a loyalty to both, but lacks the orthodox novelist's confidence in the possibility of reconciling them. He makes the difficulty of his task, in a sense, his subject.

The father and mother of this kind of novel is *Tristram Shandy*—to say which is to concede that we are not dealing with a totally new phenomenon. But it is significant that, while it is difficult to think of anything (apart from feeble imitations) comparable to *Tristram Shandy* in the eighteenth and nineteenth centuries, when the realistic novel developed into maturity, it is not so hard to think of parallels in modern literature. Take, for example, J. D. Salinger's Glass stories. When one puts them mentally beside *Tristram Shandy* the essential similarity of each writer's undertaking is striking: the loving, minutely circumstantial evocation and celebration of a richly eccentric family, observed mainly in domestic life, with extraordinary attention to detail of speech, mannerism and gesture, recorded by a narrator who is himself a member of the family (though with certain very pointed, teasing resemblances to the actual, historic author), who is partly dependent on the other members for his information, who addresses the reader directly in a whimsical, garrulous, digressive flow of complex reminiscence and reconstruction, commenting freely on the difficulty of his undertaking, and incorporating into the narrative an account of his personal circumstances at the time of composition. Salinger's stories, it seems to me, have been received with increasing disfavour because they have been taken too much at their face value as disingenuous gospels of a new religion, to the neglect of their literary experimentation. This feature, though less obvious than in *Tristram Shandy*, is clear enough when one reads the stories through in the order of their composition. Then, one cannot fail to notice how, as the record of the Glass family comes more and more to follow the shapelessness and randomness of actuality, as the tone of the narrator (Buddy Glass) becomes more and more personal, idiosyncratic, non-literary—as, in short, the narrator begins to appeal to our interest more and more at the level of anecdote about 'real' people, so a subtly growing amount of highly unusual, objectively improbable and in fact irrational information is conveyed. Thus, in *Raise High the Roofbeam, Carpenters*, Franny Glass is said to remember her brother Seymour (the family *guru*) reading to her when she was ten months old, and Seymour records in his diary the experience of stigmata from touching certain things. In *Seymour; an Introduction* Buddy tells us how he eased the pain of pleurisy by placing 'a perfectly innocent-looking Blake lyric in my shirt pocket', and claims that from early childhood till he was thirty he seldom read fewer than 200,000 words a day, and often 400,000. In other words, as the manner of the saga inclines more and more to that of non-fictional narrative, the matter becomes more and more 'fictive'. There is a similar tension between the bizarre obsessions and eccentricities of the Shandy family and the minutely faithful, realistically particular rendering of them by Tristram. In both cases the normal conventions of narrative fiction are exposed and undermined by the narrator himself, and the stability of the reader's stance towards the experience of the book is always threatened.

It is in fact the transference of the writer's own sense (which may be humorous or deadly serious) of the problematic nature of his undertaking—making the reader *participate* in the aesthetic and philosophical problems the writing of fiction presents, by embodying them directly in the narrative—that characterizes the 'problematic novel'. I would want to make this a large enough category to include such works as Gide's *The Counterfeiters*, Flann O'Brien's *At Swim Twobirds*, Nabokov's *Pale Fire*, Sartre's *La Nausée*, the labyrinthine fables of Jorge Luis Borges, Waugh's *The Ordeal of Gilbert Pinfold*, Amis's *I Like It Here*, Muriel Spark's *The Comforters*, and Doris Lessing's *The Golden Notebook*. No doubt the reader can think of other examples, if not of the fully developed problematic novel, at least of novels that incorporate to some degree its characteristic note of self-consciousness. As Elizabeth Hardwick has written recently:

> Many good novels show a degree of panic about the form. Where
> to start and where to end, how much must be believed and how
> much a joke, a puzzle; how to combine the episodic and the
> carefully designed and consequential . . . the mood of the writer
> is to admit manipulation and design, to exploit the very act of
> authorship in the midst of the imagined scene.[4]

A very 'pure' example of the problematic novel was published in England in 1968, which I think deserves closer attention than it generally received. It is not, to be sure, a neglected masterpiece, but it is a very representative and deeply interesting 'case' for the understanding of the contemporary novelist's (particularly the English novelist's) situation at the crossroads. Indeed Julian Mitchell's *The Undiscovered Country* touches on almost all the problems and topics discussed in this essay, and for that reason I want to consider it at some length.

I hope Mr Mitchell will not be offended if I suggest that he is as 'typical' a post-war British novelist as one could hope to find. Perhaps for complete representativeness he should have gone to a good grammar school rather than to a public school, and have taken his Oxford First in English rather than History; but from that point onwards his career—academic research, a fellowship to America, the decision to become a freelance writer, supporting himself by reviewing, broadcasting, writing film scripts, living in Chelsea—is a very familiar one. (The reasons for this discussion of Mr Mitchell's private life will become evident in a moment.) With a precocity that is also representative of his generation of writers he published his first novel, *Imaginary Toys* (1961), at the age of twenty-five and has since published five others. Apart from the most recent (*The Undiscovered Country*) these novels have been fairly conventional, realistic novels about the kind of life he knows from experience—middle-class family life (*A Disturbing Influence* (1962)), the University (*Imaginary Toys*), the Englishman in America (*As Far As You Can Go* (1963)), the London 'scene' (*The White Father* (1964)). They are well written, technically accomplished, intelligent and observant, and have, on the whole, been very warmly received by English reviewers. They are also, on any really demanding scale of literary value, and by the author's own admission in *The Undiscovered Country*, minor novels.

There is no reason why the term 'minor' should be dismissive. Experience tells us that less than one per cent of novels published are likely to be 'major' works, and therefore to be a *good* minor novelist is no dishonourable ambition and no mean achievement. Evelyn Waugh (who, it might be said, brought the minor novel to its peak of perfection) expressed this point of view in *The Ordeal of Gilbert Pinfold*:

> It may happen in the next hundred years that the English novelists of the present day will come to be valued as we now value the artists and craftsmen of the late eighteenth century. The originators, the exuberant men, are extinct, and in their place subsists and modestly flourishes a generation notable for elegance and variety of contrivance.

Waugh, however, learned and practised his craft at a time when the novel still enjoyed the status of being, by general agreement, the most sensitive artistic register of contemporary experience. At a time like the present, when the status of—not only the novel, but the written word itself—is being disputed by other forms and media, the writer is apt to feel that only a major achievement can justify the process of continuing to write at all. For the American novelist, brought up to pursue the Grail of the Great American Novel, such an aspiration is natural; and American fiction probably includes more failed major works than successful minor ones. But to the contemporary English novelist, conditioned by the shrinking power and status of his country in the world, and by the psychological defence-mechanisms—irony, modesty, cynicism, 'commonsense'—we have developed to adjust to that circumstance, such ambition does not come naturally. The nearest he is likely to come to a really ambitious fictional enterprise is by stringing a number of minor novels together in a *roman à fleuve*.

In the 'fifties, indeed, unambitiousness was built into the literary programme of the Movement. 'It will have become noticeable', Kingsley Amis wrote in the course of his novel-reviewing stint for the *Spectator*, 'that I am being much less nasty to the unambitious novelist than to the ambitious.'[5] Useful as such an attitude may be in purging literary pretentiousness, it can obviously degenerate very quickly into a defence of the mediocre. The contemporary English novelist, therefore, is likely to feel himself wandering between two worlds, one lost, the other powerless to be born. The great tradition of the realistic novel, or the early modernist developments of it by writers like James, Conrad, Forster, Joyce, Mann, Proust, the richness of which is being busily mined by the literary-criticism industry, will sooner or later make him dissatisfied with the aesthetic of modest competence, but any alternative will seem false, pretentious, 'willed'. Translated into formal or technical terms this produces an impatience with the literary decorums of the 'well-made' realistic novel, combined with an inability to commit oneself wholeheartedly to any radical alternative, such as fabulation or the non-fiction novel.

Some such syndrome, I suspect, lies behind *The Undiscovered Country*. The book is in two parts. The first part is a memoir, written in his own person by Julian Mitchell, of a friend, the gifted and charming, but wayward and unstable Charles Humphries. We are told that they formed a friendship at prep-school that survived, precariously, into adulthood, despite Charles's wild experiments in vocation, ideology, sexuality and general life-style. Julian Mitchell disapproved of most of these experiments, but always felt at the same time an irrational kind of guilt and responsibility, as if he had somehow failed Charles by withdrawing from a full commitment to their relationship at various crucial moments. Charles became more and more neurotic and unhappy, and in 1965 killed himself, leaving behind a novel, a fragmentary satirical fantasy called *The New Satyricon*. This novel, with an introduction and commentary by Julian Mitchell, is presented in Part II of *The Undiscovered Country*.

This structure constantly teases the reader with the question (characteristic of problematic novels) of whether Charles Humphries is a fictional character or not. The average reader will probably start with the assumption that he is, for Julian Mitchell is, after all, a novelist, and the idea of disguising a fiction as a real memoir is not, of course, a new one. But Mitchell has gone to considerable lengths to persuade us to accept Part I as a document. All the facts about Julian Mitchell's own life (and this section is quite as much about himself as about Charles Humphries) are true: they correspond to the biographical note on the dust-jacket, and to any other facts the reader may happen to know about the author—for example, that he reviewed fiction for *The Sunday Times* in 1962:

> I left Oxford and went back to London, renting a basement flat in Olivia Manning's house in St John's Wood. By the sort of coincidence which makes people believe in a critical conspiracy, we were both reviewing novels for *The Sunday Times*, week and week about.

The dropping of names like Olivia Manning's—that is, names of real people whom the reader may be assumed to have heard of—with reference to their private, rather than their public lives, is exploited very elaborately in Part I, and—since it goes far beyond the normal conventions of the fictitious memoir—contributes significantly to its documentary effect. It is written in a fluent, but rather dry and flat prose that puts factual precision before literary airs and graces; and is marked off from Julian Mitchell's novels both by explicit assertion—

> This is too hard to write. Charles is dead. I am a minor novelist, telling the literal truth. I am a character in one of my own books. . . .

—and by mentioning the composition of the novels so as to stress their fictional handling of the experience being factually reported in the memoir:

> It will not come as a surprise to anyone who has read a novel called *As Far As You Can Go* that the character there called Eddie Johnson was based at some distance on Charles. . . .

Sooner or later the reader will probably decide that the expectation of reading fiction, with which he began *The Undiscovered Country*, was correct. He will observe that the mass of verifying detail which establishes the historicity of the narrator, Julian Mitchell, does not apply in the same way to Charles Humphries; and that despite all Julian Mitchell's efforts, the ways in which Charles pops up in his life have about them the unmistakable whiff of fictional economy and coincidence. The important point is, however, that the reader is never allowed to rest comfortably on this assumption: the deviations from fictional convention are too persistent for him to eliminate entirely the possibility that it might all be true. (That is why, summarizing it earlier, I used the past tense. To have used the present tense in which one customarily summarizes fictions would have been to give the whole game away at the beginning.) Part I of *The Undiscovered Country* is, therefore, a kind of non-fiction novel—fiction disguising itself as far as possible as fact, partly by incorporating a great deal of unmodified fact.

Part II is quite the reverse—fiction rejoicing in its fictiveness, the opportunities for invention, distortion, and stylistic exuberance afforded by the abandonment of realistic illusion and the properties of consistency, continuity, particularity and historicity which belong to the realistic novel. In a word, it is fabulation. Though Petronius's *Satyricon* is regarded by literary historians as an early and rare example of realistic prose fiction, and a kind of progenitor of the novel, Humphries's *The New Satyricon* is fantasy, and imitates only the fragmentary structure and satirical motives of Petronius's classic. It begins with the arrival of the narrator, Henry, at the airport of some imaginary and unspecified country. He checks into a hotel and goes by mistake into the wrong room, where he interrupts a society called the Encolpians at their strange rites. This society is dedicated to the refinement of erotic pleasure through the discovery of new sexual postures. Henry, who is something of a virtuoso in this field, is welcomed into the society. At the same time he glimpses for the second time the figure of a beautiful creature, of uncertain sex, and falls in love with him or her. The rest of the story, such as it is, follows the hero's pursuit of this ambiguous love object through the rooms and corridors of the vast hotel, which, like the University in *Giles Goat-boy*, serves as a microcosm of the modern world. Thus the Cold War is represented as a dispute between the management and the kitchen staff, and the death of Kennedy is introduced (with no great concern for analogical consistency) as the death of the King of the country in which the hotel is situated. In the rooms into which Henry blunders in pursuit of his beloved or to escape from the violent denizens of the hotel, various activities are going on which are made the occasion for parody and satire of various aspects of contemporary culture: pop music, the theatre of the absurd, theatre of cruelty, James Bond, academic literary criticism, 'with it' Christianity, psychoanalysis, pornography, etc., etc. Henry is transformed into a woman and falls into the clutches of a band of aggressive Lesbians from whom he/she escapes by telling a long, enigmatic fabulation about ducks which sends them all to sleep; but is immediately afterwards captured and raped by the Encolpians. After this experience, Henry suffers a second metamorphosis into a hermaphrodite. His quest for his similarly androgynous beloved takes him from the roof of the hotel down to its lower floors, a descent which, following a well-established literary archetype, reflects a darkening of the moral atmosphere of the story and a more intimate exploration of the narrator's own psyche. In the style of Tristram, Henry gives an account of his own birth. At a grotesquely affected gourmets' banquet he hears a man who appears to be his own father make a callous speech about the problems of under-developed countries, and at the same time is puzzled by the resemblance of his beloved to his father and also to his mother and elder twin brother and sister. A little later, after interrogation by a kind of Communist tribunal, he is asked to take part in a marriage service, only to find that the bride is his beloved, and is being given away to the leader of the Encolpians by his own father. The officiating minister gives a kind of cynical anti-sermon which brings to a crisis Henry's despair about ever finding any meaning in life. The marriage ceremony is broken off by the bride's recognition of Henry and flight; but pursuing her to the Turkish baths in the basement of the hotel, Henry is afflicted with blindness and decoyed by another woman. *The New Satyricon* ends with Henry's death, presented simultaneously as death in a Nazi gas chamber and as a ritual murder (after the pattern of Abraham and Isaac) by his own father.

It will be clear from this summary that *The New Satyricon* includes most of the constituents of fabulation as defined by Mr Scholes. The correspondences (presumably fortuitous) with *Giles Goat-boy* are particularly striking. In both works we find a similar mixture of non-realistic modes—allegorical, romantic, parodic, surrealistic—applied to a picaresque quest-story involving the search for knowledge, identity and union with a beloved. *The New Satyricon*, however, is

2*

considerably slighter and less assured than *Giles Goat-boy*. This brings us back to certain discussions about literature, especially about the novel, in Part I.

In these discussions Julian Mitchell defends a fairly orthodox aesthetic position (as regards the novel it is essentially Jamesian) against subversive attacks launched by Charles from a variety of angles. Thus Mitchell's contention that in successful fiction, as in all fully realized art, the imposition of form on the raw material of experience endows the work with a timeless and universal value, is countered by Humphries's Sartrean argument that 'the worth of a novel was to be judged by its contribution to the pleasure and understanding of the society which produced it'. On another occasion Humphries accuses Mitchell of cultivating impersonality in his writing as an excuse to evade honest and painful self-examination. 'All this phony classicism of yours, the detachment, the impersonality, even the bloody elegance of your writing—oh yes, it's depressingly elegant—the whole lot's defensive. You daren't let yourself go.' Humphries, indeed, is allowed to make some very scathing criticisms of Mitchell's work, and to accuse him of weaknesses which are often attributed (by Mr Rabinovitz, for example) to the present generation of English novelists as a group—that they are lacking in ambition, afraid to expose themselves, cut off from 'real life' by the inbred literary milieu they inhabit, apt to fritter away their energies on ephemeral journalism or other work for the mass media, etc., etc. Eventually these attacks goad Mitchell into challenging Humphries to write something himself. 'Any bloody fool can criticise.' *The New Satyricon* is the result.

The New Satyricon is radically different from the kind of fiction 'Julian Mitchell' writes, and within the internal rhetoric of *The Undiscovered Country* it seems to represent the kind of fiction Julian Mitchell is incapable of writing, and to confirm him in his disillusionment about his own work: 'I think it is unlikely that I shall write another book of my own for a long time with the fact of this one before me', he says. Of course, Julian Mitchell *has* written *The New Satyricon*, and if this work were brilliantly successful the effect would be affirmative and liberating, marking an exciting new phase in the author's development. In fact, *The New Satyricon* is not brilliantly successful and is not (I hope) meant to be. I say 'I hope' because Julian Mitchell's commentary on Charles Humphries's novel raises considerable, and perhaps insolvable problems of tone and response. Mitchell's praise of Humphries's book is acceptable and natural as long as we accept the premise that they are distinct, historic individuals. But to the extent that the reader believes or suspects that they are one and the same person, he will tend to resent the praise as a form of self-congratulation. That Mitchell also points out weaknesses in *The New Satyricon* does not entirely solve the problem, for it is not easy to assess the weight of such criticisms.

On balance, I am inclined to think that though Julian Mitchell may wish us to admire *The New Satyricon* more than we actually do, he does not offer it to us as a fully achieved work, and that the kind of criticisms he makes of it explain his own reservations, as an orthodox novelist, about fabulation. It appears that the main theme of *The New Satyricon* is a critique of 'a decadence of feeling' in modern civilization, in which truth and reality are constantly evaded by rationalization or aestheticism. But it is precisely this kind of objection to which the literary mode of fabulation—and certainly *The New Satyricon*—is most vulnerable. As Mitchell remarks in his introduction, *The New Satyricon* does not really fulfil the literary theories of Humphries himself:

> We had many discussions about the relationship between art and life, fact and fiction, and Charles was always caustic about novelists' 'unscrupulous lying'. I used to argue for the illusion of realism through the elimination of the author from his work; Charles said that the only honest thing for a writer to do was to display himself in and through his book. . . . The style he chose for *The New Satyricon* certainly puts the narrator firmly between the reader and the narrative. . . . Curiously, for me, the style fails to display the Charles I thought I knew; it is defensive rather than aggressive. But this was probably intentional, part of the counter-double-bluffing of which the novel is full.

Of course, this statement may itself be a bluff, since Mitchell is author of as well as commentator on *The New Satyricon*.

An apparently flippant remark of Charles Humphries about Julian Mitchell in Part I—'But he's my friend, my alter ego, my doppel-ganger, my secret sharer'—is a clue to the former's identity, confirmed by a piece of information not revealed in the book—namely, that the author's full name is Charles Julian Humphrey Mitchell. Charles, then, appears to represent an aspect of the author's personality which has been hidden, denied and repressed on social or moral principles corresponding to the aesthetic principles according to which Julian Mitchell's first five novels were written. Through the portrait of

Charles and his book the author has allowed this hidden side of his personality some expression, but in a way that is elaborately qualified and protected. *The Undiscovered Country* offers no solution to the conflict it deals with. On the literary level, the realistic compromise between fact and fiction is abandoned in favour of two diametrically opposed alternatives—the non-fiction novel of Part I and the fabulation of Part II—but all the counter-double-bluffing cannot conceal the fact that neither is entirely satisfactory.

Although *The Undiscovered Country* is, therefore, in its overall effect, a somewhat negative and defeatist work, I do not think we need to take its disillusionment with the conventional novel too seriously. Problematic novels are not normally valedictory, signalling the author's abandonment of his literary vocation. More often than not they are purgative or exorcistic: problems in the writer's life and/or work have accumulated to the point where they threaten a creative 'block', and only by grappling with them directly can the writer free himself from them—after which he often proceeds with restored confidence.

This brings me to my conclusion, which is a modest affirmation of faith in the future of realistic fiction. In part this is a rationalization of a personal preference. I like realistic novels, and I tend to write realistic fiction myself. The elaborate code of literary decorum that governs the composition of realistic fiction—consistency with history, solidity of specification, and so on—which to many of the writers discussed above seems inhibiting, or evasive, or redundant—is to my mind a valuable discipline and source of strength—or at least can be. Like metrical or stanzaic form in verse, which prevents the poet from saying what he wants to say in the way that comes most readily to his mind, involving him in a laborious struggle with sounds and meanings that, if he is resourceful enough, yields results superior to spontaneous expression, so the conventions of realistic fiction prevent the narrative writer from telling the first story that comes into his head—which is likely to be either autobiography or fantasy—and compel him to a kind of concentration on the possibilities of his *donnée* that may lead him to new and quite unpredictable discoveries of what he has to tell. In the novel personal experience must be explored and transmuted until it acquires an authenticity and persuasiveness independent of its actual origins; while the fictive imagination through which this exploration and transmutation is achieved is itself subject to an empirical standard of accuracy and plausibility. The problem of reconciling these two opposite imperatives is essentially rhetorical and (contrary to Mr Scholes) requires great linguistic resourcefulness and skill for its successful solution. (I am not of course denying that fabulation or autobiography or the non-fiction novel have their own internal disciplines and challenges, but merely trying to define those of the realistic novel.)

If the case for realism has any ideological content it is that of liberalism. The aesthetics of compromise go naturally with the ideology of compromise, and it is no coincidence that both are under pressure at the present time. The non-fiction novel and fabulation are *radical* forms which take their impetus from an extreme reaction to the world we live in—*The Armies of the Night* and *Giles Goat-boy* are equally products of the apocalyptic imagination. The assumption behind such experiments is that our 'reality' is so extraordinary, horrific or absurd that the methods of conventional realistic imitation are no longer adequate.* There is no point in carefully creating fiction that gives an illusion of life when life itself seems illusory. (This argument, interestingly, was used by the Marquis de Sade, writing at the time of the French Revolution, to explain the Gothic novel and by implication, his own pornographic contribution to the genre.[6]) Art can no longer compete with life on equal terms, showing the universal in the particular. The alternatives are either to cleave to the particular—to 'tell it like it is'—or to abandon history altogether and construct pure fictions which reflect in an emotional or metaphorical way the discords of contemporary experience.

The realist—and liberal—answer to this case must be that while many aspects of contemporary experience encourage an extreme, apocalyptic response, most of us continue to live most of our lives on the assumption that the reality which realism imitates actually exists. History may be, in a philosophical sense, a fiction, but it does not feel like that when we miss a train or somebody starts a war. We are conscious of ourselves as unique, historic individuals, living together in societies by virtue of certain common assumptions and methods of communication; we are conscious that our sense of identity, of happiness and unhappiness, is defined by small things as well as large; we seek to adjust our lives, individually and communally, to some

---

* See the quotation from Norman Mailer at the head of this essay. Although I have taken Mailer to represent the non-fiction novel (a vein he has continued to work in *Miami and the Siege of Chicago* (1968)), he has also produced fictions, *An American Dream* (1965) and *Why Are We In Vietnam?* (1967), which lean in the opposite direction, towards fabulation.

order or system of values which, however, we know is always at the mercy of chance and contingency. It is this sense of reality which realism imitates; and it seems likely that the latter will survive as long as the former.

Writing in 1939, at the beginning of World War II, George Orwell voiced many of the doubts about the future of the novel reviewed in this essay. The novel, he said in 'Inside the Whale' was inextricably tied up with liberal individualism and could not survive the era of totalitarian dictatorships he saw ahead. In his appreciation of Henry Miller's *Tropic of Cancer* he seems to endorse the confessional non-fiction novel as the only viable alternative ('Get inside the whale . . . Give yourself over to the world process, stop fighting against it or pretending you control it, simply accept it, endure it, record it. That seems to be the formula that any sensitive novelist is likely to adopt.') Orwell's prophecy was, however, incorrect. Shortly after the War there was a significant revival of the realistic novel in England, inspired partly by Orwell's own fiction of the 'thirties; and although none of this fiction is of the very first rank, it is not an inconsiderable body of work. Many of the most talented post-war American novelists—John Updike, Saul Bellow, Bernard Malamud and Philip Roth, for example—have worked, for the most part, within the conventions of realistic fiction. Obsequies over the novel may be as premature today as they were in 1939.

Part II Fiction and Criticism

2   Waiting for the End: Current Novel Criticism

I

Our journal takes its title and its justification from the amazing surge of interest in the novel since the last world war. . . . There has been more work on fictional theory, since the last great war, than in all the novel's previous history; and more intelligent appraisals of novels have appeared than in all its history. At the same time there has been a veritable log-jam of conflicting theories and, along with it, a disturbing increase in irrelevant criticism.

I quote from the first editorial of an enterprising new journal, *Novel: a forum on fiction* (Fall, 1967). After making allowances for the somewhat declamatory tone appropriate to such utterances, it is surely undeniable that the views advanced here are substantially true. There *has* been a remarkable shift of attention in modern literary criticism from poetry and poetic drama to prose fiction, a movement balanced roughly on the fourth decade of this century. Exactly why this has happened is not easy to explain. Is it that the critical revolution of the inter-war period, having exerted its sway over poetry, naturally expanded into the practically virgin territory of the novel? Or does the trend reflect a tardy recognition by literary academics that, in Frank Kermode's words, 'in our phase of civility, the novel is the central form of literary art'? If the latter is the case, 'tardy' might bear a double meaning; for if we are to believe the McLuhanite prophets, literature in the forms most familiar to us faces obsolescence, as we move from a print-orientated culture to an electronically revived oral-aural culture—a situation in which the novel, historically the product of the printing press, is clearly the most vulnerable of the literary genres.

The editors of *Novel* are inclined to interpret the current boom in novel-criticism as evidence of the continuing vitality of written narrative. One could, however, equally well suggest that literary intellectuals, feeling threatened by the prophets of media revolution, are instinctively rallying to the defence of that literary form which is above all consecrated to the Book. Poetry and drama, after all, have their roots (and, some would say, their very life) in oral-aural and (in the case of drama) non-verbal modes of communication.

The period in which they became frozen into the uniformity of print and consumed by the contemplative private reader can be seen as a fairly brief interregnum in man's cultural history. This period, however, spans the entire history of the novel—and also, virtually, of literary criticism as we know it and practise it. The novel is the exemplary *written* fiction, the form on which all those in the arts (among whom I number myself) who believe Gutenberg was not a cultural disaster will tend to rest their case. It is noteworthy that novels are not only read and studied more and more in an exclusively academic context, but increasingly (especially in America) written there as well.

One can perhaps take comfort from the fact that as the novel retreats into academe, academe itself is expanding fast enough to maintain stability. It is not, in any case, my purpose here to deliver another sermon on the text *Is the novel dying?*, but to take a fairly random scoop into the flood of books about the novel now pouring from the presses, with a view to identifying current trends of thought—thus, hopefully, easing the log-jam referred to by the editors of *Novel*, and discriminating what they darkly describe as 'irrelevant' criticism.

This latter task is always a difficult and invidious one. To take a commonsense view of the matter it would seem that a work of criticism must justify itself on one or both of two grounds: either (1) it is as educative and life-enhancing as some work of the imagination we might have read in its place, or (2) it is an addition to knowledge in the sense that one's understanding and appreciation of certain imaginative works would be significantly weaker without it. Of the six books under review,* only Professor Kermode's and Professor Colby's seem to me to pass this test unequivocally (mainly on grounds (1) and (2) respectively). But this is in fact a very generous proportion. We all give a great deal of our time to books which fall below this high standard, and the reason must be that works of literature being in a sense public property, no human response to them is without interest. Nevertheless we are all concerned, I suppose, by the phenomenon of over-production in literary studies, leading to

* *The Modern Confessional Novel*, by Peter M. Axthelm, Yale; *Joseph Conrad and the Fiction of Autobiography*, by Edward W. Said, Harvard; *The Sense of an Ending; Studies in the Theory of Fiction*, by Frank Kermode, Oxford University Press; *The Turn of the Novel*, by Alan Friedman, Oxford University Press; *The Truth-tellers: Jane Austen, George Eliot, D. H. Lawrence*, by Laurence Lerner, Chatto & Windus; *Fiction with a Purpose: Major and Minor Nineteenth-Century Novels*, by Robert A. Colby, Indiana U.P.

the appearance of books which seem designed to be published, reviewed, indexed and shelved, but not in an ordinary sense to be *read* with pleasure and/or profit. Mr Friedman and Mr Lerner cannot be thus accused; but I could not defend Mr Axthelm or Mr Said with any conviction.

II

It is a little unfair to say this of *The Modern Confessional Novel*, for although it has all the appearances of a post-graduate thesis committed to print for the sake of 'publication' Mr Axthelm was, in fact, an undergraduate when he wrote it and has since taken up a career in journalism. *The Modern Confessional Novel* belongs to the Yale College Series, established to publish 'some of the best work by the Honours Majors in the Senior Class'. As an undergraduate dissertation it is, needless to say, an extraordinarily assured performance; but its very assurance is curiously depressing. Beginning with a glance at Augustine's *Confessions*, Mr Axthelm plunges into Dostoevsky's *Notes from Underground*, from which he seeks to derive a modern tradition of existential confessional fiction in texts by Gide, Sartre, Camus, Koestler, Golding and Bellow. He has some evidence for postulating a continuity between these books: the frequent appearance of a 'double' figure, for instance, and the preference for an ironic and often intellectual narrator; but as so often in thematic criticism, the individual edge of each text is blunted by flat, stale and unprofitable formulations of meaning—'interpretation' in Susan Sontag's invidious sense of that term.

> Both heroes [of *Darkness at Noon* and *Free Fall*] finally reach the conclusion that cold, logical formulas for existence cannot solve the problems of our time; truth and meaning, they discover, can be found only in our understanding of the self and its relation to the world.

How banal that makes these heroes sound—and how odd that, of all things, they should sound banal. Reading such blandly approving statements as, '*The Fall* leaves us with a profound awareness of the possibility of our own guilt and a pervasive uncertainty about the value of life', I couldn't help being reminded of Lionel Trilling's wry reflections on teaching modern literature to his abler students at Columbia:

I asked them to look into the Abyss, and, both dutifully and gladly, they have looked into the Abyss, and the Abyss has greeted them with the grave courtesy of all objects of serious study, saying: 'Interesting, am I not? And *exciting*, if you consider how deep I am and what dread beasts lie at my bottom. Have it well in mind that a knowledge of me contributes materially to your being whole, well-rounded men.'

As Trilling's essay suggests, none of us who are teachers of modern literature can easily shrug off responsibility for this kind of thing; and I am not so much attacking Mr Axthelm's book as those he has taken as his model and so competently imitated.

Mr Axthelm brightens perceptibly when he comes home to his native vernacular with *Herzog*. This is easily his best chapter, conveying a sensitive and infectious appreciation of Bellow's novel and making some original observations about the mythical allusion woven into its texture. But when he misquotes Heidegger's phrase ('Dear Doktor Professor Heidegger, I should like to know what you mean by the expression "the fall into the quotidian". When did this fall occur? Where were we standing when it happened?') as 'the fall *of* the quotidian' one feels that this is more than a trivial slip of the pen, that it is symptomatic of the coarsening of responsiveness to literary language entailed in too hasty a rush into deep waters like these.

III

Mr Said has a much more sophisticated and mature mind—indeed a formidably well-informed one. Unfortunately this mind and its information always seem to be getting between us and Mr Said's subject, Joseph Conrad. The argument is that there is a close but devious relationship between Conrad's fiction and the history of his own psyche; that, burdened by an acute temperamental pessimism, Conrad took an uncompromising view of experience that allowed '*either* a surrender to chaos *or* a comparably frightful surrender to egotistic order'; that his art was the product of a lifelong struggle to find a personal equilibrium in this painful dilemma; that his art was to a large extent deliberately designed to mislead his public with the mask of a composed and straightforward personality; but that a close examination of his letters and more intimately autobiographical stories indicates the real stress and strain of his creative and inner life. So far so good. If this perspective is not completely novel (Jocelyn

Baines, for instance, threw a good deal of light on Conrad's protective self-disguises in his admirable biography) and if it is always threatening to displace attention from the major to the minor work, and from this to Conrad's personal character, nevertheless there is a valid and useful point to be made here. Unfortunately Mr Said will not make it as simply and economically as is possible. He complicates it, firstly by jargon, and secondly by a great deal of extraneous allusion.

Literary criticism, like any other highly developed intellectual discipline, cannot entirely dispense with jargon; but since its subject is human eloquence it has a responsibility to maintain as much continuity as possible with human discourse. Am I being crass in suggesting that if the following passage were stripped of its weight of solemn abstraction and vague metaphor it could be assimilated far more easily and with no loss of sense?

> Conrad's individuality resides in a continuous exposure of his sense of himself to a sense of what is not himself: he set himself, lumpish and problematic, against the dynamic, fluid processes of life. Because of this, then, the great human appeal and distinction of Conrad's life is the dramatic spirit of partnership, however uneasy or indecorous, his life exemplifies, a partnership between himself and the external world: I am speaking of the full exposure of his soul to the vast panorama of existence it has discerned outside itself. He had the courage to risk a full confrontation with what, most of the time, seemed to him to be a threatening and unpleasant world. Moreover, the outcome of this dialectic is an experiencing of existential reality at that deepest level of alternative and potentiality which is the true life of the mind. Now the vocabulary and rhetoric of this experience (which I have called its idiom) is what the letters provide us with to such a degree that we are able to discover the contours of Conrad's mind as it engages itself in a partnership with existence. For 'exposure' of the mind and soul has its literary paradigm: it is a habitual verbal exercise (hence *idiom*) whose purpose is to arbitrate the relations between a problematic subject and a dynamic object.

My point is that if one boils this down one is left with a fairly ordinary statement about the relationship of the self to the external world which is common to most artists in the modern period. What is special about Conrad is the element of deliberately-invited risk in his early life (justly noted in the fourth and most lucid sentence of the above quotation) but even this is not unique. What *is* unique (or 'individual' or 'distinguished') about Conrad is what he made of his experience artistically and imaginatively. But so far from leading us helpfully towards this, Mr Said seems to set before us a verbal obstacle course, along, over and through which we must struggle, wriggle and clamber, with ever-failing energy and zest.

The superfluous jargon goes hand in hand with superfluous allusion to other writers. *A propos* of the 'dynamic movements or structures of experience (mechanisms)' that Mr Said sees emerging from the letters, he observes:

> In one of his earliest works, *History and Class Consciousness*, Georg Lukacs has described structures similar to these: Lucien Goldmann calls them *significant dynamic structures*. . . . But the Marxist conclusion, class consciousness, does not suit this study. . . .

So these writers are not *à propos* after all. Then why introduce them? Even when such analogies are adopted and applied in some detail— Newman's concept of 'economy', for instance, or Sartre's phenomenonological theory of the emotions—one feels that they are introduced to complicate and thus dignify an imaginative achievement that is in no need of such service.

IV

I can see, ironically enough, how easy it would be to make similar criticisms of *The Sense of an Ending*. This is an extraordinarily and, it often seems, wilfully difficult book. Two or three readings are needed to get the most out of it, and what it could have been like to take it in through the ear (originally the text was delivered as the Flexnor Lectures at Bryn Mawr) defies imagination. There is a strong streak of intellectual dandyism in Professor Kermode: he is a brilliant critic who delights in exhibiting his brilliance. But the brilliance is genuine, and the obscurity is the result, not of inflation but of compression; so that instead of resenting the riddling epigrams (*e.g.*, 'if the ziggurat is a topocosm, the book is a bibliocosm'), the knowing allusions to obscure sources and esoteric scholarship, the risky excursions into theology, philosophy and physics, one recognizes that the manner is inseparable from the matter, and that one is being teased and cajoled into participating in an exciting intellectual adventure.

The Sense of an Ending has in common with the three books discussed below an area of theoretical enquiry which may be described as the problematical relationship of fictional technique to reality. The relationship of art to reality is of course the central problem of all aesthetic discussion, but it is raised in a particularly acute form by the novel, because in its origins and to a large extent in its continuing development the novel has undertaken to represent reality more faithfully and completely than any other literary genre.

The novel is only a part of Professor Kermode's enormous subject, but it is the part I shall be concentrating on here. However, in order to bring out the significance of what he has to say about the novel, some preliminary description of the book's overall subject is necessary. *The Sense of an Ending* is well described on the dust-jacket as 'a pioneering attempt to relate the theory of literary fictions to a more general theory of fiction, using the fictions of apocalypse as a model'. This begs the question: what are *non*-literary fictions? And the answer seems to be: more or less every attempt to make sense of the world we live in, whether historical, theological, philosophical, or scientific. We cannot tolerate brute, inchoate, discrete 'reality'—we have a human need to make sense of it through intellectual schemes or paradigms; but all such schemes distort or misrepresent reality and to that extent are 'fictions'. Some fictions are more plausible than others; most need revising from time to time.

The fictions of apocalypse, which Kermode takes as his model, answer a need generated by the Judeo-Christian view of history as linear, with a beginning, an end which is different from the beginning, and a middle in which we are problematically situated. (The cyclic view of history characteristic of pagan and primitive cultures offers a different kind of explanation, or consolation; though it, too, has its apocalyptic moments, as the example of Yeats suggests.) In his first chapter Kermode defines the characteristics of his model chiefly by reference to early Christian and medieval apocalyptic prophecy, which usually took the form of interpreting Revelations, often with the assistance of pseudepigrapha such as the Sibylline oracles, to determine the date of the end of the world. A representative figure was Joachim of Flora (d. 1202) who divided history into three phases, each phase heralded by a period of Transition. In this latter concept Kermode sees the progenitor of our modern sense of 'crisis': 'insofar as we claim to live now in a period of perpetual transition we have merely elevated the interstitial period into an "age" or *saeculum* in its own right.' Joachite speculation was officially condemned by the Church in 1260, but the remarkable thing about apocalyptic prophecy is that it manages to survive not only what Kermode calls 'clerkly scepticism', but 'disconfirmation' by history itself. When predictions of the end of the world fail to come true, the prophets are commonly unabashed and return to the making of new calculations, discovering new 'consonances'. The relevance of all this to literary fictions may be illustrated by the following:

> Peripeteia, which has been called the equivalent, in narrative, of irony in rhetoric, is present in every story of the least structural sophistication. Now peripeteia depends on our confidence of the end; it is a disconfirmation followed by a consonance; the interest of having our expectations falsified is obviously related to our wish to reach the discovery or recognition by an unexpected and instructive route. It has nothing to do with any reluctance on our part to get there at all. So that in assimilating the peripeteia we are enacting that readjustment of expectations in regard to an end which is so notable a feature of naive apocalyptic. And we are doing rather more than that: we are . . . re-enacting the familiar dialogue between credulity and scepticism. The more daring the peripeteia the more we may feel that the work respects our sense of reality.

'The dialogue between credulity and scepticism' would serve as a description of *Don Quixote*, and it remains a continuing preoccupation of the form that Cervantes fathered. The novelist undertakes to win our credulity by making as many concessions to our scepticism as is consistent with his desire to impose order on experience. Kermode's point is that as a result of advancing knowledge 'clerkly scepticism' grows increasingly suspicious of the paradigms which fictions, literary and non-literary (history, for example) impose upon reality. But, he argues, the paradigms persist, for they seem to be a necessary condition of human thought, and in artistic matters they are another way of describing 'form'.

The history of the novel illustrates this thesis very well. 'Its history is an attempt to evade the laws of what Scott called "the land of fiction" —the stereotypes which ignore reality and whose remoteness from it we identify as absurd.' This is certainly true. Defoe, Richardson and (to a lesser extent, because he was less bothered about scepticism) Fielding, demonstrably honour 'reality' more faithfully than their predecessors in narrative literature, but they are also demonstrably more committed to the stereotypes than, say, Jane Austen or George Eliot, who in turn impose a degree of order upon experience that would be impossible to sustain (at their level of seriousness) in the modern era. Peripeteia itself, which, Kermode suggests, originated as a concession to scepticism, comes to look, in the perspective of the novel's realistic representation of experience, like a stereotype, and is therefore to be handled carefully—domesticated, inverted, disguised or resisted altogether. (Compare Oedipus' discovery of his origins with Tom Jones's, both with Emma's discovery that she alone must marry Mr Knightley and that Harriet is only a tradesman's daughter, and all of them with the muted, precarious, ironized union of a father-without-a-son and the son-without-a-father in *Ulysses*.)

The development of the novel is thus the response to a continuing demand for 'constantly changing, constantly more subtle relationships between a fiction and the paradigms'. It is the major novelists, the innovators, who carry on this process: the run-of-the-mill writer is content to manipulate the stereotypes. Therefore 'the history of the novel is the history of anti-novels'. This judgment gets most interesting confirmation, as regards the nineteenth century, from Mr Colby. As regards the twentieth century it scarcely needs confirmation, since the difficulty of adjusting fictions to an increasingly intransigent 'reality' is the overt subject of so many modern novelists. Kermode is particularly interested in those who have self-consciously pursued this enterprise to extreme conclusions—Musil, Sartre, Burroughs, Beckett, Muriel Spark, Robbe-Grillet; but though understandably tolerant of experiments which illustrate his theory so neatly, he pulls back from endorsing those (in literature and the other arts) whose aim is to put an end to the dialogue between credulity and scepticism, destroying the former in a nihilistic surrender to the latter: in other words, the art of 'schismatic modernism' that emerges with Dadaism and currently flourishes in random music, 'found' poetry, cut-up-fold-in novels and so on. Perhaps the reason why we still cherish the art, including the novels, of the 'traditional moderns' and find it so difficult to go beyond them, is that they struck such an admirable balance between credulity and scepticism—one which still serves many of us very well.

V

It is with such novelists that Mr Friedman is concerned, in a book whose subject lies very much within Kermode's field of interest:

> The traditional premise about the design of experience which was profoundly, if variously, embodied in the eighteenth and nineteenth-century novel, was the premise of a closed experience . . . My theme and argument in this book is the existence in the novel of a gradual historical shift from a closed to an open form.

By an 'open form' Friedman does not mean the deliberate non-resolution of meanings, nor the studious avoidance of any kind of narrative climax, but the kind of ending 'that does not contain or "close off" the rising pressure of conscience in a novel'. He recognizes that the 'mutation in the form of the novel' which he is tracing 'corresponds to a mutation in the ends of culture. . . . For endings are also ends.' But although he thus hovers closely about the thesis developed by Kermode, he never quite grasps it, veering away instead into rather vague talk about the 'stream of conscience' and 'ethical process'. What emerges so persuasively from *The Sense of an Ending* is that historical changes in literary fictions correspond to historical changes in *knowledge*. Lacking this insight, Mr Friedman lacks a convincing explanation of why modern novelists have exchanged the closed form for an open one. Perhaps some consciousness of this deficiency impels him to shuffle his terminology so restlessly, and deliver his discourse in a bright, chattering style, occasionally reminiscent of a conjuror's patter, which I found the reverse of disarming.

Despite these limitations and mannerisms, Friedman displays considerable shrewdness as a critic, in studying texts by Hardy, Conrad, Forster and Lawrence to illustrate the 'turn of the novel' in its new direction. Hardy and Conrad particularly interest him for their hesitation and indecision in this respect. He is right, I think, to see the last chapter of *Tess of the d'Urbervilles*, where Liza-Lu, 'a spiritualized image of Tess', and Angel walk hand in hand out of the book to a chorus of Christian allusion, as Hardy's compromise with his audience's expectations of a closed ending, and as a betrayal of the basic rhythm and impulse of the novel; and to see a similar falsification in the marriage of Powell and Flora at the end of Conrad's *Chance*—a final twist in that ingeniously constructed novel designed, not to throw a new and interesting light on events, but to leave the reader with a comfortable, sentimental glow. The audience is, in fact, always a conservative influence. Hardy, Friedman suggests, went on to make an uncompromising break with the conventions of closed endings in the mordantly ironic conclusion of *Jude* and, notoriously, deeply offended his public. *Chance* (significantly Conrad's first popular success) represented a retreat from a more radical approach to form evident as early as *Almayer's Folly*. Friedman discerns in Conrad's career a persistent conflict between 'his effort to "close" his form morally and his refusal to do so' which 'helps to indicate the slow turn of the novel, the progressive emergence of a finally open experience as normative for fiction'. Certainly Conrad, writing on Henry James, yields him a choice quotation, one that Kermode might have made good use of, for the value it concedes to credulity, as well as to scepticism:

> . . . It is obvious that a solution by rejection must always present a certain lack of finality, especially startling when contrasted with the usual methods of solution by rewards and punishments, by crowned love, by fortune, by a broken leg or a sudden death. Why the reading public which, as a body, has never laid upon a story-teller the command to be an artist, should demand from him this sham of Divine Omnipotence, is utterly incomprehensible. But so it is; and these solutions are legitimate inasmuch as they satisfy the desire for finality, for which our hearts yearn, with a longing greater than the longing for the loaves and fishes of this earth. Perhaps the only true desire of mankind . . . is to be set at rest. One is never set at rest by Mr. Henry James' novels. His books end as an episode in life ends. You remain with the sense of life still going on. . . . It is eminently satisfying, but it is not final.

It is important to emphasize that this discussion is concerned not with endings considered in isolation, but with the kind of ending implied in every word of a given novel. Thus Friedman is prepared to defend the inconclusiveness of *The Rainbow* and *Women in Love* by maintaining that, read sensitively, these books can only arouse expectations of inconclusiveness. 'There is no absence of an inevitable close [in *The Rainbow*], only an absence of *the* inevitable close.' 'The evidence in *Women in Love* makes it safe to say that Lawrence—his critics to the contrary—regarded a conclusive ending as a corruption of the form of life *and* the form of fiction.'

This raises the question, which is never far away in one form or another in discussions of Lawrence, of how you distinguish between a good inconclusive novel and a bad one. If it is conceded that in Kermode's words, 'there is a humanly needed order we call form', then it behoves the novelist in casting out obsolete formal conventions, to devise new ones with which to convey a new vision of experience without losing the sense of order. Joyce is a classic example, as T. S. Eliot was one of the first to recognize in his essay '*Ulysses*, Order and Myth'. Now, the difficulty with Lawrence is that while possessed of a radically revolutionary vision of experience, he relied to a large extent on formal conventions which belonged to a phase of fiction his own was designed to render obsolete. 'You mustn't look in my novel for the old stable *ego* of the character.' Fair enough; but we are often

uncomfortably aware of the old stable *ego* of the authorial voice—
uncomfortably, because the two go together.

Ultimately, the problem can be reduced to one of language. Friedman suggests that Lawrence's subject was 'the unconscious' in a way
that contrasts interestingly with Joyce. Joyce renders the unconscious
as a distortion of conscious verbal activity. Friedman suggests that
'subconscious' would be a more appropriate word here. Lawrence's
'unconscious' was not verbal at all, hence there is no possibility of
verbal mimesis. 'He is attempting to render the fluid non-conscious,
or as he would say "dark" mental processes while at the same time
remaining wholly within the region of conventional and conscious
syntax.' Instead of distorting the verbal medium, Lawrence distorts
'emotional consciousness. The deep unconscious intrudes through a
tissue of correlative feelings and perceptions.' On these grounds Friedman justifies the characteristic rhapsodies of heightened sensation and
emotion which so often tremble on the brink of, if they do not actually
fall into, strained and unconvincing rhetoric. Friedman acknowledges
that it is a risky technique, requiring considerable tolerance from the
reader, but claims that in such scenes as the corn-gathering in *The
Rainbow* it pays off handsomely enough to satisfy all doubts. Whether
one is finally convinced or not, the argument seems more
persuasive and to the point than the more familiar defence of Lawrence
as an English moralist.

VI

From his title, that is exactly what one might expect of Mr Lerner: it
sounds uncomfortably like a warming-up of *The Great Tradition*. He
is, of course, far too intelligent a critic to do any such thing. Nevertheless his critical preferences and criteria are more conditioned, less
personal, than he seems willing to acknowledge. *The Truthtellers*
expounds, in a rather extreme form, an approach to fiction that is
generally characteristic of the English (as distinct from the American
or European) critical temper. One could draw analogies with the work,
not only of Leavis, but of Barbara Hardy, John Bayley, and the late,
much-lamented W. J. Harvey.

In this perspective, the relationship between fiction and reality is seen
as the more or less truthful rendering and assessment of experience.
'The great novel is that which understands, whose vision of man speaks
to us with the insistence of truth.' The essential criterion is therefore
the reader's degree of assent to the human truthfulness of fictions, a

position which (compared, say, to Kermode's) assumes a fairly stable notion of reality and a fairly firm consensus about values. Lerner tries to tease out the implications of this position in a comparative study of Jane Austen, George Eliot and D. H. Lawrence.

Thus it should follow that beneath all the obvious dissimilarities existing between these three novelists, there is something in common in their view of experience. Lerner suggests that 'none of them believed in God'—that they all treat religious experience as 'a human phenomenon . . . as a metaphor for conduct'. This, he suggests (though he does not demonstrate it), is the kind of truth which even overtly religious novelists tell us. Again, if novels are valued because they tell the truth, it follows that they contain a kind of knowledge, and therefore may be measured against more systematic forms of knowledge, such as psychology. Lerner discusses the concept of the unconscious and the novelist's dealings with it, and compares the novelist's interest in human behaviour with that of the behaviourist psychologist. What he has to say on these topics is always interesting in detail (behaviourism, particularly, is a subject rarely commented on by literary critics) but his conclusions seem to me either dubious or rather tame. I would make much the same criticism of the other, critical side of his book. There are many shrewd comments and useful insights on Austen, Eliot and Lawrence, but one does not emerge with any definable sense of an enhanced or altered understanding of any of them. This is partly due to the confusing design of the book, in which even the author seems to get lost at times. But it is also due, I feel, to the critical method adopted.

It would be disingenuous to pretend that I have an open mind about this. In his Introduction, Lerner distinguishes between two kinds of criticism, the Aristotelian and the Platonic, on grounds that may readily be guessed at. He describes *The Truthtellers* as 'a highly Platonic book—dogmatically so, some will think, polemically, even fanatically so. Its aim is to discover and compare the values of these three writers—their human, not their artistic values.' I shall not reiterate here the arguments for taking an opposite view of critical priorities, which are no more likely to convert Mr Lerner than he is to convert me, except to take up two points he makes himself: firstly, that 'a critic can be a mere Aristotelian, but to be a Platonist at all he must be something of an Aristotelian first', and secondly, that 'I have felt it necessary to ask myself constantly if what I have written is proof against the central objection to the Platonist . . . that he unwrites literature.'

On the first point, I would say that Lerner is at his best as a critic when he gives his Aristotelian side most play. This is especially evident in the section on Lawrence, where he makes some devastating analyses of failure and falsity in *The Plumed Serpent, Lady Chatterley's Lover* and *St. Mawr*. Lerner is not abandoning his Platonist stance—he claims that there is always a connection between the morally pernicious and the artistically false in Lawrence's work. This may be so; but there are critics who do not believe *The Plumed Serpent* to be pernicious, and I fancy they would find it easier to defend the book on moral than on formal grounds. It is in a discussion of Lawrence's poetry that Lerner almost transforms himself into an Aristotelian: 'there is, after all, such a thing as technique; by writing you discover just what you want to say. If you always try to get an emotion out in its own course—if you never *work* at it—you are making yourself helpless.' This seems to me to be as true of novels as of poems.

On the second point, I *do* think the 'Platonist' critic is in danger of 'unwriting literature'. Sometimes the temptation to sharpen a judgment leads to simple misrepresentation. Thus, Lerner uses a quotation from *Tender is the Night* (where Nicole goes shopping) to emphasize the superior truthfulness of George Eliot's insight, in a passage from *The Mill on the Floss*, into the economic and social injustice that underpins the pleasures of the affluent leisured classes.

> Where he sees the glamour, she sees the unfairness. Even in this shortened quotation, Fitzgerald's fascination with the colour and luxury of Nicole's shopping is evident; and we see the same romantic lure in his account of the 'ingenuity and toil' that 'drew mouthwash out of copper hogsheads'—interesting, unusual, but not, as he describes it, arduous. . . . But George Eliot has not bothered with ingenuity or romance: she writes with a firm cumulative anger of 'sweating at furnaces, grinding, hammering, weaving, under more or less oppression of carbonic acid'.

Lerner, however, has omitted some crucial lines from the Fitzgerald passage which make much the same kind of point as George Eliot is credited with:

> girls canned tomatoes quickly in August or worked rudely at the Five-and-Tens on Christmas Eve; half-breed Indians toiled on Brazilian coffee plantations and dreamers were muscled out of patent rights in new tractors . . .

One might argue that Fitzgerald's evocation of the glamour as well as the absurdity and human cost of the industrial production-consumption machine represents a more subtle and complex response than George Eliot's. In fact they are writing about different phases of the industrial revolution, with different artistic ends in view, and there is no meaningful sense in which one passage can be said to be 'truer' than the other.

The basic objection to this kind of comparative criticism is that it tears passages from the contexts in which they have their meanings. Lerner acknowledges this objection, but does not dispose of it, in commenting on the authorial defence of Elizabeth Bennet's 'change of sentiment' towards Darcy in Chapter 46 of *Pride and Prejudice*:

> If gratitude and esteem are good foundations of affection, Elizabeth's change of sentiment will be neither improbable nor faulty. But if otherwise—if the regard springing from such sources is unreasonable or unnatural, in comparison of what is often described as arising on a first interview with its object, and even before two words have been exchanged—nothing can be said in her defence, except that she had given somewhat of a trial to the latter method, in her partiality for Wickham, and that its ill success might, perhaps, authorize her to seek the other less interesting mode of attachment.

Lerner comments:

> The whole plot of *Pride and Prejudice* is a defence of the less interesting mode of attachment. And while we are reading, this paragraph is surely an unexceptionable and consistent reflection: it is only if we look at it in isolation, freed from the spell of the context, that we pause to doubt. . . . There is a resistance to emotion underlying this paragraph that it is very tempting to call old-maidish.

Tempting, perhaps, but surely unfair? One scarcely needs even to know the context to recognize that Elizabeth is defended here by an ironic undercutting—not of 'emotion'—but of emotional cliché: there is a clear allusion to the cliché of love at first sight. Such clichés are perpetuated by mediocre fictions and purged by good ones.

VII

The notion that Jane Austen defined her view of experience (not only in *Northanger Abbey* and the juvenilia, but throughout her career) by implied parodic contrast with fictional stereotypes has been pretty well assimilated by her modern critics, and it is easy enough to fit her into

Kermode's thesis that the history of the novel is the history of anti-novels. It is not so simple, at first sight, to accommodate some of the other major nineteenth-century novelists. One of the most interesting things about Mr Colby's book is that, working with a quite different method from any of the other writers discussed here, he makes this task surprisingly easy.

He is a literary historian first, and a critic second. He reminds us that we read the great novels of the past in a kind of timeless library of great books, removed from the context of competing fiction in which they were originally produced and read. This seems to me as inevitable as it is artificial—it is part of what we mean by the word 'classic'—but there is certainly much to be learned by returning the great books temporarily to their literary contexts. Colby's method has something in common with Professor Kathleen Tillotson's admirable *Novels of the 1840's*, but breaks new ground, on a wider front. He takes seven major novels—*Waverley, Mansfield Park, Oliver Twist, Pendennis, Villette, The Mill on the Floss* and *Middlemarch*—and studies their relationships with the minor fiction of the same period or with similar themes. What emerges is a complex and fascinating spectacle of major novelists borrowing, parodying, correcting and remaking the themes and conventions of minor novelists. The sense of 'purpose' which Colby sees as characteristic of the nineteenth-century novel is thus aesthetic or critical as well as ethical.

Waverley is seen—entirely plausibly—as an anti-romance, tracing the passage of the hero from romantic illusion to realistic maturity, and thus represents an implied criticism of the sensational Gothic novel. Jane Austen shares with Scott an interest in the theme of youth acquiring maturity, but in *Mansfield Park* the implied fictional context is that of the Christian didactic novel as represented, for instance, by Hannah More's *Coelebs in Search of a Wife* which was, Colby suggests (sobering thought) probably the most widely-read novel of the first quarter of the century. *Oliver Twist* is seen as a sophisticated development of the popular 'foundling tale' typified by *Fatherless Fanny*; and is shown to have a close relationship with *Hans Sloane: A Tale Illustrating the History of the Foundling Hospital* (1831) by Dickens's friend John Brownlow, to whom Dickens paid the compliment of giving his name to Oliver's benefactor. Colby also suggests that Dickens justifies his concentration on 'low' characters and behaviour by ironic allusion to characteristic features of 'Silver Fork' novels—'not merely exposing his more privileged readers to the cess-pools of London but showing them their own reflections there'. Thackeray, having a much closer temperamental affinity with Silver Fork fiction, provides a rather more subtle revision of its values and life-styles in *Pendennis*, another novel of youth's passage into maturity; and the hero's education and literary aspirations give Thackeray ample opportunity to weave a good deal of literary criticism into the texture of his novel. *Villette* belongs to the type of the 'governess novel' that Colby sees emerging from the *Fatherless Fanny* tradition in Lady Blessington's novel *The Governess* (1839). A governess novel that certainly influenced Charlotte Brontë (it was presented to her by the author) was Julia Kavanagh's *Nathalie* (1850), a story with a Continental setting in which a governess falls in love with the cynical, middle-aged uncle of the family by whom she is employed. This love ends happily, unlike that of Lucy and M. Paul—a characteristic adjustment of fictional stereotypes. Running all through *Villette* Colby finds a strong anti-romance vein that reaches its climax in Lucy's discovery that what she took to be a nun's ghost is only a *bourgeoise belle* in masquerade.

> The unholy spirits that had been driven out of the temple of fiction by Jane Austen and Sir Walter Scott are exorcised once more at mid-century. Miss Brontë's last word on the Gothic romance is a laugh, and a laugh that liberates. It also signalises a new life for her heroine. Lucy, as a living captive nun, had identified herself with fictitious ghostly nuns. In burying the empty religious vestments under her pillow she becomes the 'new' realistic heroine sloughing off the sheltered romantic heroine.

This quotation may suggest that Colby is not merely a crack-shot at source hunting (though he is undoubtedly that) but also knows how to turn his knowledge to critical advantage.

Of all the novelists discussed, George Eliot probably took herself and her art most seriously. Her letters and reviews display a keen critical nose for mediocrity in fiction and a healthy *amour propre*. 'The most ignorant journalist in England would hardly think of calling me a rival of Miss Mulock,' she wrote after a French journal had done just that, 'a writer who is read only by novel readers, pure and simple, never by people of high culture.' It is the implied thesis of *Fiction with a Purpose* that no novelist can be immune from the influence of other novelists, and Colby is able to show how George Eliot took hints from Mrs Anne Thackeray, Trollope and George Sand. However, it is entirely characteristic of George Eliot that the most interesting influences Colby discovers are from non-fictional sources, especially from the works on psychology and physiology that Lewes was preparing when George Eliot was writing *The Mill on the Floss* and *Middlemarch*.

George Eliot makes a fitting conclusion to Colby's book because she represents the high point of the development he traces through the century, whereby the major novelists continually improved upon, renewed and expanded the range of fiction while still remaining in the mainstream of national cultural life. It is no coincidence that the most 'intellectual' of the great early or mid-Victorian novelists lived at the last moment when it was possible to be highly educated without being a specialist. Henceforward the rapport established between author and audience breaks up under the pressure of expanding and fragmenting knowledge. The correction of credulity by scepticism proceeds too rapidly for a mass audience to keep pace. '*Middlemarch*', it was Henry James's opinion, 'sets a limit to the development of the old-fashioned novel.'

What followed is Friedman's subject. If we put Kermode's book besides Colby's, however, what emerges strikingly is the continuity rather than the discontinuity between traditional and modern fiction. 'Scott and his successors', says Colby—and he demonstrates his point amply—'were mockers and improvers, seeking to counteract false fictions with true, bringing art in touch with "common life" by a more detailed notation of experience.' Would this not serve as an account of Joyce's aims in *Ulysses*?

3 Towards a Poetics of Fiction: An Approach through Language

Much of what I have to say under this title and subtitle will inevitably be either a defence or a qualification of what I said in a book called *Language of Fiction* (1966). This procedure is the more difficult to avoid because Malcolm Bradbury, in an article to which I am here responding,* cites my book in connection with a critical approach to the novel which he finds (while acknowledging its usefulness) to be in some ways inadequate and misleading. That approach he characterizes as 'symbolist' or 'neo-symbolist', tracing its derivation from the principles that modern criticism developed in the study of poetry, especially lyric poetry. In this perspective novels like poems 'are verbal constructs in which all the material necessary for their appreciation and elucidation is contained'. Elucidation and appreciation are conducted primarily in terms of verbal analysis, and the novelist's art is seen as one of 'presentation, rather than representation'. Bradbury finds this approach wanting in its failure to accommodate the referential character of novels or their 'attention to workaday reality'. But the kind of criticism which *does* undertake to deal with this element he finds equally unsatisfactory. This is the 'realist' approach, which characterizes the novel by its special interest in 'life', whether this is seen (as by Ian Watt in *The Rise of the Novel*) as the expression of historical changes in human experience and modes of perceiving it, or (as by F. R. Leavis in *The Great Tradition*) as the mediation by author to reader of a more or less mature and life-enhancing scale of values in concretely realized instances.

Neither of these critical approaches, in Bradbury's view, offers the basis for a 'poetics' of the novel; neither is capable of giving a comprehensive formal account of the novel's peculiar identity. To reconcile 'these two divergent poetics' Bradbury proposes a more inclusive one, which he calls 'structural'. His approach is essentially neo-Aristotelian.

* My essay was the second in a series published by the journal *Novel: a forum on fiction* under the running title, 'Towards a Poetics of Fiction'. I was responding, by pre-arrangement, to Malcolm Bradbury's essay 'Towards a Poetics of Fiction: An Approach through Structure' in the previous issue of *Novel* (I (1967), pp. 45–52).

The novel 'is a complex structure by virtue of its scale, prose-character and matter'. This, he concedes, does not yield a structural typology, but 'still, if there is no necessary structure, almost any fictional structure must necessarily consist of certain things—primarily a chain of interlinked events, unified by persuasive discourse and by those materials in life which, transliterated as discourse, take on for the author the character of interconnectedness'. It is the last part of this sentence that is crucial: Bradbury is seeking to accommodate within the concept of novel *form* that *matter* which is the special concern of the realist critics. 'If we say that the novel is determined by conditions within the medium itself and outside it in life,' he writes, 'then we may move freely between language and life, and find order and unity in the kind of working that a novel has . . . in achieving its persuasive ends; and we may further allow, by this approach, for the book's referential dimension as an account of life, its rhetorical dimension as a species of language, its sociological dimension as an exploration and crystallization of a cultural situation, and its psychological or mythic dimension as an exploration of personal or psychic experience.'

The inclusiveness of the poetics sketched here is indeed appealing, but I rather doubt whether the concept of 'structure' can be made to bear the strain of so many different applications. The word 'structure' in literary criticism is, after all, a metaphor, which describes a temporal medium in spatial and visual terms, and it can be no more inclusive analogically than it is literally. For example, to describe the structure of a cathedral is to describe its overall shape, its balancing and distribution of large masses and spaces, not the texture of its stone, or the carving of its gargoyles, or the colouring of its windows. Thus it is not surprising to find Bradbury later defining the concept of structure more narrowly as 'that devised chain of events that, presented by narration, conditions the successive choices, made sentence by sentence, paragraph by paragraph, chapter by chapter, and constitutes not only an entire narrative but an attitude towards it'. This is much more like the concept of 'plot' in Aristotelian and neo-Aristotelian criticism. Bradbury is shrewd enough to see the pitfalls inherent in such a theory, but not, I think, to avoid them altogether. 'We might project the situation back in Aristotelian terms, or neo-Aristotelian terms, in the form of a prior working-out of the action in the mind of the writer, which the compositional process then imitates; but it is only meaningful to do this if we say that the action imitated exists simultaneously as that which has to be written (that which motivates and directs the compositional process) and that which is worked, achieved, realized in the writing.' The two parts of this sentence cancel each other out: priority cannot be logically reconciled with simultaneity. Yet some notion of priority—of crucial choices and decisions being made by the novelist prior to the verbal articulation of them in the novel—is essential to Bradbury's theory, since it is in this way that he aims to incorporate an account of an author's particular engagement with 'life' into a formal poetics, by seeing selection and ordering of experience as 'the larger blocks of fictional persuasion'. As he recognizes, 'the trouble with such matters for enquiry is that, though we may accept them as a necessary condition of literary creation, there is no really satisfactory method of ascertaining what they are except *through* the words which finally express them.' This is, in fact, an argument I have used myself to urge primary attention to the novelist's use of language. Bradbury's answer is that 'successful reading of those words is surely a kind of process by which we hypothesize the sort of decisions of relevance made in order to put the material to us in this way'. He buttresses this by what I must take as an *argumentum ad hominem*: 'there are very few writers who appear to have felt that it is only through language that they are communicating. They are, I would suppose, always conscious that they are mediating verbally a devised succession of events.'

Now, whatever novelists 'feel', it is axiomatic that it is only through language that they are communicating, since there are no other means of communication at their disposal. What Bradbury means, I think, is that novelists feel it is not language *that* they are communicating: that, in other words, they are conscious of selecting and arranging non-verbal 'life-stuff', which is gradually rendered more and more concrete and particular in the process of verbalization. In this view, while it is acknowledged that only through the final verbalization do we apprehend the gross structure, the gross structure also conditions the final verbalization; and a meaning or persuasive power inheres in this gross structure which cannot be accounted for by direct reference to the language alone, but only by working back from the language to construct a hypothetical picture of the initial non-verbal process of selection and ordering.

'It is the interaction between what is prefigured and the obligations of achieving it that creates a novel,' is Bradbury's elegant formulation. But that second 'it' is an ambiguous word. As Bradbury says, 'any novelist will admit that the prefigured novel is not the same as the novel achieved'. And this difference, it must be emphasized, is not merely a matter of detail or density—it is also in Bradbury's terms 'structural'.

If we are to appeal to the experience of novelists (my own certainly bears this out) it will be found that in many, if not most cases, major decisions regarding the pattern of events, the behaviour of characters and so on, are made or significantly revised at an advanced stage of composition—at the point, very often, when the ongoing process of composition compels a decision upon the writer.

The prefigured structure of a novel seems less like the framework of pillars and arches which holds a building in a certain shape, than like the scaffolding, without which indeed the building cannot be started, but which is altered and dismantled in the process of construction. Instead of saying 'it is the interaction between what is prefigured and the obligations of achieving it that "creates" a novel', one might say that 'the interaction between what is prefigured and what is achieved creates a novel'. In this interaction what is achieved is certainly conditioned to some extent by what is prefigured, but in a more significant sense what is achieved, as it is achieved, *displaces* what has been prefigured, and alters the prefiguration of what is not yet achieved.

Furthermore, the devising of a chain of events is accorded very different degrees of priority by different novelists and is by no means as constant a feature of the prefiguring process as Bradbury's theory seems to require. His theory would probably fit *Tom Jones* very well, but hardly *Madame Bovary*:

> Flaubert said to us today: 'The story, the plot of the novel is of no interest to me. When I write a novel I aim at rendering a color, a shade. For instance, in my Carthaginian novel, I want to do something purple. The rest, the characters and the plot, is a mere detail. In *Madame Bovary*, all I wanted to do was to render a grey color, the mouldy color of a wood-louse's existence. The story of the novel mattered so little to me that a few days before starting on it I still had in mind a very different Madame Bovary from the the one I created: the setting and the overall tone were the same, but she was to have been a chaste and devout old maid. And then I realized that she would have been an impossible character.[1]

The genetic study of works of literature is indeed a fascinating and rewarding branch of literary criticism, but the processes of composition vary so much between one writer and another (and often between books by the same writer) that genetic study will not yield enough reliable generalizations on which to erect a poetics of the novel.

It will be noted that I am not denying that novelists make choices and decisions regarding the kinds and disposition of characters, events, backgrounds, themes, moods to be handled in a given novel, nor that these decisions are (in a provisional and variable sense) made prior to their articulation in the actual work. What I am denying is that these things have any substantive existence somehow 'outside' language, that in Bradbury's words, 'the structure . . . can be distinguished from the discourse as a species of imitation'. To make this point clear I must dissociate myself both from certain assumptions about language implied in Bradbury's theory, and from those he attributes to 'symbolist' criticism.

To begin with the latter point, I would reject the symbolist theory as he describes it, as 'anti-causal or solipsistic'—and not only with regard to the novel, but with regard to verse. I take language to be a shared system of sounds and written symbols for sounds, by which meaning is conveyed between people who share the system. This excludes the possibility of a private language and of a literature of 'pure' sound (sound without meanings). It means that I would not regard a novel as 'something which can be analysed only as an image system or a rhetoric independent of writers and readers'. In fact, I am in complete agreement with Bradbury in seeing the art of the novelist as 'persuasion'—as effects achieved in order to persuade the reader to view experience in a certain way. But I must protest when he says that 'these effects exist less in the realm of style *per se* than in the realm of persuasion'. If style means (as I presume) literary language here, there can be no such thing as style *per se* (that is, words considered apart from the meanings they bear and the persuasive purposes they serve) and no persuasion without style. In my view the crucial fallacy in Bradbury's argument, and in most neo-Aristotelian theory, is that it regards language as, in his words, 'one of a variety of elements which the writer must dispose of in producing a work', and not as the all-inclusive medium in which whatever 'elements' we may choose to discern and categorize in a work of literature are contained and communicated.

Fundamentally, my position rests on the assumption that consciousness is essentially conceptual, i.e. verbal. There is of course such a thing as non-verbal or pre-verbal *experience*—the whole life of sensation, for example—but we cannot be conscious of that experience without verbal concepts. This position would only imply solipsism if language was a private and arbitrary affair. It is not, but the notion that, in Wittgenstein's words, 'the limits of my language are the limits of my world' is apt to be resented because it seems to deny the reality of non-verbal experience. In this latter view meaning resides in experience, in things, in 'life', which we use language merely to refer to. But this is to confuse meaning with reference, it is, as Wittgenstein says, to confound the *meaning* of a name with the *bearer* of a name. Meaning, we might risk saying, resides in the application of a concept to a thing in particular circumstances. 'Just as a move in chess doesn't consist merely in moving a piece in such and such a way on the board—nor yet in one's feelings and thoughts as one makes the move: but in the circumstances that we call "playing a game of chess", "solving a chess problem", and so on.'*

It is true that this leaves us problematically situated in relation to 'reality'. We 'know' that there is a reality outside language, but we have no means of describing it except through language: language, as someone succinctly put it, is an experiment without a control. This makes the practice of criticism particularly difficult, but it is evidently the price we pay for being human.

It follows from what I have been saying that there is no mental act involved in the creation of a novel, however far one projects back, which is not conducted in language. There is no point at which we can say: up to this point the author was sorting out the basic life-stuff, and then afterwards he began to put it into words; because it has been in words all the time. To be sure, the words change, and are incremented, as the novel acquires body and definition in the ongoing process of composition, but 'it' is changing and being incremented *pari passu*. There is in fact no substantive 'it' which remains constant throughout the creation of a novel. 'It' is only available for observation when the compositional process is temporarily or finally arrested, and 'it' is never the same at any two such points. The final text of a novel is not therefore evidence from which we infer how the author saw, and how he meant us to see, a certain complex of experience; it is the criterion—the only criterion—of what he is seeing, and how he is seeing it, and how he means us to see it.†

I must emphasize that I do not wish to prohibit Bradbury or anyone

---

* Wittgenstein again. I have taken these philosophical hints at second hand from John Casey's *The Language of Criticism* (London, 1966), pp. 2–3. For a fuller argument that consciousness is dependent on verbal concepts see J. M. Cameron's essay 'Poetry and Dialectic' in *The Night Battle* (London, 1962), especially pp. 142–6.
† I borrow this formula from John Casey (*op. cit.*, p. 106): 'Shakespeare's language is (in some wide sense) a *criterion*—the central criterion—of how he is seeing and feeling, not evidence on the basis of which we can make an inference. When what is seen and felt is essentially bound up with a mastery of language, the language is the only criterion. Macbeth's capacity to feel as he does when he hears of his wife's death is bound up with his capacity to speak as he does: the feelings "expressed" by the "tomorrow and tomorrow and tomorrow" lines are inseparable from a

else from discussing the 'structure' of novels; I am merely affirming that he can usefully do so only by virtue of his responsiveness to their language, and that, conversely, explicit critical attention to language does not, as he implies, involve the neglect of 'structure', and what he includes under that category. Let me take the question of the 'devised chain of events' to which he attaches cardinal importance, or in other words, plot. Plot I take to denote the invention and arrangement of events to show their sequence in time and their connections of cause and effect. In a sense every work of literature must have a plot, since language, being itself extended in time, cannot stand still, despite the efforts of some modern poets to create that illusion. Plot, however, is especially significant in narrative literature, where it characteristically operates to arouse and appease our hopes, fears and curiosity about the fortunes of certain characters. At first sight plot, and the skill necessary to create one, seem to have nothing to do with language, but this is an illusion. It is certainly possible to communicate a plot by non-verbal means—in a silent movie, for example—but scarcely without the assistance of language. For, to take the example of the silent movie, by what other means is the story to be devised and the contributions of those concerned to be co-ordinated?

The case of the novelist is still more clear-cut. He is committed to language all along the line: the first glimmer of an idea, the first hesitant vague shaping of a possible story, requires not only a lexis with which to name things, but a grammar with which to relate them, and this dependence on language can only become more pressing as the compositional process proceeds. We might indeed in a stylized way describe the prefigured plot as a single, simple sentence which in the creative process quickly becomes a complex sentence through the insertion of subordinate clauses carrying further ramifications until the weight of subordination makes these clauses break off into independent complex sentences of their own, which in turn produce further sentences, and so on, each new development burgeoning and branching from another, not evenly or predictably, but (the favourite organicist analogy is irresistible) like a tree, until it stands, fully grown, one huge complex feat of language from root to blossom.

O chestnut tree, great-rooted blossomer,
Are you the leaf, the blossom or the bole?

mastery of language. To try and speak about these feelings apart from their expression would be to try and talk about a non-entity.' In the theatre, of course, the 'expression' is not entirely linguistic. But this problem does not concern the novel.

Well, we all know the answer to that one, and it certainly isn't the seed. So that when, for the purposes of describing a plot, we try to reduce the innumerable sentences through which it is communicated—if not to a single, simple sentence, at least to a few complex ones—we shall not produce anything resembling those first *ur*-sentences of the fore-shadowed novel. Nor shall we produce anything that in itself conveys the quality or value of the reading experience.

Thus, if we say that it was very clever of Jane Austen to invent a ituation in which Emma thinks that Mr Elton is courting Harriet when he is really courting Emma, and Mr Elton thinks that Emma is leading him on when she is merely officiously trying to promote Harriet's prospects, we can't mean that this situation is inherently significant, has any persuasive power, merely as a situation in which any three people might find themselves. We can only mean that it is significant and persuasive because it happens to three characters who have been richly realized for us in other ways, because it grows out of and adds to what we already know of them, and because it is not presented to us as a bald fact, as it appears in our summary, but as a process, subtly and delicately rendered for us in a sequence of small, perfectly-judged effects. And if pressed to substantiate this argument we should inevitably end up by indicating and analysing linguistic manœuvres on the author's part.

Now in actual critical practice such explicit demonstration is not necessarily binding on the critic, but it must always be implicit and, as it were, producible on demand. Consider, for example, Percy Lubbock's justly esteemed book *The Craft of Fiction* (1921). This follows what one might call a structural approach, in that Lubbock takes 'the whole intricate question of method in the craft of fiction . . . to be governed by the question of the point of view—the question of the relation in which the narrator stands to the story', and that question is one that, usually, is decided early in the compositional process and conditions the range of effects available in a given novel. (I say *usually* because it is always possible to introduce a new point of view at a late stage—as late as an epilogue—and thus open up an entirely new range of effects.) Using this approach, Lubbock examines very perceptively a dozen or so major novels and enhances our understanding and appreciation of them in the process. He does so without, I believe, giving a single illustrative quotation from his texts. Yet we cannot say that the narrative strategies he is examining have any life except insofar as they are embodied in these texts, in language; and he carries us with him precisely to the degree that his own sensitive and delicate use of language conveys to us, or revives in us, a sense of that life. Similarly, our differences with him must appeal to the same criteria, in matters both major and minor. When Lubbock asserts that we never for a moment move outside Strether's point of view in *The Ambassadors*, we must point, for instance, to the explicit appearance of an authorial 'I' in the first chapter, and the description of Strether's physical appearance through the eyes of Maria Gostrey in the same place. And when Lubbock claims that the narrative method of *The Ambassadors* is the 'ideal' method, implying that it has some inherent virtue which would be conferred upon any novel that used the same basic strategy, we must protest, no, you have only shown us that it is the ideal method for *The Ambassadors*.

To summarize: my position is that all good criticism is a response to language—that it is good insofar as it is a sensitive response—whether or not there is any explicit reference to language in the way of quotation and analysis. This applies not only to the 'structural' approach, but to the moral, mythical, historical, psycho-analytical and thematic approaches too; and it explains, I believe, why we can profit from criticism using radically different approaches from our own. Does this mean that any approach is as good as any other? Not quite—I must believe that criticism responsibly aware of its engagement with language is less likely to go seriously wrong than criticism which is not so aware, or which denies the primacy of language in literary matters. But I think we have to admit that any given method is justified by the use made of it by a particular critic. Critical methods do not compete with each other *as methods* (they may of course conflict over the interpretation and evaluation of a particular work)—they complement each other. We can see them as competing only if we pursue some phantom of total accounting. There is no satisfactory total account of a work of literature except the work itself. It is only the work itself that presents *all* its meanings in the most significant and assimilable form. We therefore cannot ask the critic to tell us the 'whole truth' about a novel, any more than we can ask a novelist to tell us the whole truth about life. Criticism does not—cannot—aim to reproduce the work it contemplates. It sets beside this work another work—the critical essay—which is a kind of hybrid formed by the collaboration of the critic with the artist, and which, in this juxtaposition, makes the original yield up some of its secrets.

Criticism, then, cannot avoid being partial and selective. Percy Lubbock's discussion of *The Ambassadors*, for example, which slices a thin layer off the whole surface of the novel, is no less selective than Ian Watt's article on 'The First Paragraph of *The Ambassadors*' which cuts deep into one small part of it. They are selecting differently, to different ends. Furthermore, Watt's article presupposes a knowledge of Lubbock's, or rather an equivalent acquaintance with and understanding of the novel's total scope and narrative strategy.

'We are inclined to assume', Bradbury complains, 'that if we can show that the imagery of cash and legality runs through a Jane Austen novel, or a whiteness-blackness opposition runs through *Moby Dick*, we can show more about the real being of the book than by showing that it deals with a society, with dispositions of character and relationship, so as to create a coherent moral and social world and an attitude towards it, steadily worked from page to page.' I would say, rather, we assume that the fact that each novel deals with a society, with dispositions of character and relationship, can be taken as common ground between readers; and that the 'steady working from page to page' by which the social and moral world is created and by which our responses are controlled is precisely what the tracing of iterative imagery and the like is designed to explain and illustrate. Such tracing can give us a model, a clue, a key—call it what you will—that enhances our response to the complex original.

It will be evident that a rather misleading flag is flying over this essay. Perhaps it should have been called 'Against a Poetics of Fiction'. I am certainly sceptical of the possibilities of formulating a poetics of the novel analogous to that which Aristotle formulated for the tragic drama of his time, not only because the novel is a much more amorphous genre than fifth-century Greek tragedy, but because so many of the philosophical assumptions underlying Aristotle's descriptive apparatus have been undermined. Furthermore, in the present state of modern knowledge, we cannot expect to agree upon any descriptive or analytic scheme which will serve all the purposes literary criticism may apply itself to. I am far from claiming that the fundamental axiom that novels are verbal constructs yields any foolproof or exclusive prescriptions for critical procedure.

I do believe, however, that if, in Aristotelian fashion, we try to define the novel as a genre by reference to its distinguishing characteristics, we shall find its way of using language the most promising area for enquiry. Bradbury suggests that the novel is distinguished as a genre by 'its scale, prose character and matter'. It is evident, however, that there is nothing we can say about the scale and matter typical of novels that cannot be matched in poems (like *Don Juan*) or in non-literary narrative fictions such as movies and TV serials. We are left, then, with 'prose-character'.

Now, of course, the use of prose for narrative is not peculiar to the novel, but I think we can say that the emergence of the novel as a literary phenomenon—the way it defines itself against earlier forms of prose fiction and, once established, exerts a magnetic attraction over all forms of prose fiction—is closely associated with the use of a certain kind of prose language, designed to render experience in a certain way, for which our handiest term is 'realism'. This, of course, is Ian Watt's argument in *The Rise of the Novel*, and it seems to me substantially correct. It is, I think, reconcilable with the scheme more recently proposed by Scholes and Kellogg in *The Nature of Narrative*, according to which the novel is seen as a modern synthesis of 'fictional' and 'empirical' modes (romance and allegory on the one hand, history and fictional realism on the other) which were originally held together in the synthesis of the primitive oral epic, but which fragmented and developed separately in late classical and medieval literature. For while the novel certainly includes all these modes in various ways, and therefore cannot be properly regarded as antithetical to any of them, there is little doubt that realism (what Scholes and Kellogg call, rather confusingly, 'mimesis') is the dominant or synthesizing mode. Modern prose fictions with a marked romantic or allegorical character (*The Blithedale Romance*, *The Trial*, and *Giles Goat-boy*, for example) are distinctly different, in the kind of response they invite, from classical or medieval allegories and romances, even when the latter are written in prose. And this difference, I suggest, resides in the kind of 'illusion of life' with which such modern texts invest their actions, however fantastic, and which they derive from the more orthodox novel tradition and the kind of language used in that tradition. I am not saying that all novels are realistic; I am saying that realism conditions all novels.

Let me return to something I said earlier: that the notion that consciousness is dependent on verbal concepts is resented because it seems to deny the reality of non-verbal or pre-verbal experience. This is because as living, acting, responding individuals we are conscious of our sensations, desires, fears, and choices, but we are not usually conscious of our consciousness of them, and to be doubly conscious in that way, at least all the time, would appear to dissipate the unique significance of what we are experiencing. Thus when we fall in love, we are not conscious that it is only by virtue of possessing a common concept of 'falling in love' that we do so, and if this is pointed out to us we are likely to feel that the spontaneity and integrity of our emotion is impugned. This is a natural reaction, and it may well be that without the illusion from which it derives we should be paralysed as regards action. It does not, however, affect the actual state of affairs.

The case of literature is rather different. In most traditional literature, especially poetry and poetic drama, the 'double consciousness' I have spoken of is deliberately brought into play—the verbal conceptualization of experience is overtly stressed in verbal artifice; so that in reading a Shakespeare sonnet, or beholding a Shakespeare play, for instance, we are simultaneously conscious of being put in touch with a bit of life, and of having this bit of life presented to us in a particular way, which imposes aesthetic distance on it. Among the various literary forms, this distance is, notoriously, most foreshortened in the novel. No other literary form immerses us so completely in the life it presents; no other form takes such pains to disguise the fact that it is an artefact. There is no need to dwell on the devices and strategies it uses to this end—solidity of specification, continuity with history, etc.—except to note that they naturally require as medium that kind of written language which we use to record and describe actual events, namely the prose of historiography, essays, letters, diaries, and so forth.

At the same time, the novel, being fictive, is committed to rendering experience with an enhanced sense of order and harmony, and this obligation pulls the novelist in the opposite direction, towards a heightened version of experience and a heightened use of language. Thus the novelist is constantly divided between two imperatives—to create and invent freely, and to observe a degree of realistic decorum.* And it is precisely this dynamic tension that has made the novel the dominant literary form in an age when, as Frank Kermode has pointed out,[2] the paradigms that we impose—that we *must* impose—upon discrete 'reality' come under the maximum degree of sceptical scrutiny.

* What I mean by this second imperative can be illustrated by another quotation from Flaubert, writing to a friend in 1856: 'Try, my good fellow, and send me by next Sunday, or sooner if you can, the following morsels of medical information. They are going up the slopes, Homais is looking at the blind man with the bleeding eyes (you know the mask) and he makes him a speech; he uses scientific words, thinks that he can cure him, and gives him his address. It is, of course, necessary that Homais should make a mistake, for the poor beast is incurable. If you have not enough in your medicine-bag to supply me with the material for five or six sturdy

Arnold Kettle has called these two opposing tendencies within the novel 'life' and 'pattern',[3] and the history of the novel is very much the history of the compromises novelists have struck between them. 'Pattern' certainly includes those deliberate arrangements of events to which Bradbury attaches great importance, but as I have already argued, we cannot ultimately dissociate such arrangements from verbal arrangements. It is language—specifically the language of prose—which has to bear the strain of reconciling the life and the pattern; and the great novelists are those who in very different ways have managed to stretch their medium to encompass both ends simultaneously. I therefore maintain that the explicit analysis of the language of novels is likely to be a particularly fruitful approach. In the case of those novels (perhaps the majority) which accord a high degree of respect to the demands of realistic decorum, such analysis will be mainly concerned with demonstrating how language that appears to serve only the purpose of 'life' also serves the purpose of 'pattern'. (This might take the form of, for instance, exposing the submerged imagery of cash and legality in a Jane Austen novel. But imagery is only one—perhaps the most obvious and accessible—kind of linguistic patterning which we can examine: the more closely we look, the more apparent it becomes that there is no aspect of Jane Austen's language that is innocent of persuasive purpose, that her choices of diction and syntax are at every point creating, ordering and judging the experience she offers to us.) As, particularly in the twentieth century, the notion of 'reality' on which the novel's realism was based, is called more and more into question, that kind of prose language which, I have suggested, is the staple of the novelist's medium, is more and more thickly overlaid with 'poetic' kinds of linguistic patterning, in an effort to render the flow of interior consciousness, or the operation of the individual and collective unconscious, or the life of visions, hallucinations and dreams. Joyce's progress from *Dubliners* to *Finnegans Wake* epitomizes the movement, and with fiction that belongs to the latter end of this spectrum there is not likely to be any argument that the critic is dealing with verbal artefacts. Indeed, with many such works, the critic is likely to find his earlier task inverted: that is, he may now be concerned to show that language which appears to serve only the purpose of 'pattern' also serves the purpose of 'life'. I hope this makes it clear that in

---

lines, draw from Follin and send it to me.' From J. C. Turner, *Gustave Flaubert as seen in his Works and Correspondence* (1895), reprinted by Ellmann and Feidelson, *op. cit.*, p. 243.

recommending an approach to the novel through language I am not seeking to deny or sever its connection with 'life', but merely asking that the crucial role of language in presenting life to us in literary fiction be adequately recognized.

4   Choice and Chance in Literary Composition: A Self-analysis

I

> I have often thought how interesting a magazine paper might
> be written by any author who would—that is to say who could—
> detail, step by step, the processes by which any one of his com-
> positions attained its ultimate point of completion. Why such a
> paper has never been given to the world, I am much at a loss
> to say—but, perhaps, the authorial vanity has had more to do
> with the omission than any one other cause. Most writers—poets
> in especial—prefer having it understood that they compose by a
> species of fine frenzy—an ecstatic intuition—and would positively
> shudder at letting the public take a peep behind the scenes, at
> the elaborate and vacillating crudities of thought—at the true
> purposes seized only at the last moment—at the innumerable
> glimpses of idea that arrived not at the maturity of full view—
> at the fully matured fancies discarded in despair as un-
> manageable—at the cautious selections and rejections—at the
> painful erasures and interpolations—in a word at the wheels and
> pinions—the tackle for scene-shifting—the step-ladders and
> demon traps—the cock's feathers, the red paint and the black
> patches, which, in ninety-nine cases out of a hundred,
> constitute the properties of the literary *histrio*.

With these words Edgar Allan Poe introduced an account of how he
composed his most celebrated poem, 'The Raven'. This essay, 'The
Philosophy of Composition', has teased several generations of readers
with the question of how far its author was being either serious or
truthful. 'The Raven', according to Poe, originated in the intention to
write 'a poem that should suit at once the popular and the critical
taste'. The ideal extent of such a poem, permitting sustained
intensity and pleasure, was estimated at approximately one hundred
lines. The effect aimed at was one of beauty, tinged with melancholy—
'the most legitimate of all the poetical tones'. The structural 'keynote'
or 'pivot' of the poem was to be a refrain ('the universality of its
employment sufficed to assure me of its intrinsic value'), ideally a
single word susceptible of variation in application, possessing the

sonority of the long 'o' in connection with 'r', and suggestive of melancholy. 'In such a search it would have been absolutely impossible to overlook the word "Nevermore". In fact, it was the very first which presented itself.' Only a non-rational creature could plausibly reiterate this single word and, after thinking first of a parrot, Poe decided on the more poetically appropriate raven. Grief for the death of a beloved woman suggested itself as a topic preeminently combining beauty and melancholy. And so on.

'The Philosophy of Composition' is highly disconcerting (and was clearly meant to be) to readers who admire 'The Raven' and at the same time subscribe to an inspirational and/or expressive theory of poetic creation. 'It is my design', Poe writes, 'to render it manifest that no one point of ['The Raven's'] composition is referable either to accident or intuition—that the work proceeded step by step to its completion with the precision and rigid consequence of a mathematical problem.' One need not, however, literally believe poetry to be the 'spontaneous overflow of powerful feelings' to feel a certain scepticism about Poe's essay: about, in particular, the omission of any kind of personal source for the poem, and about the absence (with a few minor exceptions, like the parrot) of any reference to the false starts, the selections and rejections of possibilities, the hesitations and last-minute discoveries, which Poe himself, in the passage first quoted, accuses other writers of wishing to conceal. Poe not only denies the operation of *chance* in literary composition—he also severely restricts the element of *choice*. He claims to have begun with an abstract, impersonal aim which was attained by a series of exclusive artistic decisions, each of which logically and inexorably dictated the next. If this were true, it would follow that every time Poe sat down to write a poem that 'should suit at once the popular and the critical taste' he would inevitably produce 'The Raven'.

Yet it must be admitted that much modern criticism of the kind that concentrates on rhetorical analysis (certainly much of my own) implies a model of the creative process not so far removed from Poe's. That is, in analysing a poem or prose work one is inevitably talking about effects; and effects imply a cause and a cause implies a causer. Even the most rigorous anti-intentionalist can scarcely avoid crediting, either implicitly or explicitly, the literary effects he admires, and the linguistic manœuvres by which they are obtained, to the mind of an author—seeing them as in some sense the product of deliberate choice. It is almost as difficult to avoid giving the impression that one's analysis re-enacts the process of composition, like a slow-motion replay in a sports telecast. In this way criticism implies a 'philosophy of composition' which is certainly unrealistically logical and economical.

There are, however, good reasons why criticism may do this without being compromised—why in most cases it cannot really do anything else. Except for those cases where the author's drafts, revisions and notebooks are available, the critic is bound to assume that the work was put together in the same orderly and deliberate manner in which he has taken it apart. This is not really to flatter or misrepresent the artist, because the artist is usually aiming for just that impression. He knows all the hesitations, omissions, revisions, all the possibilities considered and discarded in the process of composition; he may have embarked on his work without any clear idea of how it would develop, or with ideas which were repeatedly exchanged for new ones; but he aims at a finished product which will appear to have been planned and executed in a single flawless design; for it is this sense of a perfectly realized unity, each part fitting in with the other parts and with the whole, and apparently achieved with effortless grace and economy, that characterizes, for their readers, the great works of literature.

> I said, 'A line will take us hours maybe;
> Yet if it does not seem a moment's thought,
> Our stitching and unstitching has been naught.'

Edgar Allan Poe seems to have been anxious to give such an impression in 'The Philosophy of Composition'; but when the writer explicitly invites us into his workshop we are, perhaps, entitled to a little more candour. In this spirit I propose to comment briefly on the genesis and composition of a short story of my own called 'The Man Who Wouldn't Get Up'. I choose this example not because I am particularly proud of it (though it is, I think, moderately successful within its very narrow limits) or because it is representative of my fiction (for I am primarily interested in the very different form of the novel), but because it is short enough to be reproduced here. There is an additional reason: that this story happened to be quite significantly changed as the result of an outside intervention—an occurrence which raises the question of choice and chance in writing in a particularly pointed form.

II

The Man Who Wouldn't Get Up

His wife was always the first to get up. As soon as the alarm rang she threw back the bedclothes, swung her legs to the floor and pulled on her dressing gown. Her self-discipline filled him with guilt and admiration.

'Now don't go lying in bed,' she said. 'I'm fed up with having your breakfast spoil.'

He made no reply, feigning sleep. As soon as she had left the room he rolled over into the warm trough that her body had left in the mattress, and stretched luxuriously. It was the most sensually satisfying moment of his day, this stretch into a new, but warm part of the bed. But it was instantly impaired by the consciousness that he would soon have to get up and face the rest of the day.

He opened one eye. It was still dark, but the streetlamps cast a faint blue illumination into the room. He tested the atmosphere with his breath, and saw it turn to steam. Where one of the curtains was pulled back he could see that ice had formed on the inside of the window. In the course of the morning the ice would melt and the water would roll down to rot the paintwork on the window frame. Some of the water would trickle under the window frame where it would freeze again, jamming the window and warping the wood.

He closed his eye to shut out the painful vision of his house corroding and disintegrating around him. He couldn't, of course, suppress his knowledge of what was wrong with it—of what was wrong, for instance, with the room he lay in: the long jagged crack in the ceiling that ran like a sneer from the electric light fixture to the door, the tear in the lino near the chest of drawers, the cupboard door that hung open because the catch had gone, the wallpaper that bulged in patches where the damp had detached it from the wall, so that it seemed to breathe gently in and out with the opening and shutting of the door. . . . He could not suppress his knowledge of all this, but while he was snug under the blankets, with his eyes shut tight, it was all somehow less oppressive, as if it had nothing to do with him personally.

It was only when he left the protection of the warm bed that he would stagger under the combined weight of dissatisfaction with his environment and despair of ever significantly improving it. And, of course, it wasn't just the bedroom. As he passed through the house the evidence of decay and disrepair would greet him at every turn: the dribbling tap in the bathroom, the broken banister on the staircase, the cracked window in the hall, the threadbare patch in the dining-room carpet that would be just a tiny bit bigger than yesterday. And it would be so cold, so cold. Icy draughts needling through keyholes, rattling the letter box, stirring the curtains.

And yet here, in bed, it was so warm and comfortable. The most luxuriously furnished, gas-fired centrally-heated, double-glazed and insulated ideal home could not make him more warm and comfortable than he was at this moment.

His wife rattled the poker in the dining-room grate: the dull, metallic sounds were borne to every corner of the house through the water-pipes. It was the signal that breakfast was laid. From the room opposite his own Paul and Margaret, his two children, who had been playing in the cold and the gloom with the cheerful imperviousness to discomfort of the very young, issued boisterously on to the landing and thumped heavily down the stairs. The broken banister creaked menacingly. The dining-room door opened and slammed shut. From the kitchen he heard the distant clamour of cutlery and cooking utensils. He pulled the bedclothes more tightly round his head, muffling his ears and leaving only his nose and mouth free to breathe. He did not want to hear these sounds, harsh reminders of a harsh world.

When he looked beyond the immediate problem of getting up, of coping with the tiresome chores of washing, shaving, clothing and feeding his body, he saw no more inviting prospect before him: only the long walk to the bus stop through streets of houses exactly like his own, the long wait in line, the slow, juddering progress through the choked city streets, and eight hours' drudgery in a poky office which was, like his home, all full of broken things, discoloured, faded, chipped, scratched, grimy, malfunctioning things. Things which said as plainly as the interior of his house: this is your lot; try as hard as you like, but you will never significantly improve it; count yourself ucky if you can prevent it from deteriorating more rapidly.

He tried to gird his spirits preparatory to getting up by reminding himself how fortunate he was compared to many others. He forced his mind to dwell upon the sick and the dying, those in need, those in mental anguish. But the spectacle of human misery thus conjured up merely confirmed his helpless apathy. That others were able to bear these burdens with cheerful resignation gave him no encouragement: what hope had he of emulating them if his present discontents were enough to deprive his life of joy? What comfort was it that his present dreary existence was a fragile crust over an infinitely worse abyss into which he might plunge at any moment?

The fact was, he no longer had any love of life. The thought pierced him with a kind of thrill of despair. I no longer love life. There is nothing in life which gives me pleasure any more. Except this: lying in bed. And the pleasure of this is spoiled because I know that I have got to get up. Well, then, why don't I just not get up? Because you've got to get up. You have a job. You have a family to support. Your wife has got up. Your children have got up. They have done their duty. Now you have to do yours. Yes, but it's easy for them. They still love life. I don't any more. I only love this: lying in bed.

He heard, through the wadding of bedclothes, the voice of his wife calling.

'George.'

She called flatly, expressionlessly, ritualistically, not expecting an answer. He gave none, but turned over on to his other side, and stretched out his legs. His toes encountered an icy hot-water bottle at the foot of the bed and recoiled. He curled himself up into a foetal posture and withdrew his head completely under the bedclothes. It was warm and dark under the bedclothes, a warm dark cave. He inhaled the warm, fusty air with pleasure, and when it became dangerously deoxygenated he created cunning air-ducts in the bedclothes which admitted fresh air without light.

He heard very faintly his wife calling 'George'. More sharply, imperatively this time. It meant that his family had already consumed their corn-flakes and the bacon was now cooked. Now the tension began to build between the longing to stay in bed and the urgency of rising. He contracted his limbs into a tighter coil and wriggled deeper into the mattress as he waited for the third summons.

'George!'

This meant he was now too late for breakfast—might with luck manage to swallow a cup of tea before he rushed out to catch his bus.

For what seemed like a long time, he held his breath. Then he suddenly relaxed and stretched out his limbs. He had decided. He would not get up. The secret was not to think of the consequences. Just to concentrate on the fact of staying in bed. The pleasure of it. The warmth, the comfort. He had free will. He would exercise it. He would stay in bed.

He must have dozed for a while. He was suddenly conscious of his wife in the room.

'It's a quarter past eight. Your breakfast's spoiled . . . George . . . are you getting up? . . . George?' He detected a note of fear in her voice. Suddenly the bedclothes were lifted from his face. He pulled them back, annoyed that all his cunning air-vents had been disturbed. 'George, are you ill?'

He was tempted to say, yes, I'm ill. Then his wife would tip-toe away, and tell the children to be quiet, their father was ill. And later she would light a fire in the bedroom and bring him a tray of tempting food. But that was the cowardly course; and the deception would only earn him, at the most, a day's respite from the life he hated. He was nourishing a grander, more heroic plan.

'No, I'm not ill,' he said through the bedclothes.

'Well, get up then, you'll be late for work.'

He did not answer, and his wife left the room. He heard her banging about irritably in the bathroom, calling to the children to come and be washed. The lavatory cistern flushed and refilled noisily, the pipes whined and hummed, the children laughed and cried. Outside in the street footsteps hurried past on the pavement, cars wheezed, reluctant to start in the cold morning air, fired and moved away. He lay quiet under the bedclothes, concentrating, contemplating. Gradually he was able to eliminate all these noises from his consciousness. The way he had chosen was a mystical way.

The first day was the most difficult. His wife thought he was being merely idle and delinquent, and tried to make him get up by refusing to bring him any food. The fast caused him no great distress, however, and he stuck to his bed all day except for discreet, unobserved visits to the bathroom. When his wife retired that night she was angry and resentful. She complained because she hadn't been able to make the bed properly, and she held herself cold and rigid at the very edge of the mattress furthest from himself. But she was puzzled and guilty too, because he hadn't eaten. There was a note of pleading in her voice when she hoped he would have had enough of this silly nonsense by the next morning.

The next morning was much easier. He simply went off to sleep again as soon as the alarm had stopped ringing, untroubled by guilt or anxiety. It was blissful. Just to turn over and go to sleep again, knowing you weren't going to get up. Later, his wife brought him a breakfast tray and left it, wordlessly, on the floor beside his bed. His children came to the door of the bedroom and stared in at him while he ate. He smiled reassuringly at them.

In the afternoon, the doctor came, summoned by his wife. He marched breezily into the room and demanded,

'Well, now, what appears to be the trouble, Mr Barker?'

'No trouble, Doctor,' he replied gently.

The doctor gave him a brief examination and concluded: 'No reason at all why you shouldn't get out of bed, Mr Barker.'

'I know there isn't,' he replied. 'But I don't want to.'

The next day it was the vicar. The vicar begged him to think of his responsibilities as a husband and father. There were times, one knew only too well, when the struggle to keep going seemed too much to bear, when the temptation simply to give in became almost irresistible ... But that was not the true Christian spirit. 'Say not the struggle naught availeth. ...'

'What about contemplative monks?' he asked. What about hermits, solitaries, column-squatters?

Ah, but that kind of religious witness, though possibly efficacious in its own time, was not in harmony with modern spirituality. Besides, he could hardly claim that there was anything ascetic or penitential about his particular form of retreat from the world.

'It isn't all roses, you know,' he told the vicar.

And it wasn't. After seven days, he began to get bed-sores. After a fortnight, he was too weak to walk unaided to the bathroom. After four weeks he remained permanently confined to his bed, and a nurse was employed to care for his bodily needs. He wasn't sure where the money was coming from to pay for the nurse, or indeed to maintain the house and his family. But he found that simply by not worrying about such problems, they solved themselves.

His wife had lost most of her resentment by now. Indeed he rather thought she respected him more than ever before. He was, he gathered, becoming something of a local, and even national, celebrity. One day a television camera was wheeled into his bedroom, and propped up on the pillows, holding the hand of his wife, he told his story to the viewing millions: how one cold morning he had suddenly realized that he no longer had any love of life, and his only pleasure was in lying in bed, and how he had taken the logical step of lying in bed for the rest of his life, which he did not expect to be protracted much longer, but every minute of which he was enjoying to the full.

After the television broadcast, the trickle of mail through the letter box became a deluge. His eyes were growing weak, and he relied on volunteers from the parish to help him with the correspondence.

Most of the letters pleaded with him to give life another chance, enclosing money or offers of lucrative employment. He declined the offers politely, and banked the money in his wife's name. (She used some of it to have the house redecorated; it amused him to watch the painters clambering about the bedroom; when they whitewashed the ceiling he covered his head with a newspaper.)

There was a smaller, but to him more significant number of letters sending him encouragement and congratulations. 'Good luck to you, mate', said one of them, 'I'd do the same if I had the guts.' And another, written on the notepaper of a famous university, said: 'I deeply admire your witness to the intolerable quality of modern life and to the individual's inalienable right to opt out of it: you are an existentialist saint.' Though he wasn't clear about the meaning of all these words, they pleased him. Indeed, he had never felt so happy and so fulfilled as he did now.

And now, more than ever, he thought it would be sweet to die. Though his body was washed and fed and cared for, he felt vitality slowly ebbing away from it. He longed to put on immortality. It seemed as if he had solved not only the problem of life, but the problem of death too. There were times when the ceiling above his head became the canvas for some vision such as the old painters used to draw on the roofs of chapels: he seemed to see angels and saints peering down at him from a cloudy empyrean, beckoning him to join them. His body felt strangely weightless, as if only the bed-clothes restrained it from rising into the air. Levitation! Or even . . . apotheosis! He fumbled with the blankets and sheets, but his limbs were weak. Then, with a supreme effort, he wrenched the bedclothes aside and flung them to the floor.

He waited, but nothing happened. He grew cold. He tried to drag the blankets back on to the bed, but the effort of throwing them off had exhausted him. He shivered. Outside it was getting dark. 'Nurse,' he called faintly; but there was no response. He called his wife, 'Margaret', but the house remained silent. His breath turned to steam on the cold air. He looked up at the ceiling, but there were no heads of angels and saints looking down: only a crack in the plaster that ran like a sneer from the door to the light fixture. And suddenly he realized what his eternity was to be. 'Margaret! Nurse!' he cried hoarsely. 'I want to get up! Help me up!'

But no one came.

III

Most writers (and I do not mean only imaginative or professional writers, but anyone who has grappled seriously with the problems of communicating *via* the written word) could point to things in their writing attributable to either chance or choice. Whenever one hesitates over a word, or changes a word, one clearly makes a conscious choice; when one gratefully accepts a misprint or typing error (as, in my own experience, a description of mountain peaks and glaciers 'rolling into the blue distance' came out of the typewriter, much improved, as 'reeling into the blue distance') one makes use of chance. But most of the process of composition goes on in an intermediate, twilight area between these two poles, in which the writer is neither making deliberate choices nor being simply the medium of chance (or of the Muse or the Collective Unconscious or his own unconscious). What he is doing, I believe, is in fact making choices—but making them so quickly that he is not conscious of doing so. Language is such a complex system of communication that it is virtually impossible to employ it and at the same time to be aware of *how* one is employing it without bringing communication to a grinding halt. The experience of painfully constructing a sentence in a foreign language in which one is not fluent gives some idea of how unnatural it is to be conscious of the grammatical rules one is operating in making the simplest utterance—rules which the native speaker of the language has learned so thoroughly that he employs them 'instinctively' or 'intuitively'. The writer is concerned not merely with the simple rules or structures which permit functional communication, but also with rhetorical delicacies and subtleties; but he too is drawing all the time from a reservoir of verbal concepts, and methods of connecting them, which he has learned: and he does so, when he is in full spate, with the same kind of instinctive or intuitive reflex action. What rhetorical analysis does for the poem or novel, therefore, is comparable to what the grammar does for a language: giving a logical, linear, deliberate account of a process which in practice is largely intuitive and instantaneous and unreflective. Hence the common phenomenon of critics finding things in works of literature which their authors were not conscious of putting there. It is equally possible for the author himself to find in his own work things he was not conscious of putting there at the time of composition, and this is partly my own experience with respect to 'The Man Who Wouldn't Get Up'.

For example: it seems to me that the effectiveness (if this is granted) of the passage in which George is called by his wife and disobeys the summons is partly dependent on the fact that the summons is repeated three times—that a thrice-repeated summons is more effective here than two repetitions or four would have been, because the number three is traditionally associated with moments of crisis, challenge or existential choice (the most obvious examples are Christ's temptation by Satan, and Peter's denial of Christ, but there are many instances in romance, myth, and in popular folk-lore, as in the notion that one sinks three times before drowning). I was certainly not conscious of this when I wrote the passage, but I do not think that it was therefore fortuitous, or 'inspired', or the operation of the Collective Unconscious. I would prefer to call it an instinctive choice of an archetypal narrative device which I have learned through reading and possibly employed before, which came readily to hand in the act of writing and seemed to fit so well that no conscious formulation of cause and effect was entailed.

It must be admitted that testimony of this kind is never entirely trustworthy because of the natural fallibility of the human memory, and also because in the case of creative writing there seems to be a tendency for a choice, once made, to suppress or erase the memory of other possible choices, presumably in the interests of concentration. One of the most crucial choices involved in the composition of my story, as of any story, was the choice of narrative method, telling the story from George's point of view in the third person. Clearly the story would have a quite different effect if the 'same' events were related by an omniscient, intrusive author, or by George himself in the first person or from the point of view of his wife. In retrospect it seems that the method used is the only possible one that would communicate the character's extreme and obsessive state of mind both sympathetically and yet with a certain ironic distance, and I cannot recall having entertained any other possibilities; but it may be that my memory is at fault. Looking up the first draft manuscript of the story I find that I originally began it with the first passage of dialogue:

'Now don't go lying in bed,' said his wife as she pulled on her
dressing gown. 'I'm fed up with having your breakfast spoil.'

These words are crossed out in the ms., and the story begins, as printed:

His wife was always the first to get up. . . .

In the original opening the phrase 'his wife' implies that at the outset George was to be the observing and recording consciousness of the story, but this implication is much more emphatic in the revised opening, which characterizes the wife not as an independent person speaking her own mind, but as a reflector of George's depressed and guilty consciousness. The wife's spoken words (exactly the same words) have a slightly but significantly different effect coming after this narrative perspective has been established—they belong more obviously to the alien outside 'life' George is going to reject.

This emendation seems to be the result of a conscious choice. But the point I want to make is that the kind of explanations a writer may make about his own work, about artistic intention, cause and effect, are very much the kind of explanations a critic makes about a text, and are almost as far from the realities of the creative process.

Looking over my story with a critical eye I note various features: for example, that the pace of the narrative accelerates markedly in the second half, after a fairly leisurely exposition in the first half; that there is a good deal of slightly unorthodox or 'deviant' handling of direct and indirect speech; that the last two full-length paragraphs are in marked stylistic contrast. And I can provide reasons for all these features. The first half of the story is leisurely because the character's situation and mood have to be established in some depth and density to make his subsequent behaviour persuasive, but once established, events can move fast—and must move fast if the reader's scepticism about their plausibility is to be allayed. The incorporation of direct speech into indirect speech without conventional punctuation ('He was tempted to say, yes, I'm ill'), the use of interior dialogue in the same form ('Well, then, why don't I just not get up? Because you've got to get up . . .') in the first part of the story, emphasizes the location of the experience in the obsessed consciousness of the main character; and the rapid elisions from direct speech to indirect speech and back again in the interview with the vicar have a similar effect and at the same time usefully permit a high degree of condensation and an element of caricature. The penultimate full-length paragraph shows the hero indulging in delusions of grandeur, while the following paragraph shows the collapse of these delusions and the revelation of a bleak and uncomfortable truth. It is, therefore, expressively appropriate that the former paragraph is characterized by literary allusion, rhetorically patterned syntax and grandiloquent diction, while the latter is characterized by short sharp sentences mainly of a simple subject-predicate construction using simple diction referring to physical objects and sensations.

I can say fairly confidently that I was not, at the time of writing the story, conscious *in these terms* of employing these devices; but the explanations I have given seem to me to be valid ones and to reflect, albeit in an overly logical and orderly way, choice rather than chance.

IV

Even the elements in literary composition most obviously governed by chance (like the useful misprint) come within the province of the author's choice, since he is at liberty to accept or reject such windfalls. The original *donnée* of any work is in some sense the product of chance since it is dependent on the largely fortuitous circumstances of the author's own life. If Conrad hadn't taken that job in the Belgian Congo, if Henry James hadn't gone to that dinner party with Archbishop Benson, we should not have had *Heart of Darkness* and *The Turn of the Screw*. But for every such 'idea' that a writer has and works on, he probably has a hundred others which he rejects and forgets; and the one that 'takes' immediately raises multiple problems of choice, some of which are resolved deliberately and some 'intuitively'.

My own story had its origin in a period of depression I suffered some years ago, occasioned chiefly by acute dissatisfaction with the house I was then occupying and frustration of my attempts to find another of the kind I wanted at a price I could afford, but also due partly to 'withdrawal symptoms' following a return to England after a fairly euphoric year in the United States. One of the most cardinal symptoms of mental depression, in my experience, is that at the moment of awakening from sleep one is at once reminded of the immediate cause of the depression, which seems to poison the whole of one's existence; one desires more than anything else to return to the oblivion of sleep; one puts off as long as possible the moment of rising, and yet even as one clings to the warmth and passiveness of the dozing state one's pleasure is spoiled by feelings of guilt and the knowledge that eventually one will have to get up and face the day.

It will be fairly obvious how this experience developed into the idea of a story about a man who *didn't* get up—whose dissatisfaction with his life and environment and craving for the womb-like warmth and passivity of bed reached a sufficiently intense pitch as to encourage him to violate all the sanctions which impel us, in the end, to get up. It will be obvious, too, how the particular occasion of my own depression at this time—my house—has become the chief focus of my character's depression. Yet of course what happens in the story—the hero's decision to stay in bed, and the consequences—has no analogy in my own experience; and I have never, I am happy to say, seen my life in such bleak terms of irredeemable banality and impoverishment as my character sees his. The story had its origin in a kind of wish-fulfilment fantasy of escape, and the writing of it was in a sense therapeutic; but I would like to think that the imaginative exploration of the possibilities of my personal experience has more representative, public, significance than any strictly factual account of that experience would have had.

At the end of the story the hero is dying and realizes that his eternity—his hell, if you like—is going to be a room in just the state—cold and neglected—in which his bedroom was at the beginning of the story, representing a return to a state of being he thought he had escaped from for ever. In the original draft, however, the story had ended like this:

> He fumbled with the blankets and sheets, but his limbs were weak. Then, with a supreme effort, he wrenched the bedclothes aside and flung them to the floor. He was aware of cold and darkness. He was in space.
>
> 'What do you think you're doing?' said his wife. 'The alarm clock hasn't gone yet.'

In other words, the whole experience described in the story had been a dream: all the enormous effort and eventual triumph of the man who wouldn't get up had been an illusion and he was back where he had started, at the beginning of another intolerable day.

I cannot remember at this date at what point in the composition of the story I decided on this ending. It was certainly not at the outset, and I was not happy with it when I had finished the story mainly because the awakening from a dream is such a narrative cliché. But I couldn't see any other way of plausibly ending a story that, to my mind, was always hovering on the edge of fantasy. I sent off the story and heard a few weeks later that the editor of *The Weekend Telegraph* liked it, except for the ending. Was I prepared to change the ending? Couldn't the man die, the editor suggested, or just get fed up with the whole business and decide to get up? This latter suggestion didn't appeal to me at all. For George to get up and return to normal life would be too banal—it is what, after all, we all do in the end; and the effect of the story would then be to diminish the intensity of the man's utter disenchantment with life, his total withdrawal. I wanted to make the story a forceful, and up to a point sympathetic, account of the disenchantment and withdrawal, but I wanted an ironic ending which would leave the hero confronting a deeper, bitterer awareness of the hopelessness of his situation than he had to begin with. Hence the original idea of the dream, which left him exactly as he started but taunted by the memory of his illusory victory over circumstances.

The editor's other suggestion, however, that the man should die on the end, attracted me. The reason I hadn't considered it before was, I think, that I hadn't sufficient faith in the credibility of the story, especially its second half, to believe that it could sustain an ending on the same level of reality—it seemed to me that the illusion and the reader's assent were bound to crack eventually, and that it was best to accommodate this by the dream device. What interested me about the editor's suggestion was that he evidently did find the main story persuasive and credible enough to accept an ending on the same level of reality. But that level of reality wasn't, by the end of the story, quite the commonsense reality of everyday experience, and the death would therefore have to have some quality of ambiguity and even the uncanny. Eventually I decided that awareness of death should come to him in the shape of the physical environment with which he had started: 'And suddenly he knew what his eternity was to be.' I then added the words, '—a cold room that needed redecorating'. But I found this over-explicit, so I returned to a detail of the original description of the room, one that had pleased me most: the crack in the ceiling plaster that ran like a sneer from the door to the light fixture. To make the point clearer, I inserted a passage earlier about the bedroom, and specifically the ceiling, having been redecorated. The reappearance of the crack in the ceiling thus brought in the hint of the supernatural that I wanted as well as enhancing the unity of the story by connecting the beginning with the end in a fairly unobtrusive way.

Some readers may feel that this anecdote merely reveals that I am prepared to alter my work to suit my publishers. But, though I don't deny that I was anxious to get the story published, I believe that I improved the story by changing its ending. It is not, now, of course, the same story as the one I originally wrote. The revised ending significantly modifies the total effect—roughly speaking I would say that it punishes the hero more severely than the original ending, and turns it in the direction of a macabre, cautionary tale rather than a wry anecdote. But this was always, I think, a potential meaning of the basic situation and once discovered it seemed to me the right one. So I chose it.

Part III Fiction and Catholicism

5 Graham Greene

A buzzard flaps across a dusty Mexican square and settles heavily on a tin roof . . . in Brighton the lights go out above the black struts of the Palace Pier and the dark shifting water . . . in Saigon old wrinkled women in black trousers squat gossiping on the landing outside the *urinoir* . . . over Clapham Common solitary walkers move with bowed heads through the slanting rain . . . in West Africa the laterite roads turn a fragile pink at sundown, then are swallowed by darkness.

These are some characteristic scenes from a country of the mind known internationally as Greeneland. No one interested in modern literature has failed to explore it; but the explorers have brought back conflicting reports. The reception and reputation of Graham Greene's fiction is, indeed, a subject in itself. Briefly, he enjoys the admiration of reviewers, fellow novelists, and 'general readers', who praise particularly his 'craftsmanship', his ability to 'tell a story'; and of some critics with a vested interest in Christian or specifically Catholic literature. But in the mainstream of Anglo-American literary criticism his reputation does not ride so high. The bibliography of Greene studies grows longer and longer, but the proportion of unfriendly and depreciative criticism is enough to force Greene's admirers into a characteristically defensive stance.

It is difficult not to see behind a good deal of the hostile comment on Greene a certain academic suspicion of the popularly successful writer. But there is evidence that Greene himself is far from complacent about the kind of praise he has received. Frank Kermode has pointed out[1] that the sardonic fable of the jeweller, maker of ingenious jewelled eggs, in *A Burnt-Out Case* (1961) fits Greene himself as well as the character of Querry, the famous Catholic architect, to whom it is applied in the novel:

> Everyone said he was a master technician, but he was highly praised too for the seriousness of his subject-matter because on the top of each egg there was a gold cross set with chips of precious stones in honour of the King.

The popular image of Greene as a master technician with a crucifix hidden behind his back (or up his sleeve) obviously will not do. But his work does not fit into the categories that orthodox literary criticism has evolved in its appraisal of serious modern fiction. While the mass media of entertainment have figured as the villains in most contemporary cultural discussion, Greene has not only enjoyed popular success as a writer of thrillers and stories (like *The Third Man*) designed for the movies, but has drawn extensively on their conventions in his most ambitious work. In a period when the most influential school of criticism in England has proclaimed the duty of the novelist to be 'on the side of life', Greene has spoken eloquently on the side of death. Belonging by language and nationality to a tradition in the novel based essentially on the values of secularized Protestantism, Greene has adopted the alien dogmatic system of Roman Catholicism, and put it at the very centre of his mature work. Eschewing the 'poetic' verbal texture, the indifference to 'story', and the authorial impersonality of most of the accredited modern masters of fiction, Greene has cultivated the virtues and disciplines of prose, favoured involved and exciting plots, and reasserted the right of the novelist to comment on his characters and their actions.

The result of all this, one can't help thinking, is that Greene has represented for many critics a temptation of a kind to which criticism of the novel is always susceptible: the temptation to abstract from fiction the author's version of reality, measuring this against a supposedly normative version, rather than assessing the persuasiveness with which the novelist realizes his version. 'We must grant to the artist his subject, his idea, his *donnée*: our criticism is applied only to what he makes of it,' said Henry James (a novelist, incidentally, for whom Greene has enormous admiration). But many critics have not been prepared to grant Greene so much: in their view Greene's technical skill is not legitimate rhetoric, but a kind of trickery.

Part of the trouble, no doubt, is that Greene's *données* are often based on Catholic dogma and belief, on such assumptions as that there is such a thing as 'mortal' sin, that Christ is 'really and truly' present in the Eucharist, that miracles can occur in the twentieth century. The fictional endorsement of such ideas in the context of a pluralist and largely secular culture presents very real artistic problems. In seeking to convey to his non-Catholic audience a technical and emotional understanding of Catholic experience, the Catholic novelist risks arousing in this audience whatever extraliterary objections and suspicions it entertains about the Catholic Church as an active, proselytizing institution; while on his own part he has to grapple with the problem of retaining his artistic integrity while belonging to a

Church which has never accepted the individual's right to pursue intellectual and artistic truth in absolute freedom.

George Orwell argued in *Inside the Whale* (1940) that any kind of ideological orthodoxy was inimical to the production of good fiction. 'How many Roman Catholics have been good novelists?' he asked. 'Even the handful one could name have been bad Catholics.' Not a few of Greene's critics have implied that his conversion to Roman Catholicism was his undoing as a writer. Yet Greene's religious convictions were late in rising to the surface of his fiction, and they did so in precisely those novels that are, by general agreement, his best. This evidence does not, however, completely falsify Orwell's opinion. In an exchange of letters with Elizabeth Bowen and V. S. Pritchett (*Why Do I Write?* (1948)) Greene admitted that loyalty to his own imagination involved him in a certain 'disloyalty' to his Church. By this he meant that in pursuing his artistic aims he could not consult the counsels of religious prudence or the interests of ecclesiastical propaganda. The result has been that Greene's novels have offended Catholics at least as much as non-Catholics. *The Power and the Glory* (1940), for instance, provoked a condemnation from the Holy Office itself. The passing of time and, one hopes, the deepening of understanding have made the novel acceptable to Greene's co-religionists; but in the meantime he has found new ways of demonstrating his 'disloyalty'.

It is obvious that no writer subscribing to the Catholic faith could prevent it, even if he wished to, from invading his most deeply felt creative work. But Catholicism as a public system of laws and dogmas is far from being an adequate key to Greene's fiction. There is a good deal of evidence, internal and external, that in Greene's fiction Catholicism is not a body of belief requiring exposition and demanding categorical assent or dissent, but a system of concepts, a source of situations, and a reservoir of symbols with which he can order and dramatize certain intuitions about the nature of human experience— intuitions which were gained prior to and independently of his formal adoption of the Catholic faith. Regarded in this light, Greene's Catholicism may be seen not as a crippling burden on his artistic freedom, but as a positive artistic asset.

Graham Greene was born in 1904, the son of C. H. Greene, the headmaster of an English public school, Berkhamsted, which he himself attended as a pupil before entering Balliol College, Oxford. Greene read history but, like many Oxford undergraduates, he wrote poetry, publishing a 'slim volume', *Babbling April*, in 1925. In the same year he graduated from Oxford, and after a number of false starts, began a career in journalism, working first for the Nottingham *Journal*. It was in this industrial Midland city that Greene, an Anglican by upbringing, was received into the Catholic Church, in 1926. He moved to London to work as a sub-editor on the London *Times*, a post he resigned after the publication of his first novel, *The Man Within* (1929). Since that time Greene has been a freelance writer, except for brief spells of journalistic work in the 'thirties, and service with the British Government during World War II.

Greene has not yet published an autobiography, but he has made some interesting autobiographical revelations in his essays, prefaces, travel books, and other miscellaneous writings. Some of these revelations are so obviously dropped in the critic's path as clues to the fiction that, knowing Greene's reputation as an accomplished hoaxer and practical joker, one hesitates to pick them up. But the temptation to do so is irresistible. Of particular interest is the information about Greene's childhood and youth, for he frequently insists on the lasting effect of early experience on adult life.

'There is always a moment in childhood', comments the authorial voice of *The Power and the Glory*, 'when the door opens and lets the future in.' For Greene himself, we learn in his Mexican travel book *The Lawless Roads* (1939), the door was a real door, a door that crops up here and there in his fiction, the green baize door that separated his family's quarters, smelling of 'books and fruit and eau de cologne', from the corridors and dormitories of Berkhamsted school; and what it let in for the young Greene was nothing less than evil.

> In the land of . . . stone stairs and cracked bells ringing early, one
> was aware of fear and hate, a kind of lawlessness—appalling cruelties
> could be practised without a second thought; one met for the
> first time characters, adult and adolescent, who bore about them
> the genuine quality of evil . . . And so faith came to one—
> shapelessly, without dogma, a presence above a croquet lawn,
> something associated with violence, cruelty, evil across the way.
> One began to believe in heaven because one believed in hell, but
> for a long while it was only hell one could picture with a certain
> intimacy.

In the youthful Greene's gloomy intimations of immortality, it is easy to see the origin of that Manichaean or Jansenist colouring which critics have detected in the religious perspective of his fiction, in his vision of a fallen world for which the chances of redemption seem slender and difficult. Greene seems to confirm this analysis in the title essay of *The*

Lost Childhood, where he describes the effect of reading Marjorie Bowen's historical novel *The Viper of Milan* at the age of fourteen: 'she had given me my pattern—religion might later explain it to me in other terms, but the pattern was already there—perfect evil walking the world where perfect good can never walk again. . . .'

It may be doubted whether Greene has altogether done himself a service by these fascinating confessions. It is true that they echo or foreshadow views to be found in the fiction, but they do so more crudely and extravagantly; and they have perhaps given too much encouragement to critics anxious to apply to Greene his own observation (in an essay on Walter de la Mare) that 'every creative writer worth our consideration . . . is a victim: a man given over to an obsession'. Greene, like most writers—and perhaps most men—has more than one obsession, and in his fiction generally has them well under control.

One of these obsessions—the impact of childhood experience—has already been mentioned. Another is certainly death. A prey to boredom, melancholy, and disgust from an early age, Greene has evidently found death an alluring prospect or one whose imminence can revive the will to live. In his remarkable essay 'The Revolver in the Corner Cupboard' he describes various suicidal experiments he made in youth. Years later, sick and lost in Liberia, he discovered in himself 'a thing I thought I had never possessed: a love of life'. In the Introduction to a new edition of *It's a Battlefield* he writes, 'as one approaches death one lives ahead; perhaps it is a hurry to be gone'. Many of Greene's characters seem to be in a hurry to be gone. With the unimportant exception of *Loser Takes All* (1955), all Greene's novels and entertainments involve the death—usually violent, sometimes suicidal—of one or more of the chief characters. If 'hurry' is a misnomer it is because these characters have religious misgivings about the afterlife, or, like Fowler in *The Quiet American* (1955), they find that 'though my reason wanted death, I was afraid like a virgin of the act'. The last image reminds one of another Greeneian obsession: the association of death with the 'little death' of sexual love.

Then there is the obsession with treachery and betrayal—the 'Judas complex' which Greene has detected in Henry James, but which is far more evident in his own work. To betrayal we may add other moral and emotional abstractions that haunt Greene's imaginative writing: trust and distrust, justice and injustice, pity, responsibility, innocence, jealousy. Beyond this there is Greene's fascination with squalor and failure, with what he has himself called 'seediness'. Then there is his obsession with the theme of pursuit, of the relationship between hunter and hunted. Already we have reviewed too many items to be talking in terms of 'obsession', but the list is far from complete. There is his obsession with dreams: John Atkins counted sixty-three dreams in Greene's fiction up to and including *The Quiet American*.[2] (I agree with Atkins, incidentally, in finding them, for the most part, oddly unconvincing.) There is his obsession with dentistry and dental decay. There is his obsession with a certain kind of waif-like heroine. There is his obsession, particularly evident in the short stories, with resurrection and animated corpses. There is his obsession with his own name, which Philip Stratford has documented in a witty and ingenious article, 'Unlocking the Potting Shed'.[3] Stratford investigated a number of books and stories by and about other Greenes or Greens, and found several highly plausible sources for Graham Greene's own work. Though the article is not entirely serious, it is a useful caution against interpreting Greene too rigidly in terms of personal trauma and psychological obsession, and encourages us to put more emphasis on the creative, inventive, and rhetorical side of his work. That, at least, will be the aim of the remainder of this essay.

In his travel book *Journey Without Maps* (1936) Greene described Liberia as a country 'saved from melodrama by its irony', and the same might be said of his own fiction, particularly the earlier work. It is melodramatic insofar as moral choice is dramatized by extreme circumstances, often arising out of crime, war, revolution, and espionage, and the narrative aims to excite and engage very basic emotions: horror, compassion, fear, admiration. The irony resides in the fact that in Greene's stories the conventions of melodrama are handled with a sophisticated and very personal sense of values so as to displace the usual melodramatic distribution of sympathy and antipathy. We are led to identify, not with the honest and brave, but with the criminal and cowardly; not with the rich and beautiful, but with the poor and ugly; and there is rarely an unequivocally happy ending. In Greene's own words: 'The little duke is dead and betrayed and forgotten: we cannot recognize the villain and we suspect the hero and the world is a small cramped place' (*The Ministry of Fear* (1943)).

Sometimes the irony is not sufficiently subtle and controlled to transform the melodramatic stereotypes. That would seem to be the trouble with Greene's first novel, *The Man Within*, though the hero is, to be sure, an anti-hero. Set in a vaguely defined historical past— eighteenth- or nineteenth-century England—this novel centres on the plight of a young man called Andrews, who has betrayed to the authorities a gang of smugglers (previously led by his father, now by a man called Carlyon) of which he himself has been a member. The betrayal is an act of perverse self-assertion by Andrews, who has always felt himself to be despised and neglected. Carlyon and three others escape, and are pursued by the law, while they in turn, intent on revenge, pursue Andrews across the bleak, befogged Sussex Downs. Andrews takes refuge in the cottage of a solitary young girl, Elizabeth. Failing to impress her in the role of desperate and unscrupulous outlaw, Andrews is himself impressed by Elizabeth's courage and self-possession, and becomes more keenly aware than ever of 'the man within me that's angry with me' (the phrase is Sir Thomas Browne's). Elizabeth seeks to redeem Andrews from his self-disgust by encouraging him to testify against the smugglers at the local assizes. This he does, but not before he has been unfaithful to Elizabeth with Lucy, the seductive mistress of counsel for the prosecution. In the denouement Elizabeth dies protecting Andrews from Carlyon's men, and Andrews atones for all by surrendering himself as her murderer.

Some of Greene's most characteristic themes and devices appear in his first book: betrayal (' "He's a sort of Judas," [Carlyon] said softly'), pursuit ('He saw himself friendless and alone, chased by harsh enemies through an uninterested world'), and the yearning for death ('He felt no fear of death, but a terror of life, of going on soiling himself and repenting and soiling himself again'). Though immature, *The Man Within* is by no means a bad novel. There are some exciting scenes that already bear the Greene imprint—notably one where Andrews stands motionless in the middle of a road obscured by fog while his would-be murderers pass within a few feet searching for him. But the vaguely sketched, rather dream-like setting of the story lacks the authenticating particularity of Greene's later work, and gives him too much room for a rather self-indulgent romanticism in the presentation of his hero. Elizabeth and Lucy, the sexual extensions of Andrews's inner dualism, are crude stereotypes of pure and carnal love, untouched by saving irony.

Similar, but more damaging criticisms can be levelled at Greene's second and third novels, *The Name of Action* (1930), which describes a young Englishman's rather gratuitous involvement in a Ruritanian revolution, and *Rumour at Nightfall* (1931), which is set against the background of the Carlist wars in Spain. Greene has excluded these two novels from the Uniform Edition of his works, and there seems no justification for resurrecting them in a study as short as the present one.

4*

The literary and financial failure of these two books occasioned a serious crisis in Greene's career, from which he recovered with his first 'entertainment', *Stamboul Train* (1932). Greene later wrote of it: 'One had never really taken the book seriously, it had been written hurriedly because one had desperately needed the money.' Yet there are strong indications that for Greene the novelist it was *Stamboul Train* that opened a door and let the future in. Greene followed it up with two 'novels' whose literary pretensions are more serious; but what is successful in them derives from *Stamboul Train* rather than from *The Man Within*. Correspondingly, it is in the early entertainments rather than in the early novels that we may observe most clearly the genesis of Greene's mature art.

Stamboul Train follows the fortunes of a number of travellers on the Orient Express, which runs from Ostend to Istanbul. The main characters are Dr Czinner, a disappointed Communist revolutionary; Myatt, a Jewish merchant; and Coral Musker, a young dancer, who in her combination of courage and vulnerability and her minimal expectations of happiness foreshadows many future Greene heroines. In her brief liaison with Myatt there is, characteristically, more pathos than pleasure: 'helpless and sick under the dim unsteady lamp of the corridor, her body shaken by the speed of the train, she woke a painful pity'. There are a number of minor characters: a murderer on the run, a Lesbian journalist, a clergyman of the muscular Christianity school, a best-selling novelist, and some dim English tourists. The structural device that weaves these diverse strands together, involving the characters wittingly or unwittingly in each other's destinies, is the journey itself. Time and place are marked by the progress of the train between the various stations on its route, which supply the titles of the five parts of the novel.

The railroad train is one of the few products of the industrial revolution to have acquired a certain mythic quality; and in its headlong rush across Europe the Orient Express provides just the right combination, for Greene's purposes, of the familiar and the unfamiliar. Greene has admired this combination in the work of John Buchan, entertainer of an earlier era, quoting from Buchan's *The Power House* a line that might well stand as an epigraph to any of his own entertainments: 'Now I saw how thin was the protection of civilization.' In *Stamboul Train* the protection is as thin as the walls and windows of the train. Once she leaves its safety Coral is helplessly involved in the callous trial and condemnation of Czinner, and separated from Myatt. She is rescued only to fall into the clutches of the Lesbian, Mabel Warren.

Greene's next entertainment, *A Gun for Sale* (1936), is particularly
interesting as being a kind of secular rehearsal for *Brighton Rock* (1938),
his first overtly Catholic novel. Both novels explore, through their
warped, murderous 'heroes', a paradox that is crucial in Greene's work,
a paradox most forcefully put by T. S. Eliot in his essay on Baudelaire,
which Greene has quoted in his own essays:

> So far as we are human, what we do must be either evil or good;
> so far as we do evil or good we are human; and it is better, in a
> paradoxical way, to do evil, than to do nothing: at least we exist.
> It is true to say that the glory of man is his capacity for salvation;
> it is also true to say that his glory is his capacity for damnation.
> The worst that can be said for most of our malefactors, from
> statesmen to thieves, is that they are not men enough to be damned.

If in theological terms this view leads to the celebration of the sinner
as one perversely aware of supernatural values, in secular terms it leads
to the celebration of the criminal, who becomes the symbolic scapegoat, victim and scourge—the existential hero in fact—of a society
characterized by moral anarchy. So it is with Raven, the harelipped
killer of *A Gun for Sale*. At the beginning of the novel we see him
commit the brutal murder of a rather saintly European politician, yet
by the end we have come to identify and almost to sympathize with
him. Raven is paid for the assassination with stolen notes and the action
of the novel describes his flight from the English police on this account
while he himself seeks revenge on those who have double-crossed him
—a group of wealthy armament manufacturers who stand to profit by
a European war. Raven's violence is thus an extension of a much larger
public violence ('There's always been a war for me', he says) and his
guilt is diminished by juxtaposition with those who kill with clean
hands. The conventions of the thriller are precariously maintained—
Raven is shot down at last, and the heroine Anne is reunited with her
policeman-fiancé—but not before Raven, rather in the style of a
Jacobean revenger, has purged society of corruption in high places.
In *A Gun for Sale* Greene calls attention to the theme of treachery
and betrayal more insistently than ever before. At the outset of the
story the only value Raven cherishes is a belief in honour among
thieves, and it is his disillusionment on this score that awakens in his
twisted mind (itself partly excused by traumatic childhood experience)
the first glimmerings of moral awareness. His sense of grievance colours
his interpretation of Christmas, the season that forms a sad, ironic

background to the story. Raven looks at a crib in a shop window, 'staring at the swaddled child with a horrified tenderness, "the little bastard", because he was educated and knew what the child was in for, the damned Jews and the double-crossing Judas and only one man to draw a knife on his side when the soldiers came for him in the garden'— a passage anticipating Greene's startling and unconventional use of religious allusion in later fiction.

The reiteration of the betrayal motif in *A Gun for Sale* exemplifies a characteristic feature of Greene's fiction, in which the properties of realism—the sharp visual images presented through cinematic devices of montage and close-up, the catalogues of significant particulars, the keen rendering of sensation, the touches of local colour laid on with so skilled a hand—seem to cluster around the nucleus of some ambiguous moral concept which is 'the heart of the matter' and which is represented by some word or words recurring as insistently as a drum beat. One is reminded of the narrator of *Under Western Eyes* (by Joseph Conrad, a writer Greene abandoned in 1932 because 'his influence on me was too great'), who speaks of the necessity of finding 'some key word ... a word that could stand at the back of all the words covering the page, a word which, if not truth itself, may perchance hold truth enough to help the moral discovery which should be the object of every tale'.

The key word of *The Confidential Agent* (1939), for instance, is *trust*, or its negative forms *distrust* and *mistrust*: even the 'trust-system' for buying newspapers contributes significantly to the plot. This, the third of Greene's entertainments, describes the mission of D., a confidential agent representing a foreign government (which is pretty obviously the Republican side in the Spanish Civil War) who is sent to England to negotiate a coal contract. Pacing the deck of the cross-channel steamer as it nears Dover, D. thinks:

> You could trust nobody but yourself, and sometimes you were uncertain whether you could trust yourself. *They* [i.e. his own government] didn't trust you. . . . He wasn't certain that he wasn't watched at this moment. He wasn't certain that it wasn't right for him to be watched. . . . And the watcher—was he watched? He was haunted by the vision of an endless distrust.

In the subsequent action D.'s mission, and his life, are constantly threatened by the intervention of his own side as well as that of his political enemies. He is caught up in a web of intrigue and violence, plausibly unravelled against the background of an outwardly calm and reassuring England. The irony of the title is clear: D. is a confidential agent in whom no one has confidence, and who can have confidence in no one.

All three entertainments discussed above concern political crisis of one kind or another, and depict Europe as a place of tyranny, violence, and unrest. In this respect Greene's early fiction clearly belongs to the 'thirties. It presents a vivid picture of that period of economic depression and the threat of war, a picture made up of people anxiously watching news flashes, people demonstrating, people looking for jobs, people turning over secondhand clothes, jerry-built housing estates, TO LET and FOR SALE signs, desolate slag heaps, the pervasive evidence of decline and despair. The writers of the 'thirties characteristically confronted these circumstances by committing themselves to Marxist political solutions, and by adopting a more open, robust, and popular literary style than that of the 'aesthetic' 'twenties. Greene was a Party member for only four weeks in early youth, but the sympathies in his fiction go out to the underprivileged and the characters who are ideologically on the left. His rejection, after a few unsatisfactory experiments, of the 'stream of consciousness' technique, and his development of a fictional mode that was serious without being high-brow, using devices of journalism and the cinema, shot through with the sense of social and political crisis, were in accord with the literary programme of Auden, Isherwood, and their associates.

Greene, however, avoided the cruder kind of political simplifications that characterize much of the writing of the 'thirties: Czinner is a flawed character, and D. is by no means convinced of his side's ideology. Greene's whole fictional world seems ripe for dissolution rather than revolution. This may be accounted for by reference to his Catholicism, and his own innate pessimism. Increasingly there flows into his work the current of anti-humanism that runs so strongly through most Christian and specifically Catholic writing from the Decadence onward; so that by 1939 we find Greene (in *The Lawless Roads*) declaiming against 'Progress, Human Dignity, great empty Victorian concepts that life denies at every turn'. Greene, however, never moved toward the political right, though for his generation of intellectuals this was the logical consequence of conversion to Catholicism.

In Greene's best writing, in fact, there is always a fruitful tension between two systems of value. As he neatly puts it in *Journey Without Maps*: 'I find myself always torn between two beliefs: the belief that life should be better than it is and the belief that when it appears better it is really worse.' In his mature fiction this dialectic is deepened by being placed in a Christian and hence 'eternal' perspective; but in his earlier work we are conscious of a secular despair stifling creative achievement.

This seems particularly true of the 'novel' *It's a Battlefield* (1934), in which Greene is also labouring under Conrad's excessive influence. This novel has its key word—*justice*—but does not get much further than the discrediting of all ideas of justice as it follows, through a cross-section of metropolitan London, the repercussions of a Communist bus driver's conviction for the murder of a policeman. The possibility of divine justice is not introduced; and we are left with the depressing spectacle of rootless, unhappy, or culpably complacent individuals co-existing without communicating, impotent contenders on a befogged battlefield.

Greene's next novel, *England Made Me* (1935), is much more successful. Set mainly in Stockholm, it concerns a number of characters associated with a Swedish millionaire tycoon (modelled on Kreuger, the match king), particularly his mistress, Kate Farrant, and her ne'er-do-well brother, Anthony. Kate persuades Krogh to give Anthony a job, but there is no *rapport* between these two 'hollow men': the tycoon whose colossal financial power has cut him off from human values, and the social failure sheltering behind a bogus Harrow tie. When Anthony threatens to expose the crooked basis of Krogh's empire, he is murdered by Krogh's faithful henchman, Hall. Minty, the genuine Harrow article, but even more down-at-heel, provides another, jaundiced perspective on events.

England Made Me is the most carefully wrought of Greene's novels of the 'thirties, but its success seems to represent a kind of dead end for his particular talent. The characters are drawn with brilliant observation, but the brilliance is all on the surface: Greene's attempts to penetrate their minds through interior monologue are not happy. The characters seem trapped, deprived of free will and of the capacity to develop, by the very finality and authority with which Greene categorizes them. The analysis, which they illustrate, of the disorder of society as a whole is thus drawn inevitably to a defeatist conclusion. Several critics have pointed out that Greene's view of human destiny has always tended to the deterministic, and his characterization to caricature. But in his 'religious' novels the determinism is checked by the mysteries of Christianity, and the caricature becomes a generally legitimate and highly effective means of dramatizing the interplay of the divine and the human.

Explaining, in *Journey Without Maps* (1936), why he made the first long journey of his life to so unpromising a place as Liberia, Greene writes: 'There seemed to be a seediness about the place you couldn't get to the same extent elsewhere, and seediness has a very deep appeal: even the seediness of civilization.' Greene draws a daunting picture of the boredom, fear, disgust, and physical discomfort he experienced in the uncharted depths of Liberia, but it all weighed more heavily in the balance for him than 'the smart, the new, the chic, the cerebral'. Throughout the book Africa is contrasted with England by means of a kind of cultural synecdoche very common in Greene's writing:

> It isn't a gain to have turned the witch or the masked secret dancer, the sense of supernatural evil, into the small human viciousness of the distinguished military grey head in Kensington Gardens with the soft lips and the eyes which dwelt with dull lustre on girls and boys of a certain age.

Too honest to be an exciting travel book, and too confused to be a satisfying spiritual journal, *Journey Without Maps* is nevertheless a curiously fascinating work, and one that helps to explain his next, *Brighton Rock* (1938), in which 'the sense of supernatural evil' and 'the seediness of civilization' are imaginatively fused.

Briefly, *Brighton Rock* describes the decline and fall of Pinkie Brown, a teenage criminal who has inherited the leadership of a gang of racecourse hoodlums operating from the popular seaside resort of Brighton. At the outset of the novel they murder the associate of a rival gang, making one small slip which is observed by a young waitress, Rose. In order to secure his own safety, Pinkie befriends the girl and marries her in a registry office. Since they are both Catholics this means they are living in sin—a source of perverse satisfaction to Pinkie, who despises and revolts from sexuality. Meanwhile Ida Arnold, a big, cheerful, irrepressible Cockney, who made a chance contact with the murdered man just before he was killed, undertakes her own private investigation of the crime. Harried by Ida, by his distrust of Rose, and by the machinations of the rival gang, Pinkie is driven to committing another murder and unsuccessfully conniving at a third. But the net closes in inexorably, and he seeks to escape it by the most diabolical act of all: disposing of Rose by luring her into a faked suicide pact with himself. In the end it is Pinkie who dies, when, blinded by his own vitriol, he dashes over a cliff.

Such a synopsis, suggestive merely of a violent and sensational crime story, scarcely conveys an idea of the extraordinary displacement of conventional values and sympathies which Greene effects in *Brighton Rock*. In this novel he explores the Eliot-Baudelaire paradox in its most extreme form. Pinkie is self-consciously man enough to be damned, yet Greene persuades us to respect him more than Ida Arnold, who with her cheerful humanism and sense of fair play, represents secular values in the novel. He does this partly by stressing the loyalty and devotion of Rose to Pinkie. Rose, Greene's most successful 'waif' character, is as good as Pinkie is evil; but as Ida discovers, good and evil have more in common with each other than with the code of 'right and wrong' that is always on her own lips:

> Good and evil lived in the same country, came together like old friends, feeling the same completion, touching hands beside the iron bedstead. 'You want to do what's Right, Rose?' she implored.

Like Charles Péguy, the French Catholic writer (often mentioned by Greene) who challenged the idea of eternal punishment by deliberately remaining in a state of mortal sin, Rose 'had chosen her side; if they damned him, they'd got to damn her too'. In the end she resists the temptation to damn herself by suicide, or rather she succumbs to what François Mauriac has called 'the good temptation to which many men succumb in the end'—God. Pinkie resists the good temptation, which, like Francis Thompson's Hound of Heaven, presents to his tormented mind the aspect of some incomprehensible disaster:

> An enormous emotion beat on him; it was like something trying to get in, the pressure of gigantic wings against the glass. *Dona nobis pacem.* He withstood it, with all the bitter force of the school bench, the cement playground, the St. Pancras waiting room, Dallow's and Judy's secret lust, and the cold, unhappy moment on the pier. If the glass broke, the beast—whatever it was—got in, God knows what it would do. He had a sense of huge havoc—the confession, the penance and the sacrament—an awful distraction, and he drove blind into the rain.

As at the climax of *A Gun for Sale*, a certain pity and understanding is solicited for the criminal hero by recapitulating his appalling social background. But there is more of the tragic and less of the pathetic spirit about Pinkie. With a desperation reminiscent of Macbeth, he asks himself, 'Had he got to massacre a world?'; and his lawyer Drewitt is given to quoting *Hamlet*, *Othello*, and *Dr. Faustus*.

But the paradox on which *Brighton Rock* is based cannot be sustained to its logical conclusion. It is plainly better to do nothing than to damn yourself. In other novels Greene acknowledges this by holding out the hope of mercy for his sinners, but hardly in *Brighton Rock*. The priest at the end of the novel seeks to console Rose by suggesting there was some love, and hence some good in Pinkie. But we leave her walking towards 'the worst horror of all'—the phonograph record on which, unknown to her, Pinkie had recorded: 'God damn you, you little bitch, why can't you go home and let me be?'

The effort of sustaining this bleakly pessimistic vision leads Greene into some falsities (as when Pinkie improbably intones '*Credo in unum Satanum*') but on the whole the novel holds us appalled and fascinated in its coil. Its popularity may be accounted for by reference to Greene's utterly authentic evocation of Brighton and what it stands for in British 'folk' culture, and to the fact that on a very superficial level it can be read as an entertainment (which it was called in some editions). On a deeper level of literary appreciation, however, one has to acknowledge the force of the book's demonic rhetoric: the pervasive poison imagery (Pinkie's veins run with poison, and even the sea is 'poison-bottle green'), the perverse sexual imagery ('a prick of sexual desire disturbed him like a sickness'), the bizarre emblems of cruelty (Pinkie dismembering a fly, murmuring, 'She loves me, she loves me not . . .'), the sensational religious allusion ('She was good, but he'd got her like you got God in the Eucharist—in the guts').

In *Brighton Rock*, indeed, Greene may be said to have finally discovered his personal style, his artistic *métier*, though the excitement of the discovery leads him into a certain extravagance. I have already remarked on the way he shapes a vividly particularized narrative around a thematic abstraction. The same kind of effect is to be observed in microcosm in his use of language, his employment of synecdoche, oxymoron, metaphor, simile, and other tropes in which the abstract and the concrete are brought into arresting conjunction, often enforced by alliteration: 'the music drifting landward, grief in the guts'; 'she felt responsibility move in her breasts'; 'Camaraderie, good nature, cheeriness fell like shutters before a plate-glass window'; 'A dim desire for annihilation stretched in him, the vast superiority of vacancy.' As Richard Hoggart has observed,[4] Greene sometimes reverses the normal figurative relationship of abstract to concrete. Thus, the priest in *The Power and the Glory* 'drank the brandy down like damnation'. Greene might say with Mauriac, 'I am a metaphysician who works in the concrete'.

It was in an essay on the French novelist that Greene took the opportunity to question the modern prejudice against authorial comment in fiction. Greene reasserted 'the traditional and essential right of a novelist to comment, to express his views', which he associated particularly with the 'religious sense' lost to English fiction in its post-Jamesian phase. Authorial comment is certainly an important element in Greene's own fiction, though he is enough of a 'modern' to employ it more subtly and more unobtrusively than a Victorian novelist. His method is usually to develop his commentary out of the thoughts and situation of one of his characters, so that we are scarcely aware of the transition, and accept the comment almost as an articulation of the character's consciousness, though at the same time we feel the force of the superior expressiveness and deeper perspective which the authorial voice commands.

In *The Lawless Roads*, the record of a journey through Mexico in 1938, when the Catholic Church was subject to persecution in some states, Greene frequently alludes to the growing cult of the martyred priest, Father Pro, who died heroically, praying for his enemies; but it is entirely characteristic that his imagination was fired by the casual mention of a much less impressive priest:

> I asked about the priest in Chiapas who had fled. 'Oh', he said, 'he was just what we call a whiskey priest.' He had taken one of his sons to be baptized but the priest was drunk and would insist on naming him Brigitta. He was little loss, poor man . . . but who can judge what terror and hardship and isolation may have excused him in the eyes of God?

The Power and the Glory (1940) is an imaginative exploration of that final question.

The story is very simple, and divides into four sections. In the first we are introduced to the whiskey priest, trying to escape from the state in which he is the last representative of the Church, and to a number of other characters, Mexican and European, who become associated with him. In the second part, he returns to his native village, where he has an illegitimate daughter (Brigitta) and narrowly escapes detection by the Lieutenant of Police, who is looking for him. Later he turns up in the town looking for wine with which to celebrate Mass, and is ironically arrested for violating the anti-liquor laws. In the third part, having been released, unrecognized, from prison, he is on the point of escaping to a safe state when he is called back to minister to a dying gangster—a call he obeys though he knows it is a trap. He is executed, and the effect of his death on the other characters is studied in the fourth part.

The structural devices developed in the entertainments are therefore still in evidence: the story of a chase thrown across a vividly authentic background, drawing in a number of characters who dramatize the theme by their involvement or indifference. But the eschatological perspective that struggles against the conventions of the thriller in *Brighton Rock* is all-pervasive here. Only the whiskey priest's belief in his sacramental powers saves him from utter despair:

> Now that he no longer despaired, it didn't mean of course that he wasn't damned—it was simply that after a time the mystery became too great, a damned man putting God into the mouths of men.

It is the priest's wavering, undignified but persistent loyalty to his vocation that makes him a genuine martyr, even though he has to be carried to the place of execution, his legs buckling under the influence of fear and alcohol.

In this novel Greene challenges conventional ideas of sanctity and of the priesthood. The picaresque progress of the whiskey priest is deliberately contrasted with the conventional saint's life that a Mexican mother reads to her son and daughters; but it is the former that has the breath of life—and more in common with the passion of Christ. The relationship between the priest and the half-caste who betrays him, for instance, parallels the story of Christ and Judas; and the climax of the brilliant scene in which the *Jefe* and his cousin greedily consume the priest's precious wine recalls the death of Christ on the cross. (Trying to explain his tears the priest says that when he is drunk he sees ' "all the hope of the world draining away. . . ." Lightning filled the windows like a white sheet and thunder crashed suddenly overhead.') The sentimentality of the hagiographical account alienates the little Mexican boy, and throws him temporarily into allegiance to the atheistic Lieutenant of Police; but the death of the whiskey priest restores the boy's loyalty to his faith.

It is this boy who welcomes the new priest who arrives at the end of the novel to fill the vacuum left by the death of the whiskey priest. We are told that 'the boy had already swung the door open and put his lips to his hand before the other could give himself a name'. The new priest thus shares the anonymity of the whiskey priest, which underlines the fact that his priestly ministry transcends his personal imperfections. This is also stressed by the fact that he is the last frail source of religious consolation in a place otherwise characterized by a desolating sense of abandonment. In his Mexican travel book Greene wrote of Villahermosa (the 'port' of *The Power and the Glory*): 'One felt one was drawing near to the centre of something—if it was only of darkness and abandonment', and 'abandon' is a word that recurs significantly throughout the novel. Padre José, for instance, figures the earth rolling 'heavily in space under its fog like a burning and abandoned ship', and Mr Tench, the dentist, reflects, when his ether cylinder fails to arrive, that 'a little additional pain was hardly noticeable in the huge abandonment'. The priest's personal sense of abandonment is, however, associated with his shedding of the conventional attitudes of his station in life, a stage in his self-discovery. After his night in the prison (that brilliantly evoked microcosm of the Greeneian world, 'overcrowded with lust and crime and unhappy love') the priest 'had passed into a region of abandonment—almost as if he had died there with the old man's head on his shoulder and now wandered in a kind of limbo because he wasn't good or bad enough. . . .'

With deliberate irony, enforcing the novel's thesis, the Lieutenant of Police appears, in every respect except faith, much more like an ideal priest. He is chaste, honest, ascetic, and dedicated. His room is 'like a monastic cell' and 'there was something of a priest in his intent observant walk—a theologian going back over the errors of the past to destroy them again'. His zeal in hunting down the whiskey priest is purely ideological, and he twice acts with real generosity towards his victim. 'I have nothing against you, you understand, as a man,' he says to the priest, who replies, 'Of course not. It's God you're against.' When the priest is shot the Lieutenant's feelings echo the words of the former when his wine is consumed: 'He felt without a purpose, as if life had drained out of the world.'

As the above remarks may suggest, *The Power and the Glory* is a highly schematic novel, which perhaps explains why, although it is the most widely respected of his books, and his personal favourite among them, it stands up to repeated reading less well than some of the later works. But I have not had sufficient space to do justice to those aspects of the book which largely conceal its simplifications and carry it to the success of a *tour de force*: the gallery of vividly drawn minor characters, and Greene's remarkable skill in evoking the physical and metaphysical atmosphere of his Mexico.

Published inauspiciously at the beginning of World War II, *The Power and the Glory* had to wait for the reputation it deserved until interest was revived by the international success of *The Heart of the Matter* (1948). In the meantime Greene published an entertainment,

The Ministry of Fear (1943), a rather uneven work which applies the devices of the pre-war thrillers to the circumstances of the London blitz and the activities of fascist spies, with an effect that sometimes comes near self-parody. The book also looks forward, however. The background of wartime London and the comic exploitation of a private detection agency were to reappear in *The End of the Affair*. More significantly, the organization of *The Ministry of Fear* around the concept of pity (the hero has murdered his incurably ill wife out of pity) makes it a kind of rehearsal for *The Heart of the Matter*. The entertainment was written during Greene's service for the Foreign Office in Freetown, Sierra Leone, during the war—the time and place of the novel's action.

I intend to short-circuit the theological debate, which the novel provoked in some quarters, about whether the hero is damned or not. The novel leaves us in little doubt that the answer should be in the negative, and a theological approach to the novel is limiting. Scobie's case is that of a man with an overdeveloped sense of pity and responsibility (both words recur in the novel with about the same frequency) and neither quality is a prerogative of Catholics. The effect of Scobie's Catholicism is to enlarge and intensify the implications of a situation that *could* have been treated in purely secular terms (though not, so powerfully, by Greene). Scobie's distress at the spectacle of innocent suffering is a familiar human trait, but his belief in a benevolent God gives an extra turn of the screw to his anguish and bewilderment. The plot of the novel turns on one of the most hackneyed situations in literature—adultery; but Scobie's Catholicism means that the moral issues of adultery are present, for all their complexity, in terms that are precise and inexorable, while at the same time it introduces into the 'eternal triangle' a fourth character whose claims to love and loyalty have to be considered. In this way, a story of essentially ordinary people acquires some of the moral and metaphysical dimensions of high tragedy.

We are first introduced to Henry Scobie as the Assistant Commissioner of Police in a British West African Colony, married to a rather unlovable wife, Louise, and childless since the death of a daughter. He is at the right age for promotion, but although Scobie is an honest and efficient policeman (Greene establishes this with great skill and economy) he lacks the qualities of a successful careerist. In the small, spitefully intimate colonial society, Louise feels the slight keenly, and vents her spleen on the long-suffering Scobie. He promises her a holiday in South Africa, though this involves him in an imprudent debt to a Syrian merchant, Yussef. Greene comments (his use of comment is both bold and wonderfully assured in this novel):

> He would still have made the promise even if he could have foreseen all that would come of it. He had always been prepared to accept the responsibility for his actions, and he had been half aware too, from the time he made his terrible private vow that she would be happy, how far *this* action might carry him. Despair is the price one pays for setting oneself an impossible aim. It is, one is told, the unforgivable sin, but it is one the corrupt or evil man never practises. He always has hope. He never reaches the freezing-point of knowing absolute failure. Only the man of goodwill carries always in his heart this capacity for damnation.

The Eliot-Baudelaire paradox is given a new, and perhaps more interesting twist. Scobie's 'capacity for damnation' has already been hinted at by his conduct during a routine inspection of a Portuguese cargo boat, when he discovers a contraband letter. Scobie resists the captain's attempts to bribe him, but succumbs to his appeals for pity. Shortly afterwards, Scobie has to report on the suicide of a young district commissioner. The episode foreshadows Scobie's own end, and establishes the doctrinal framework within which he makes his desperate decision.

By the time Louise leaves, therefore, the stage is set for Scobie's tragedy, the fall of a good man. He has to assist in the reception of a number of survivors from a ship torpedoed in the Atlantic. Most of them are in bad shape, and some die. The group includes two children and a young woman widowed by the sinking. The manifestation of meaningless and undeserved suffering makes enormous demands on Scobie's sense of pity and responsibility.

> It was as if he had shed one responsibility [i.e. Louise] only to take on another. This was a responsibility he shared with all human beings, but there was no comfort in that, for it sometimes seemed to him that he was the only one who recognized it.
>
> Outside the rest-house he stopped again. The lights inside would have given an extraordinary impression of peace if one hadn't known, just as the stars on the clear night gave also an impression of remoteness, security, freedom. If one knew, he wondered, the facts, would one have to feel pity even for the planets? if one reached what they called the heart of the matter?

Both passages, while they do credit to Scobie's humanity, indicate that he is guilty of a kind of emotional egoism, a compulsion to take the whole load of cosmic suffering on his own shoulders. This leads him, as he watches beside the little girl who is in agony, to make a generous but rash vow: 'Father . . . give her peace. Take away my peace for ever, but give her peace.' The prayer is answered, ambiguously, by the little girl's death.

It is perhaps because the young widow, Helen, with her schoolgirl idiom and her stamp album salvaged from the sinking ship, is more like a child than a woman that Scobie succumbs so easily to her claims on his protectiveness. They become lovers. Scobie is not spared an immediate awareness of the impossible situation he has created for himself, as we learn in a passage notable for its delicate religious allusion:

> He had sworn to preserve Louise's happiness, and now he had
> accepted another and contradictory responsibility. He felt tired by
> all the lies he would some time have to tell: he felt the wounds of
> those victims who had not yet bled. Lying back on the pillow he
> stared sleeplessly out towards the grey early morning tide.
> Somewhere on the face of those obscure waters moved the sense
> of yet another wrong and another victim, not Louise, not Helen.
> Away in the town the cocks began to crow for the false dawn.

Scobie's efforts to keep secret his liaison with Helen wreak havoc with his professional integrity: he is blackmailed by Yussef into assisting the latter's diamond smuggling, and even connives, half willingly, in the murder of his boy, Ali, who is reporting on him to a British security agent, Wilson. Ironically, Scobie survives the investigation and is rewarded by the belated promise of promotion. But with the return of Louise the possibilities of any human happiness are closed to him.

It is at this point that Scobie's Catholicism becomes crucially important, for even if he can, by deception, keep both Louise and Helen relatively happy, it is only at the expense of 'another wrong, another victim'. Addressing God, Scobie says, 'I've preferred to give you pain rather than give pain to Helen or my wife because I can't observe your suffering. I can only imagine it.' But when, in order to convince Louise of his fidelity, he is driven to make a sacrilegious communion, Scobie's imagination is very vivid: 'the punch-drunk head of God reeling sideways . . . his damnation being prepared like a meal at the altar . . . God was lodged in his body and his body was corrupting outwards from that seed.' Such images, in which the doctrines of

Catholicism are brought startlingly—even shockingly—to life, indicate that Scobie's sense of pity and responsibility has acquired a new dimension, a new depth of perception. His decision to commit suicide, rather than choose between injuring Louise, Helen, or God, is in a perverse way an act of generosity, of sacrifice, illustrating Péguy's apothegm, which furnishes the epigraph to the novel: 'The sinner is at the heart of Christianity. . . . No-one is as competent in the matter of Christianity as the sinner. No-one, unless it is the saint.'

Greene was to push this idea a stage further in his next novel, *The End of the Affair* (1951), which has a similar kind of epigraph from Léon Bloy: 'Man has places in his heart which do not yet exist, and into them enters suffering, in order that they may have existence.' By this stage in his career Greene's work shows the influence of the French Catholic literary tradition very clearly. Beginning with Huysmans, and continuing in such writers as Bloy, Péguy, Bernanos, and Mauriac, this tradition reveals its Decadent origins in its fascination with evil, its rejection of optimistic materialism, its stylistic tendency to epigram (weaving Pascalian *pensées* into the fabric of narrative), and its interest in extreme religious situations: vows, conversions, challenges to God, miracles, and the idea of 'mystical substitution' (when an individual takes upon himself the suffering and guilt of others). With the exception of Mauriac, however, there is no evidence that Greene greatly admires the literature produced by this tradition. He draws on it for ideas, but domesticates these in fiction that owes much more to his native literary tradition. Indeed, one is conscious of how much that is finely realized in *The Heart of the Matter* one overlooks by concentrating on Scobie and his dilemma: the superb realization of time and place, of the petty, exhausting tensions in colonial society, of racial conflicts and contrasts, of the work men do. The minor characters are kept in their place but in their different ways they are as memorable as Scobie: Harris keeping the public-school spirit alive with his cockroach hunts; Wilson, the poet and lover doomed to absurdity; the smooth, ambivalent Yussef; even Robinson the bank manager, brooding over books on diseases of the urinary tract.

Although Scobie believes that 'we [Catholics] know all the answers', this certainly makes life more, not less, difficult for him. In all Greene's work there is a powerful tension between the imperatives of religious orthodoxy and the human impulses (rendered with deep sympathy and understanding) that run counter to them. In *The End of the Affair* Greene presents this conflict in the character of a woman to whom religious faith comes unbidden but irresistibly, wrenching her from the one relationship she values in life; and further dramatizes it by using as narrator her lover, a novelist and an agnostic.

When Sarah Miles abruptly broke off her affair with Maurice Bendrix, shortly after he had narrowly escaped death in a wartime bomb explosion, Bendrix assumed the rivalry of another lover. Two years later he meets her husband, Henry, who is, belatedly it seems to Bendrix, suspicious of his wife's behaviour. Still deeply jealous, Bendrix arranges to have Sarah investigated by a private detective, Parkis, and is put in possession of her journal. From this he learns that Sarah had been convinced that he had been killed by the bomb, and had prayed to a God in whom she did not really believe, promising to give up Bendrix in return for his life. Since that time, convinced that her prayer was answered, she has resisted the severe temptation to return to him, and has moved, despite herself, towards positive belief in God through the Catholic faith. Thus enlightened, Bendrix begs her to return to him, but she refuses, and dies shortly afterwards. Bendrix is bitterly resentful of the destructive effect of religion on their happiness, but he is disturbed by the aura of sanctity that surrounded Sarah at the end of her life, by information which establishes that Sarah, unknown to herself, had been a baptized Catholic, and by certain phenomena that have the appearance of miracles performed through her intercession.

Such a summary scarcely indicates the complexity of the novel's structure and time scheme. Sarah's journal of her dramatic conversion is embedded in Bendrix's account, which itself reflects his progress from disbelief to a kind of exhausted defiance of God. On one level, *The End of the Affair* is an enormously complicated—and deeply absorbing—detective story, in which a divine culprit is pursued by a godless detective. It is also the story of an 'eternal triangle' in a highly significant sense: Bendrix's rival for Sarah's love is not another man, not Henry, but God. There can be no end to this 'affair'. Moreover, God is not only divine culprit and divine lover, but divine novelist, as Frank Kermode was the first to point out. Bendrix, the professional novelist, comes to see himself as a character in a plot more ingenious than any human imagination could contrive:

> We are inextricably bound to the plot, and wearily God forces us,
> here and there, according to his intention, characters without
> poetry, without free will, whose only importance is that somewhere,
> at some time, we help to furnish the scene in which a living
> character moves and speaks, providing perhaps the saints with the
> opportunities for their free will.

There is no mistaking, of course, which human novelist God most resembles.

The End of the Affair illustrates Greene's use of key words more strikingly than any other novel: it rings with the repetition of *love* and *hate*. For the statistical record, these words or forms of them recur about three hundred and one hundred times respectively in this short novel. The effect is not monotonous because Greene is continually exploring new dimensions and interrelationships of love, hate, and the mixture of love and hate that is jealousy. Both Bendrix and Sarah become aware that love and hate are equally strong evidence that the defences around simple selfhood are down. Towards the end of his narrative Bendrix writes:

> If I hate her so much as I sometimes do, how can I love her? Can one really hate and love? Or is it only myself that I really hate? . . .
> I took her journal and . . . read, 'Oh God, if I could really hate you, what would that mean?' And I thought, hating Sarah is only loving Sarah, and hating myself is only loving myself. I'm not worth hating. . . . Nothing, not even Sarah, is worth our hatred, if You exist, except You.

Of equal importance with the play on love and hate is the correspondence established between human (i.e. sexual) love and divine love. Bendrix interprets a fragment stolen from Sarah's wastepaper basket— 'I know I am only beginning to love, but already I want to abandon everything, everybody but you'—as part of a love letter, though it is in fact part of a prayer. 'Reading her letter to my unknown successor would have hurt less if I hadn't known how capable she was of abandonment', comments Bendrix. The irony of his misunderstanding, however, is not total, for Sarah's love of God proceeds from her capacity for carnal love. This connection is subtly employed to make credible Sarah's orientation to Catholicism, with all its literalist dogmas and materialistic trappings. When Sarah first entered a Catholic Church she 'hated the statues, the crucifix, all the emphasis on the human body'; she seeks a God that is 'vague, amorphous, cosmic . . . like a powerful vapour moving among the chairs and walls'. But the recollection of Bendrix's body makes her wish for its resurrection and the resurrection of her own.

> And of course on the altar there was a body too—such a familiar body, more familiar than Maurice's, that it had never struck me before as a body with all the parts of a body, even the parts the

loin-cloth concealed. . . . I looked at that material body on that
material cross and I wondered, how could the world have nailed a
vapour there?

With *The End of the Affair* Greene seems to have finally rid himself
of Manichaeism. In other respects, too, the novel represents his art at
its most mature; but at the time of publication it was difficult to say
who were the most scandalized—non-Catholic readers at the
introduction of miracles into realist fiction, or Catholics at the attribution of miracles to a woman like Sarah. There was, therefore, a general
sigh of relief when in his next novel Greene turned away from explicitly
Catholic subject matter. Yet *The Quiet American* (1955) is far from being
a purely secular novel. Set against the background of the French war
in Indo-China, it is concerned overtly with political and ideological
conflict. But the conflict is dramatized and analysed in terms that are
consistent with Greene's earlier theological perspective; and the
agnostic narrator, Fowler, is left in the end, like Bendrix, troubled and
dissatisfied with any purely human explanation of experience.

The elected stance of Fowler, the British journalist covering the
war in Indo-China, is one of complete detachment. 'The human
condition being what it was, let them fight, let them love, let them
murder. I would not be involved.' Thus, when Fowler begins to feel
irritation with Pyle, a young American working ostensibly with a
medical mission in Saigon, his reasons are at first personal: a general
dislike of Americans 'with their private stores of coca-cola and their
portable hospitals and their not-quite-latest guns', and a resentment of
Pyle's attempts to woo his oriental mistress Phuong away from him.
But when Pyle proves responsible for a bomb outrage, Fowler decides
that his enthusiasm for the idea of a Third Force breaking the deadlock
between Colonialism and Communism is not merely foolish but
dangerous. In consequence, Fowler becomes 'involved' to the point of
conniving, half willingly, at the murder of Pyle by the Communists.

Fowler's judgment of Pyle's character is formulated in terms of
'innocence'. The menace of Pyle's kind of innocence is expressed in a
beautifully moulded image, its force cunningly held back until the
last moment:

> Innocence always calls mutely for protection, when we would be so
> much wiser to guard ourselves against it: innocence is like a dumb
> leper who has lost his bell, wandering the world, meaning no harm.

This judgment is consistent with Greene's suggestions, in earlier novels,
that the recognition of evil, in oneself and in others, is a necessary part

of any proper understanding of life. 'I wish sometimes you had a few bad motives,' says Fowler to Pyle. 'You might understand a little more about human beings. And that applies to your country, too, Pyle.' Fowler himself, however, by his act of involvement burdens himself with a sense of guilt for which his cynicism provides no relief. His guilt and uneasiness destroy the happiness he would otherwise have enjoyed when his wife agrees to divorce him, allowing him to marry Phuong. The last words of the novel are:

> Everything had gone right with me since [Pyle] had died, but how I wished there existed someone to whom I could say that I was sorry.

Greene impresses one as being a 'professional' writer in the best sense of the word. While working on *The Quiet American* he made four trips to Indo-China, staying there twelve months in all, and this careful preparation is evident in the complete authority with which he establishes the novel's setting. We never doubt that Fowler is a reliable reporter of the South-east Asian scene, of the war, and of the conflicts and interests behind it; while certain repeated motifs—the old trousered women squatting on the landing, Phuong's dexterity with an opium pipe—give the whole picture the characteristic mood and colouring of Greeneland.

The novel has acquired a certain notoriety as an expression of venomous anti-Americanism. While it is true that Greene has never been enraptured by the public face of American civilization, in contrasting American innocence and European experience he is following a long line of American writers; and if he comes down hard on the Americans, it is on behalf of the Asians, not of the European colonialists. On one level the novel certainly suggests that American intervention in South-east Asia is both impolitic and unjustifiable; but in the light of subsequent events this seems a prophetic rather than a prejudiced judgment.

In the chronology of Greene's work, *The Quiet American* is flanked by two plays, *The Living Room* (1953) and *The Potting Shed* (1957), in which the author's interest in religious themes is still much in evidence. The first of these ends with the suicide of the heroine, provoked by the irreconcilable claims of her lover (non-Catholic, middle-aged, and unhappily married) and her faith, as forbiddingly represented by her two aged aunts and a crippled priest, their brother. In *The Potting Shed* the son of a once famous rationalist discovers after his father's death that at the age of fourteen he (the son) committed suicide and recovered life by an apparent miracle, obtained by his uncle, a Catholic priest, who sacrificed his faith to this end in a vow. The parallels with *The Heart of the Matter* and *The End of the Affair* are obvious; but, denuded of Greene's narrative resources, the dramatic plots creak somewhat. The conventions of the realistic 'well-made play' which he adopts impose an improbable and unseemly hurry on the characters in their spiritual and emotional development, and the dialogue is liable to seem either too flat or too solemnly epigrammatic. There are some fine things in both plays (such as the ritual closing of rooms by which the old aunts in *The Living Room* deny both life and death); and they are certainly superior to the average product of the commercial theatre. But, even when the far more successful comedy, *The Complaisant Lover* (1959) is taken into account, it does not seem likely that Greene will add a significant chapter to the history of British drama.

Greene's excursion into the theatre is in one way characteristic of the latter part of his career. During this time his work seems to be directed by a restless search for new themes or new modes of exploring familiar themes; and beneath it all one detects a certain impatience with the categories with which critics have sought to define his literary identity. The dedication to *Loser Takes All* (1955), a slight comic novella about gambling, contains a wry allusion to 'some of my Catholic critics'; and in this and his next entertainment, *Our Man in Havana* (1958), Greene takes a light-hearted view of marital and sexual behaviour that is, by Catholic standards, highly irregular. 'Catholic critics' consoled by the uncompromising supernaturalism of *The Potting Shed* must have been disconcerted by *The Complaisant Lover*, in which the adulterous situation so productive of misery in Greene's previous work is resolved by the bland acceptance of a *ménage à trois*. In these years, Greene is giving his humorous vein, subdued though wholly delightful in such characters as Harris and Parkis, its full chance. *Our Man in Havana* is an extravagant burlesque of the British Secret Service—and also, incidentally, of the apparatus of Greene's early entertainments.

These and other new developments in Greene's work—such as his renewed interest in the short story, a form in which he has never excelled—naturally provoked a number of questions in the minds of his audience. Had he worked out the vein of Catholic inspiration for his work? If so, what would replace it? Would he, in fact, produce any more novels of real consequence? *A Burnt-Out Case* (1961) intensified the debate without settling it. But it does suggest that

Greene had been asking himself the same questions, and had decided to objectify them in an imaginative form.

I referred, at the beginning of this essay, to the parallel that can be drawn between the hero of this novel and his creator: between Querry, the Catholic architect who comes to a remote leprosarium in the Belgian Congo, no longer believing in religion or love or art, in flight from *Time*-style celebrity and from official adoption by his Church; and Greene, the Catholic novelist, known for his unconventional travels, his melancholia and pessimism, his dislike of publicity, and his controversial standing among co-religionists. It is worth taking note, however, of Greene's words in the Dedication: 'This is not a *roman à clef*, but an attempt to give dramatic expression to various types of belief, half-belief and non-belief.' The most important feature of Querry, as his name suggests, is that he is a mystery. In his fascinating Congo journal, *In Search of a Character* (1961), Greene describes his decision to restrain the authorial voice from penetrating the thoughts of any character in the novel: 'This makes for the mood of mystery which I want to catch.' One might suggest, therefore, that insofar as Greene is using himself as a lay figure for the character of Querry, it is not in a confessional way, but by drawing back and regarding his own public image and what others make of it. *In Search of a Character* is full of such reflections.

Given, as the subject for a novel, the discrepancies between the real character of a famous man and the character others ascribe to him, the ironies inherent in the situation will be intensified if he has virtually no character at all—if he is in the painful process of shedding his identity and finding a new one. This is precisely Querry's situation. Dr Colin correctly diagnoses Querry as a 'burnt-out case', like one of 'the lepers who lose everything that can be eaten away before they are cured'. But even the perceptive doctor had at first suspected Querry of being a leprophile; and others are not so ready to abandon their theories.

Rycker, the odious *colon*, is the first to discover that Querry is *the* Querry, and takes it upon himself to proclaim the architect a new Schweitzer. This suggestion is eagerly endorsed by Father Thomas, an insecure priest who finds the rather hearty and humdrum community life at the leprosarium lacking in spirituality. Parkinson, the syndicated journalist, contributes his own theory that Querry is atoning for a lurid past. Something like a cult begins to grow around the exasperated Querry. The ironies are extremely well managed. Querry's denials of missionary zeal are put down to humility, and his protestations of disbelief are attributed to the mystical symptom of 'aridity'. In the end, of course, Querry's admirers cannot tolerate his refusal to play the roles they require. Rycker, wounded by Querry's rebuffs, flies into a jealous rage when Querry imprudently takes pity on the man's pathetic young wife; and Parkinson, also stung by Querry's scorn, passes Rycker false but circumstantial evidence of adultery. When the scandal reaches the leprosarium, Father Thomas is the first to believe it.

Meanwhile the ambiguous concept of the 'cure' of the burnt-out case has been taking on a more positive aspect. Querry begins to find a way of life at the leprosarium, and to talk 'as a hungry man eats'— particularly with Dr Colin. Colin is easily the most sympathetic non-believer in Greene's work. Unlike the Lieutenant in *The Power and the Glory*, whom he remotely resembles in his austere devotion to duty, Colin does not see his humane vocation as opposed to the religious vocation. 'Sometimes I think that the search for suffering and the remembrance of suffering are the only means we have to put ourselves in touch with the whole human condition,' he says. 'With suffering we become part of the Christian myth.' Religious faith has often been associated with suffering in Greene's work, but never before with the relief and conquest of suffering. Yet Colin proceeds, with the obvious approval of the author, to develop an essentially optimistic theory of human development, in which evolutionary progress is identified with the spirit of Christian love. Greene has acknowledged the influence of Teilhard de Chardin's *The Phenomenon of Man* on *A Burnt-Out Case*; and it says much for the openness of his mind and imagination that he responded enthusiastically, at a fairly late stage of his career, to a philosophical argument which in some ways runs against the grain of his most characteristic fiction. In *A Burnt-Out Case* 'the belief that life should be better than it is' seems to be slowly winning over 'the belief that when it appears better it is really worse'.

But the issue is left in some doubt: Querry retains his mystery to the last. He has reached the point of recognizing suffering, and hence identity, in himself; of 'fingering' his lack of faith, in Marie Rycker's words, 'like a sore you want to get rid of'. But his self-discovery is interrupted by a bullet from the demented Rycker. Querry dies murmuring, 'This is absurd or . . .'. 'This' presumably refers not only to his tragi-farcical death, but to his whole life, in which the public appearances of success and fulfilment have been hollow and deceptive. Either this life and death are 'absurd'—i.e., meaningless—or (we may tentatively complete the thought) they acquire meaning only in some transcendent pattern: the pattern offered by religion, or the less orthodox pattern expounded by Dr Colin.

The idea, deriving from existentialist thought, of human life as 'absurd' is a familiar one in contemporary literature, where its effect has been to break down traditional genre categories and to displace potentially tragic materials toward disquieting forms of comedy. Greene's latest novel is significantly entitled *The Comedians* (1966), and is pitched, in tone, somewhere between *The Quiet American* and *Our Man in Havana*, mingling laughter with pity and fear.

Brown, the rootless, cosmopolitan, middle-aged narrator, meets on board a ship bound for Haiti a rather dubious 'Major' Jones with claims to an adventurous and heroic war record, and an American called Smith who once ran obscurely for the American Presidency on a vegetarian ticket. The absurd convergence of these three overworked names establishes the note of a story in which the characters are mostly denied the luxury of dignity as they contend with the vicissitudes of life. The vicissitudes are supplied in ample measure by Haiti, 'the shabby land of terror', in which the action is largely set, an impoverished and desperate country languishing under the tyranny of a ruthless dictator and his secret police, the 'Tontons Macoutes', whose inscrutable malice is chillingly symbolized by the black sunglasses they wear night and day. Brown is returning to Haiti to look after the hotel he has failed to sell, and to pick up the threads of a rather joyless love affair with Martha, wife of a South American ambassador and daughter of a German war criminal. Smith and his wife are hoping to set up a vegetarian centre in Haiti. Jones's mission is more obscure, but proves to be some kind of financial swindle involving government funds. Brown's association with Smith and Jones, and his discovery in his swimming pool of the corpse of the Secretary for Social Welfare, Dr Philipot, who has cut his throat to avoid arrest, draws him into the dangerous world of political intrigue. More from personal than ideological motives Brown collaborates with a group of pathetically ineffective guerrillas led by Philipot's nephew, and at the end of the story narrowly escapes to Santo Domingo, where he adds to an already varied career the profession of undertaker.

Like the Liberia of *Journey Without Maps*, Haiti gives the lie to liberal optimism. Thus, the experience of a Negro police state is a cruel blow to the civil-rights idealism of the Smiths. Greene, however, has lost his old zest for attacking Pelagians. The Smiths are in many ways admirable characters, and the narrator explicitly denies that he

finds them comic. For in this novel the words *comedy* and *comedian*
are used in a traditional, theatrical sense, denoting the improvisation
of roles and the wearing of masks. The theme of the book seems to be
that in an era in which cruelty and injustice in the public life have
grown to uncontrollable proportions (and it is emphasized that Haiti
is representative, not abnormal in this respect) the private pursuit of
happiness is inevitably attended by absurd incongruities and inde-
corums that compel the individual into the resigned adoption of a
'comic' role. The alternative is some kind of irrational commitment—
to force, to vegetarianism, to voodoo—which is validated by defeat,
and ultimately by death. Thus, Brown comments on the Negro lover
of his mother, when he commits suicide after her death: 'perhaps he
was no *comédien* after all. Death is a proof of sincerity.' In these terms
Jones is the arch-comedian. His role is the most outrageous deception
of all; yet he has the gift of amusing people and winning their
affection. And when Brown, out of misplaced jealousy, forces him to
make good his boasts and take over the leadership of Philipot's
guerrillas, he has the courage to go through with his performance to
the point of dying for it.

Early in his narrative, Brown (a lapsed Catholic) remarks:

> When I was a boy I had faith in the Christian God. Life under
> his shadow was a very serious affair; I saw Him incarnated in
> every tragedy. He belonged to the *lacrimae rerum* like a gigantic
> figure looming through a Scottish mist. Now that I approached
> the end of life it was only my sense of humour that enabled me
> sometimes to believe in Him. Life was a comedy, not the tragedy
> for which I had been prepared, and it seemed to me that we
> were all . . . driven by an authoritative practical joker towards
> the extreme point of comedy.

Without interpreting this passage as a personal confession we may
perhaps see it as some kind of gloss on Greene's progress from fiction
based on a 'tragic' conflict between human and divine values, to
fiction conceived in terms of comedy and irony in which the
possibility of religious faith has all but retreated out of sight in the
anarchic confusion of human behaviour. In Bendrix a secular and
cynical view of life is still powerfully challenged by the divine order,
but in Fowler, Querry, and Brown the challenge is progressively
weaker, and more oblique. There is evidence, here, of a greater
capacity for imaginative development than Greene is usually given
credit for. But the permeation of his later work with negative and

5

sceptical attitudes, characteristically filtered through the consciousness of a laconic, disillusioned narrator, has resulted in some loss of intensity. Fowler, Querry, and Brown are all created with Greene's accustomed skill, and the actions in which they are involved never fail to interest; but they do not possess the imagination and linger in the memory as do Pinkie, or Scobie, or the whiskey priest.

'Patronizingly in the end he would place me probably a little above Maugham,' Bendrix, the novelist, sourly predicts of his critic, Waterbury, thus cautioning critics intent on 'placing' Greene himself. Let it merely be suggested that among his own generation of British novelists it is difficult to find his equal; and that he has produced a number of novels that seem certain to live, by the force with which they embody a highly individual, genuinely challenging view of life. Finally, there is something disarming about an eminent author who has twice won *New Statesman* competitions by parodying himself. 'Fame falls like a dead hand on an author's shoulders,' Greene has written; but few have borne its weight with more self-possession than he.

6 The Uses and Abuses of Omniscience: Method and Meaning in Muriel Spark's *The Prime of Miss Jean Brodie*

I

First, then, we warn thee not too hastily to condemn any of the incidents in this our history as impertinent and foreign to our main design, because thou dost not immediately conceive in what manner such an incident may conduce to that design. This work may, indeed, be considered as a great creation of our own; and for a little reptile of a critic to presume to find fault with any of its parts, without knowing the manner in which the whole is connected and before he comes to the final catastrophe, is a most presumptuous absurdity. The allusion and metaphor we have here made use of, we must acknowledge to be infinitely great for our occasion, but there is, indeed, no other, which is at all adequate to express the difference between an author of the first rate and a critic of the lowest.

Henry Fielding *Tom Jones* Bk. X Chap. I

The 'allusion and metaphor' employed by Henry Fielding is of course the analogy between the novelist and the God of creation; and it is no coincidence that the convention of the omniscient and intrusive narrator in fiction (of which Fielding was a supreme exponent) began to lose favour at about the time that Nietzsche announced the death of God, or that most of the significant modern novelists who have persevered with this convention have been professed Christians. Jean-Paul Sartre's well-known attack on François Mauriac illustrates the point:

in a true novel, as in the world of Einstein, there is no place for the privileged observer. . . . M. Mauriac preferred his own way. He chose divine omniscience and omnipotence. But a novel is written by a man for men. In the eyes of God, which see through appearances without dwelling on them, there is no novel, no art, since art lives by appearances. God is not an artist; neither is M. Mauriac.[1]

Graham Greene, naturally enough, struck exactly the opposite note in his essay on Mauriac:

M. Mauriac's first importance to an English reader . . . is that he belongs to the company of the great traditional novelists: he is a writer for whom the visible world has not ceased to exist, whose characters have the solidity and importance of men with souls to save or lose, and a writer who claims the traditional and essential right of a novelist, to comment, to express his views. For how tired we have become of the dogmatically 'pure' novel, the tradition founded by Flaubert and reaching its magnificent tortuous climax in England in the works of Henry James. One is reminded of those puzzles which take the form of a maze. The child is encouraged to trace with his pencil a path to the centre of the maze. But in the pure novel the reader begins at the centre and has to find his way to the gate. He runs his pencil down avenues which must surely go straight to the circumference, the world outside the maze, where moral judgments and acts of supernatural importance can be found . . . but the printed channels slip and twist and slide, landing him back where he began, and he finds on close examination that the designer of the maze has in fact overprinted the only exit. . . . The exclusion of the author can go too far. Even the author, poor devil, has the right to exist, and M. Mauriac re-affirms that right.[2]

Graham Greene reaffirmed that right in his own novels, though like Mauriac he made some concessions to modern scepticism, preserving a continuity of tone between the rendering of his characters' consciousness in indirect speech and authorial comment, so that the reader is scarcely aware of the transitions. In *The End of the Affair* Greene neatly turned the tables on Sartre's argument, for this story is narrated in the first person (the least privileged mode of narration, and one used by Sartre in *La Nausée*) by a sceptical, professional novelist who discovers from the journals of his mistress and from other sources that he has been caught up in the plot of a rival and divinely omniscient plot-maker. But this was Greene's last un-equivocally 'Catholic' novel. In subsequent novels—*The Quiet American*, *The Comedians*, and *Travels with my Aunt*—he has used the first-person method in a much more conventional way, to render a limited, sceptical and largely secular vision of experience. In *A Burnt-Out Case*, where the secular and religious world-views are evenly balanced, and the interpretation of events is left deliberately open, we find third-person narration, but with no authorial comment. In short, looking at the whole canon of Greene's fiction, it is not difficult to establish a normative correlation between omniscient authorial narration and an explicitly Christian perspective on events; and, correspondingly, between limited narrators and a more secular, humanist perspective.

II

Mr Greene was, I seem to remember reading somewhere, one of the literary figures who encouraged Muriel Spark to begin writing novels. Her first, *The Comforters* (1957) was written not long after her reception into the Roman Catholic Church and is about a young woman in the same situation. This heroine, Caroline, finds that 'the True Church was awful, though unfortunately, one couldn't deny, true'. She is also subject to hallucinations in which she hears a narrator tapping out on a typewriter an account of her actions in the style of a novelist, sometimes an intrusive one. She explains, 'It says, "Caroline was thinking or doing this or that"—then sometimes it adds a remark of its own.' Her friends think she is mad; Caroline herself fears diabolic agencies, until she decides that she and her friends are being used as characters in a novel by a writer in 'a different dimension'. She resists the determinism of the plot being contrived by the invisible and 'irresponsible' novelist, but at the same time she wants to put it to the test of truth. 'I intend to stand aside and see if the novel has any real form apart from this artificial plot. I happen to be a Christian.'

The objections to orthodox Christian belief and to authorial omniscience in fiction are, as we can see in Sartre's comment on Mauriac, essentially the same: that both involve a denial of human autonomy, of human freedom. In writing her first novel about the experience of conversion to Catholicism (an experience which we know, from external sources, was one of considerable psychological strain for the author herself),[3] Muriel Spark wittily combined the two issues: the heroine's subconscious resentment of the sacrifice of individual freedom entailed in conversion is projected in the fantasy of an omniscient and intrusive narrator who seems to be directing her life.

At the end of *The Comforters*, the heroine, confirmed in her faith and restored to health, goes off to write a novel 'about characters in a novel'. Mrs Spark herself went on to write several novels distinguished by, among other things, a highly original and effective exploitation of the convention of authorial omniscience. In *The*

Comforters, it would seem, she worked out—or worked off—the problems of reconciling literary values and religious convictions, of showing the operation of God's providence in the world while protecting herself from Sartre's accusation of thus falsifying the world.[4] She reserves the right to comment and explain as author, but she does so sparingly, often cryptically, with a deceptive lightness of touch; and for most of the time her stories are narrated from some human, limited point of view. She shows her hand as author in extraordinarily daring time-shifts backwards and forwards across the chronological span of the action, and it is perhaps in this respect that authorial omniscience most closely mimics the omniscience of God, who alone knows the beginning and the end. Yet the prophetic glimpses of the future fate of her characters which are one of the distinctive features of Mrs Spark's narrative method do not serve the purposes of a pat moralism or a reassuring providential pattern. They unsettle, rather than confirm, the reader's ongoing interpretation of events, constantly readjusting the points of emphasis and the principles of suspense in the narrative. Thus the experience of reading Muriel Spark can be appropriately described in terms of the 'maze' analogy applied by Greene to the 'pure' novel, though her novels are based on quite different philosophical and aesthetic assumptions. 'The reader begins at the centre and has to find his way to the gate.' That is, we begin in the confusion and muddle of human experience and try to find our way, with the help of the novelist, out to the clear light of understanding. But the route is not easy to find, the hints and clues given by our guide are elusive and ambiguous. It is not that the author has overprinted the exit—those abrupt authorial interventions and glimpses into the future have exactly the effect Greene describes, of finding ourselves suddenly 'in the world outside the maze, where moral judgments and acts of supernatural importance can be found'. But the precise import of those shifts of perspective is, as I have said, never simple or straightforward. Mrs Spark denies solipsism and posits the existence of some divine providence at work in the world; but this providence remains ultimately mysterious and incomprehensible because the world is a fallen one and not even the novelist can claim to understand it fully. The effect is rather different from Greene's brooding pity, and quite different from Fielding's genial reassurance. In *Tom Jones*, Fielding keeps the fate of his principal characters in suspense until the very end of the book, and takes pride in the fact that every little incident in the narrative, even those which seem quite gratuitous, contribute in some way to the final denouement. Though we do not know exactly *how* the story will be resolved, the personality of the narrator encourages an expectation that it *will* be resolved, happily for the sympathetic characters, and less happily for the unsympathetic. The whole novel thus serves as a metaphor for the providence of a just and benevolent God who, in the end, in His own way and in His own good time, may be trusted to make an equitable distribution of rewards and punishments. Muriel Spark, in contrast, uses the privilege of authorial omniscience to 'give away' in advance the surprises and reversals of her plots, and admits into the latter a degree of what, by normal aesthetic criteria, looks like calculated irrelevance. In *The Prime of Miss Jean Brodie* (1961), for instance, two twelve-year-old schoolgirls are reflecting on their sudden loss of interest in sex:

'There's not much time for sex research in the Senior School,' Sandy said.

'I feel I'm past it,' said Jenny. This was strangely true, and she did not again experience her early sense of erotic wonder in life until suddenly one day when she was nearly forty, an actress of moderate reputation married to a theatrical manager. It happened she was standing with a man whom she did not know very well outside a famous building in Rome, waiting for the rain to stop. She was surprised by a reawakening of that same buoyant and airy discovery of sex, a total sensation which it was impossible to say was physical or mental, only that it contained the lost and guileless delight of her eleventh year. She supposed herself to have fallen in love with the man, who might, she thought, have been moved towards her in his own way out of a world of his own, the associations of which were largely unknown to her. There was nothing whatever to be done about it, for Jenny had been contentedly married for sixteen years past; but the concise happening filled her with astonishment whenever it came to her mind in later days, and with a sense of the hidden possibilities in all things.[5]

This passage does not seem totally pointless because it is one of a series of glimpses into the future which punctuate the novel, through which a story about a group of schoolgirls is framed and deepened by a sense of these same girls as adult women. Furthermore, it can be seen, on reflection, as one of many variations, in the novel, on the theme of the loss of innocence. But there is no obvious cause-and-effect link between this experience of Jenny and her experiences as a child, nor is the episode referred to again in the book. Its abrupt introduction is for the reader, as for Jenny herself, not an explanation of anything, but a reminder of the 'hidden possibilities in all things', of the ultimate inscrutability and unpredictability of the shapes human lives assume.

I propose to examine the relationship between method and meaning in Muriel Spark's fiction by detailed analysis of *The Prime of Miss Jean Brodie*. It is conveniently short, and is perhaps the most widely-known of her books; but the choice is also a personal act of amends, for when I reviewed the novel on its first appearance I confessed myself 'beguiled . . . but not really stirred or involved or enlightened'.[6] This disappointment now seems to me to have been entirely my own fault, but not, I believe, unique among readers who expect more from a novel than 'comic observation and spicy dialogue' (to quote the blurb on the Penguin edition of 1969). It will not, I hope, be entirely redundant to indicate just how much more there is to this novel.

III

Set in the Edinburgh of the 'thirties, *The Prime of Miss Jean Brodie* concerns a group of schoolgirls, Monica Douglas, Rose Stanley, Eunice Gardiner, Sandy Stranger, Jenny Gray, and Mary Macgregor, who are chosen and groomed for discipleship by the formidable and eccentric schoolmistress who gives the novel its title. The narrative begins in 1936, when the girls are aged sixteen, but quickly reverts to the year 1930, when they began their memorable two years' tuition by Miss Jean Brodie in the Junior division of Marcia Blaine School. Miss Brodie dominates their lives and fantasies in many ways, but they are particularly intrigued by the question of her relationships with the two men on the teaching staff: the art master, Mr Lloyd, who is a Catholic and married, and the singing master, Mr Lowther, a bachelor and an Elder of the Church of Scotland. Mr Lloyd, who lost his arm in the Great War (in which Miss Brodie's first love fell), is the more romantically dashing, and Monica Douglas sees him embracing Miss Brodie, but the latter also appears to be deeply involved with Mr Lowther. As the girls move up through the Senior School (still disapprovingly known as the 'Brodie set' because of their continuing discipleship) it becomes evident that Miss Brodie is in love with Mr Lloyd, but has 'renounced' him because he is married. However, she continues the romance vicariously through Rose, who models for Mr Lloyd (though his portraits always bear an eerie resemblance to Miss Brodie). Miss Brodie conducts an affair, in her own domineering style, with Mr Lowther, but refuses to marry him, and he despairingly marries the science mistress. At about this time (the point at which the novel opens) a new girl called Joyce Emily Hammond, with a record of delinquency, joins the school, and tries unsuccessfully to join the set. Later, however, Miss Brodie befriends her. The Headmistress impotently plots Miss Brodie's removal. One day Joyce Emily disappears and it is learned that she has been killed in an attack on a train in Spain. It is assumed she was trying to join her brother who is fighting against Franco in the Spanish Civil War. Miss Brodie continues to nourish the idea that Rose will have an affair with Lloyd, but it is in fact Sandy who does so, while Miss Brodie is enthusiastically touring Hitler's Germany, in the summer of 1938. Through Lloyd, Sandy gets interested in the Catholic faith. One day Miss Brodie reveals to Sandy that she knew of and encouraged Joyce Emily's escapade, though she persuaded her to switch her allegiance to Franco. Sandy goes to the Headmistress and tells her that if she wants to get rid of Miss Brodie the charge should be, not sexual irregularity, but fascism. In the summer of 1939, Miss Brodie is forced to resign, by which time Sandy has been received into the Catholic Church.

This is the main line of the narrative, but there are many loops in it through which events both before and after the climax of the betrayal, and the betrayal itself, are anticipated. The events *after* the climax are particularly interesting. We learn on page 14 that Mary Macgregor was killed in a hotel fire in 1943 or 44; on page 55 that Miss Brodie died of cancer in 1946; and on page 35 that Sandy entered an enclosed order of nuns and, by the late 'fifties, had achieved considerable distinction with a psychological treatise on 'The Transfiguration of the Commonplace'. To arrange the sequence of events in chronological order is indeed no easy task, so complex is the web of cross-reference, anticipation and retrospect. On first reading, however, the effect is not so much one of complexity as of a blithe insouciance, as if the author were ordering events intuitively and even haphazardly. It is quite unlike the experience of reading, say, Conrad, where we are always conscious that the shifts of time and point-of-view have been engineered for specific effects, and where a strenuous effort is required from the reader to follow the story. It is very easy to read *The Prime of Miss Jean Brodie* quickly and lightly as nothing more than a collection of wry anecdotes about

5*

an eccentric schoolmistress and her pupils. It is, of course, highly effective and entertaining on this level: as a kind of Theophrastian 'character', Miss Brodie is completely convincing, and so is the impression she makes on the sensibilities of her pupils. The ethos of the Marcia Blaine school and the quality of middle-class life in Edinburgh between the Wars are beautifully caught and communicated. In brief, the 'world' of the novel, especially that part of it concerned with school-life, though rendered with extreme economy, is authentically observed and quite acceptable as realistic fiction. This was shown by the ease with which the novel was adapted to the screen in the recent film-version.

That film, however, though made with considerable care and well-acted, was not entirely satisfactory, precisely because it rendered *only* the literal and linear dimension of the story. The film was, paradoxically, more like a conventional novel than the novel itself, particularly in narrative method. It begins with the girls in Miss Brodie's class and relates the main action in a straightforward, chronological sequence, concluding with Sandy's betrayal of the teacher; and it invites an essentially emotional, at times sentimental, response. The narrative method of the novel, in contrast—the jumps forwards and backwards in time, the pointed interventions of the authorial voice—constantly check any inclination we may have to 'lose ourselves' in the story or to sink into emotional identification with any of the characters; it detaches us from the experience presented and makes us think about its meaning, or meanings.

One can, of course, appreciate the technical difficulties of translating the method of the novel into cinematic terms, for the grammar of film seems to lack a narrative future tense. A film can move backwards in time and sideways in space, but when it moves forward in time the 'future' immediately becomes the 'present'. Thus the only way in which the adult lives of the Brodie set could have been incorporated in the film would have been by beginning with the latest point in the action—Sandy receiving her visitors in the convent—and then presenting everything else in extended flashbacks. But Muriel Spark uses a technique that can only be described as the 'flash-forward': we are not, as readers, situated in the adult lives of the Brodie set, looking back with mixed emotions on their schooldays; rather we are situated with them *in* their schooldays,[7] but able to look forward occasionally, as they cannot, at what is to happen to them later. It is difficult to see how this effect could be achieved in a film without totally abandoning realism, because it is difficult to establish within the dramatic conventions of the film a perceiving consciousness equivalent to the omniscient author of literary narrative.

It is not merely the treatment of time that is in question here. *The Prime of Miss Jean Brodie* is a novel about education and religion, and insofar as the movie lifted itself above the purely anecdotal, it touched on only the first of these themes. The religious dimension of the book was lost not merely because certain events, such as Sandy's conversion and religious vocation, were dropped out, but because the film failed to incorporate the strain of religious metaphor which is woven into the texture of the novel, largely through the medium of the authorial voice. Let us now look more closely at the meanings and methods of the novel.

IV

I say 'meanings' (plural) deliberately. It is a mistake to look for a single, simple meaning in this book, and it was because I made that mistake that I originally underestimated it. I wanted, for instance, to know whether I should approve or disapprove of Miss Brodie, and was baffled by the lack of clear directions towards either of these alternatives. The answer, of course, is that we should do neither—or rather, do both. And the key here is the character of Sandy Stranger—the shrewdest, most complex, and most interesting of the Brodie set, who is also the principal point-of-view character in the novel. Not only do we see most of the action through her eyes, but many of the authorial comments are in effect comments upon Sandy and her perceptions.

At the beginning of the book each of the girls is said to be 'famous' for something: Monica was 'famous for mathematics which she could do in her brain, and for her anger', Rose was 'famous for sex', Eunice Gardiner was 'famous for her spritely gymnastics and glorious swimming', and so on. (This method of characterizing and distinguishing between the girls with reference to particular attributes parodies and exploits the conventions of popular British schoolboy or schoolgirl fiction, like Frank Richards's *Greyfriars* stories.) Sandy, we are told, was famous for her vowel-sounds; she was 'merely notorious for her small, almost non-existent eyes'. In fact, it is these eyes that are her distinguishing mark throughout the novel; and Sandy is in an important sense the eyes of the reader. She is the only character who is interiorized to any significant extent —the only character whose thoughts we share intimately. She is marked out in this way as early as page 8, where, after Miss Brodie has firmly dismissed the interloper Joyce Emily, we are told:

> Sandy looked back as Joyce Emily walked, and then skipped, leggy and uncontrolled for her age, in the opposite direction, and the Brodie set was left to their secret life as it had been six years ago in their childhood.

There is no logical need for the words, *Sandy looked back*, here: the description of Joyce Emily skipping away could, like the preceding descriptions, have been simply authorial. The effect of the words is to make Joyce Emily an object of Sandy's perception, to establish Sandy as a perceiving consciousness in the novel, and to draw attention to her eyes ('looked back'). Three pages later we get Sandy's view of Miss Brodie's figure six years earlier:

> Some days it seemed to Sandy that Miss Brodie's chest was flat, no bulges at all, but straight as her back. On other days her chest was breast-shaped and large, very noticeable, something for Sandy to sit and peer at through her tiny eyes. . . .

We never see Miss Brodie in this way from the point of view of the other girls. And we never, of course, get inside Miss Brodie herself—we never see the action from her point of view. She is a phenomenon, a puzzle, an enigma; and as we try to make some assessment of her, we naturally use Sandy as a point of reference, because she is the only interiorized character engaged in the same task. Sandy is not, however, a totally reliable point of reference and there is an irony in the fact that she achieves fame for a treatise on 'the nature of moral perception'. Her eyes, as well as symbolizing her shrewdness and perceptiveness, also symbolize less attractive qualities. They are described as 'little pig-like eyes' (13) and as 'tiny eyes which it was astonishing anyone could trust' (100). Sandy is treacherous by nature—we see this as early as page 14 where she whispers a wrong answer to Mary Macgregor in class and gets her into trouble. And, of course, Sandy betrays Miss Brodie.

Great emphasis is put on this act of betrayal, at the expense of narrative surprise. As early as page 27 we learn that Miss Brodie was betrayed by someone: Eunice Gardiner tells her husband in the late 'fifties, ' "She was betrayed by one of her own girls, we were called the Brodie set. I never found out which one betrayed her." ' On pages 38–9 Miss Brodie says, ' "As for impropriety, it could never be imputed to me except by some gross distortion on the part of the traitor. I do not think ever to be betrayed" '—which of course, since we know she *is* going to be betrayed, strikes an ironic note of hubris, emphasized by the somewhat high-flown style of the utterance. The betrayal itself is almost the last scene of the book, and its natural climax; but the identity of the betrayer—Sandy—has been given away long ago, on page 60, when Sandy is having tea with Miss Brodie at the Braid Hills hotel in 1946:

> The whine in her voice—'betrayed me, betrayed me'—bored and afflicted Sandy. It is seven years, thought Sandy, since I betrayed this tiresome woman. What does she mean by 'betray'?

Thus, half-way through her novel, Muriel Spark throws away its main element of suspense. The interest of the reader therefore shifts from Whodunnit? to how did she do it and, more importantly, why did she do it, and with what justice? That is why Sandy is the reader's main point of reference in making a moral assessment of Miss Brodie, and why the answer to the question, 'Should we approve or disapprove of Miss Brodie?' is, 'Both'.

Sandy (as her surname, Stranger, suggests) is the most sceptical, critical and independent-minded of the Brodie set, and the one who finally takes it upon herself to 'put a stop to Miss Brodie'; but she is also the one who in mature life seems to have the keenest appreciation of Miss Brodie's positive worth. A crucial passage in this respect is one on pages 85–6, where the author is commenting on Miss Brodie's lack of guilt:

> The side-effects of this condition were exhilarating to her special
> girls in that they in some way partook of the general absolution
> she had assumed to herself, and it was only in retrospect that they
> could see Miss Brodie's affair with Mr Lowther for what it was,
> that is to say, in a factual light. All the time they were under
> her influence she and her actions were outside the context of
> right and wrong. It was twenty-five years before Sandy had so
> far recovered from a creeping vision of disorder that she could
> look back and recognize that Miss Brodie's defective sense of
> self-criticism. . . .

I think we expect the sentence to go on to say something like 'had been dangerous and harmful'. But in fact the sentence skips over that stage in Sandy's life when she turns against Miss Brodie, and concludes with her mature judgment, much more lenient towards the teacher:

Miss Brodie's defective sense of self-criticism had not been without its beneficent and enlarging effects; by which time Sandy had already betrayed Miss Brodie and Miss Brodie was laid in her grave.

This conclusion is surprising because as we read we naturally identify 'It was twenty-five years' with the preceding 'in retrospect', whereas in fact 'It was twenty-five years' introduces a retrospect of the retrospect: only in middle age can Sandy see that her perception of Miss Brodie's defects 'in a factual light', in the 'context of right and wrong', was not a true escape from the disorder generated by Miss Brodie's antinomianism, but a symptom of it, a rejection of Miss Brodie as extreme as her previous submission to the teacher's spell. The passage is typical of the way the authorial voice defeats the reader's expectation of clear and simple judgments.

Miss Brodie's 'beneficent and enlarging effects' are mainly educational. Though she is a memorably individual character, she is a not unfamiliar type: the charismatic teacher who leaves an indelible mark on her pupils. One of the functions of the 'flash-forward' technique is to present the extension of Miss Brodie's influence on the girls in their adult life simultaneously with their relationship as teacher and pupils. Was Miss Brodie a good teacher or a bad teacher? The question is no easier to answer than the question of whether she was a good woman or a bad woman. In both cases the good and the bad are inextricably entwined.

Miss Brodie's lessons are absurd in their egocentricity, their inconsequentiality, but they are very evidently fun, and the girls do learn quite a lot of useful information mixed up with the details of Miss Brodie's personal life and personal prejudices. When they transfer to the Senior School:

> These girls were discovered to have heard of the Buchmanites
> and Mussolini, the Italian Renaissance painters, the advantages
> to the skin of cleansing cream and witch-hazel over honest soap
> and water, and the word 'menarche'; the interior decoration of
> the London house of the author of *Winnie the Pooh* had been
> described to them, as had the love lives of Charlotte Brontë
> and of Miss Brodie herself. They were aware of the existence of
> Einstein and the arguments of those who considered the Bible
> to be untrue. They knew the rudiments of astrology but not the
> date of the Battle of Flodden or the capital of Finland. All the
> Brodie set, save one, counted on its fingers, as had Miss Brodie,
> with accurate results, more or less. (5–6)

On the whole, Miss Brodie's educational methods contrast favourably with the orthodoxy of the school—and they are contrasted very emphatically. When Miss Brodie is absent (suspiciously at the same time as Mr Lowther) through 'illness', her girls are taught by the forbidding Miss Gaunt, who does not bother to remember their names and uses the Romantic literature dear to Miss Brodie as a form of punishment: ' "A hundred lines of *Marmion*," Miss Gaunt flung at [Rose]' (57). The Miss Gaunt interlude is a premonition of the change the girls experience when they move from Miss Brodie's class into the Senior School, where the days were 'brisk with the getting of knowledge from unsoulful experts' (77)—experts like the science teacher, Miss Lockhart, who could 'blow up the school with her jar of gunpowder and would never dream of doing so' (114). (Miss Brodie, by implication, *would* dream of doing so.)

On the whole, Miss Brodie's teaching contrasts favourably with the dry-as-dust academic approach of the rest of the staff, and we feel a good deal of sympathy with her in her struggle with the jealously disapproving headmistress. She is a stimulating teacher. Sandy's religious name, Sister Helen of the Transfiguration, and the title of her famous treatise, suggest what Miss Brodie does for her girls: she transfigures the commonplace. Eunice remembers her warmly: ' "She was an Edinburgh Festival all on her own" ' (27). Poor, pathetic Mary Macgregor, jilted by her first, and last, boyfriend during the War, 'thought back to see if she had ever been really happy in her life; it occurred to her then that the first years with Miss Brodie, sitting listening to all those stories and opinions which had nothing to do with the ordinary world, had been the happiest time of her life' (15). Yet immediately after this passage the author describes a class-room episode in which Miss Brodie unfairly humiliated Mary, and comments 'These were the days that Mary Macgregor on looking back found to be the happiest days of her life' (16). This does not invalidate Mary's retrospect, but it does remind us that memory is highly selective, and sharply checks any inclination we may have to regard Miss Brodie in an indulgent, sentimental glow.

We cannot, indeed, ignore the fact that Miss Brodie has some very undesirable qualities as a teacher. She contrasts her own educational theory with that of the headmistress, saying that she tries to lead out the potentialities of her pupils, not to pour stuff into them, but she is of course extravagantly overbearing and tyrannical, shaping the pupils in her own image and teaching opinions as if they were facts:

'Who is the greatest Italian painter?'
'Leonardo da Vinci, Miss Brodie.'
'That is incorrect. The answer is Giotto, he is my favourite.'

She is extraordinarily egocentric, witness her obsessive harping on
her 'prime':

> 'Attend to me, girls. One's prime is the moment one was born
> for. Now that my prime has begun—Sandy, your attention is
> wandering. What have I been talking about?'
> 'Your prime, Miss Brodie.' (12)
> 'You girls are my vocation . . . I am dedicated to you in my
> prime.' (23)
> 'These are the years of my prime. You are benefiting by my
> prime.' (44)

In other words, Miss Brodie cannot allow her dedication to merely
display itself—she has continually to draw attention to it, to make it
into a legend, a myth.

Miss Brodie is a Romantic by taste and temperament, and exemplifies the defects of the uncontrolled romantic sensibility. The
literary parody in the book is important here. The whole story bears
a parodic resemblance to *Jane Eyre*, which, we are often reminded,
is one of Miss Brodie's favourite novels (she reads it aloud to the
girls while they are having sewing lessons). The love lives of Charlotte
Brontë and Miss Brodie are associated on the first page of the novel
(see quotation above). Jane, Charlotte and Jean Brodie are all
rebellious young women, teachers by profession, ardent feminists in
search of personal fulfilment. Jane falls in love with Rochester but
renounces him when she discovers he is married, and is then courted
by the austere clergyman St John Rivers. Mr Lloyd thus parodies
Rochester (both have a mutilated arm), and Mr Lowther, inhibited
and intimidated by Scottish religion (he is choir-master and the
Elder of his local church) parodies St John Rivers. There is more
overt parody of romantic literature in the fantasies of the young
Sandy, in which she translates her experience into the more exciting
terms of *The Lady of Shalott* and *Kidnapped*. But the novel's *tour de
force* in this vein is the conclusion of the romantic novel which
Sandy and Jenny compose about Miss Brodie. Miss Brodie is made
to decline a proposal from Mr Lowther in a letter which hilariously
combines the language of high romance with the sexual terminology
of newspaper court reports:

My Own Delightful Gordon,
   Your letter has moved me deeply as you may imagine. But alas I must ever decline to be Mrs Lowther. My reasons are two-fold. I am dedicated to my Girls as is Madame Pavlova, and there is another in my life whose mutual love reaches out to me beyond the bounds of Time and Space. He is Teddy Lloyd! Intimacy has never taken place with him. He is married to another. One day in the art room we melted into each other's arms and knew the truth. But I was proud of giving myself to you when you came and took me in the bracken on Arthur's Seat while the storm raged about us. If I am in a certain condition, I shall place the infant in the care of a worthy shepherd and his wife and we can discuss it calmly as platonic acquaintances. I may permit misconduct to occur again from time to time as an outlet because I am in my Prime. (73)

Fantasy is one way of 'transfiguring the commonplace', and in a child is natural and healthy. But whereas Sandy and Jenny discard their fantasies as they mature (they bury the romance about Miss Brodie in a cave) Miss Brodie continues to inhabit her own fantasies, rewriting the story of her first love to fit the circumstances of her subsequent liaisons with Lloyd and Lowther; and eventually, for her own devious psychological reasons, tries to create, in the manner of a romantic novelist, a love affair between Rose and Mr Lloyd.

> Sandy was fascinated by this method of making patterns with facts, and was divided between her admiration for the technique and the pressing need to prove Miss Brodie guilty of misconduct. (72)

Miss Brodie's sympathy for the Fascist movements of the 'thirties is not a reasoned political attitude, but an extension of her egotism and romantic sensibility:

> Miss Brodie . . . was going abroad, not to Italy this year, but to Germany, where Hitler was become Chancellor, a prophet-figure like Thomas Carlyle, and more reliable than Mussolini. (97)

Aspiring to be a charismatic leader herself, she naturally admires the successful dictators, Hitler, Mussolini and Franco. The combination of dedication, élitism, bravura style and heady rhetoric characteristic of fascist movements appeals to her. Her remark to

Sandy after the Second World War, 'Hitler *was* rather naughty', (122) shows her complete blindness to political and historical realities. On her return from a pre-war visit to Germany:

> She was full of her travels and quite sure the new régime would save the world. Sandy was bored, it did not seem necessary that the world should be saved, only that the poor people in the streets and slums of Edinburgh should be relieved. (122/3)

This reference takes us back to the episode in which Miss Brodie takes her girls for a walk through the slums of Edinburgh, the significance of which is indicated by the rather formal authorial introduction: 'It is now time to speak of the long walk through the old part of Edinburgh where Miss Brodie took her set...' (27). In one sense this expedition is a credit to Miss Brodie, since she is showing the girls an aspect of their native environment from which they have been protected. But while the spectacle of poverty makes a deep effect on Sandy, Miss Brodie seems at first oblivious to it— she 'talked of history' as the girls inhaled the 'amazingly terrible' smell of the slums—and when she explains the line of men queueing for their dole her response lacks real compassion.

> 'It is the weekly payment made by the State for the relief of the Unemployed and their families. Sometimes they go and spend their dole on drink before they go home, and their children starve. They are our brothers. Sandy, stop staring at once. In Italy the unemployment problem has been solved.' (39)

A few pages before, Sandy has mused on Miss Brodie's fondness for Mussolini, and it occurs to her that 'the Brodie set was Miss Brodie's fascisti, not to the naked eye, marching along, but all knit together for her need and in another way, marching along.' When Sandy finally betrays Miss Brodie, it is clear that she uses the charge of fascism merely as an expedient. The last straw for Sandy is the discovery that Miss Brodie connived at Joyce Emily's fatal expedition to Spain. It is not that Miss Brodie encouraged the girl to switch her allegiance to Franco that shocks Sandy (though this is how she first learns the truth of the matter), but the fact that Miss Brodie encouraged her to go at all. This is the final, decisive evidence, for Sandy, that Miss Brodie's irresponsible egotism is out of hand, and must be prevented from doing further damage.

V

This brings us to the religious aspect of the novel; for the assessment of Miss Brodie is, in the last analysis, an ethical and theological matter, not merely an educational one. As I have suggested, Sandy is our main point of reference in forming a judgment of Miss Brodie, and we find that Sandy's developing understanding of her teacher's character is formulated more and more precisely, as she grows up, in religious terms, and is inextricably connected with the growth of her own religious awareness from the secular indifferentism of her family to her conversion to Roman Catholicism. Buried in this largely comic novel there is a severe and uncompromising dogmatic message: that all groups, communions and institutions are false and more or less corrupting except the one that is founded on the truths of Christian orthodoxy—and even that one is not particularly attractive or virtuous.

The first hint of this message comes at the beginning of the walk through the old quarter of Edinburgh. Sandy is walking with Mary Macgregor, who, by the technique of the flash-forward, is already touched with the pathos of her final end.

> Sandy, who had been reading *Kidnapped*, was having a conversation with the hero, Alan Breck, and was glad to be with Mary Macgregor because it was not necessary to talk to Mary.
> 'Mary, you may speak quietly to Sandy.'
> 'Sandy won't talk to me,' said Mary who later, in that hotel fire, ran hither and thither till she died.
> 'Sandy cannot talk to you if you are so stupid and disagreeable.' (28)

Sandy continues her imaginary conversation with Alan Breck.

> 'Don't walk so fast,' mumbled Mary.
> 'You aren't walking with your head up,' said Sandy. 'Keep it up, up.'
> Then suddenly Sandy wanted to be kind to Mary Macgregor, and thought of the possibilities of feeling nice from being nice to Mary instead of blaming her. Miss Brodie's voice from behind was saying to Rose Stanley, 'You are all heroines in the making. Britain must be a fit country for heroines to live in. The League of Nations. . . .' The sound of Miss Brodie's presence, just when it was on the tip of Sandy's tongue to be nice to Mary Macgregor, arrested the urge. Sandy looked back at her companions, and

understood them as a body with Miss Brodie for the head. She
perceived herself, the absent Jenny, the ever-blamed Mary, Rose,
Eunice, and Monica, all in a frightening little moment, in unified
compliance to the destiny of Miss Brodie, as if God had willed them
to birth for that purpose.

She was even more frightened, then, by her temptation to be nice
to Mary Macgregor, since by this action she would separate
herself, and be lonely, and blameable in a more dreadful way than
Mary who, although officially the faulty one, was at least inside
Miss Brodie's category of heroines in the making. So, for good
fellowship's sake, Sandy said to Mary, 'I wouldn't be walking with
you if Jenny was here.' And Mary said, 'I know.' Then Sandy
started to hate herself again and to nag on and on at Mary, with the
feeling that if you did a thing a lot of times, you made it into a right
thing. Mary started to cry, but quietly, so that Miss Brodie could
not see. Sandy was unable to cope and decided to stride on and be
a married lady having an argument with her husband. (30–1)

On the surface this passage simply describes a familiar pattern of
behaviour in small groups, especially among children, whereby one
member of the group is assigned the role of scapegoat or butt while
continuing to enjoy the other privileges of membership, all other
members being obliged to maintain an attitude of consistent contempt
and mockery towards the butt on pain of losing caste within the group
or even being expelled from it. What is notable about the passage is
however the religious metaphor concealed within it. The Brodie set
is seen as a parody, or travesty, of the Christian Church. Sandy's
version of her companions 'as a body with Miss Brodie for the head'
is an allusion to the doctrine of the Church as the Mystical Body of
Christ ('For as the body is one and hath many members; and all the
members of the body, whereas they are many, yet are one body: so
also is Christ' I Cor. 12) of which Christ himself is the Head ('But I
would have you know that the head of every man is Christ: and the
head of the woman is the man; and the head of Christ is God' I Cor. 11).
The Church implied here is however a Calvinistic one, built on the
ideas of election and predestination: 'in unified compliance to the
destiny of Miss Brodie, as if God had willed them to birth for that
purpose.' The Calvinistic disregard for 'good works' is caricatured by
Sandy's suppression of her impulse to be kind to Mary, and her saying
instead something spiteful 'for good fellowship's sake'.
Having established her own authorial presence from the outset,

Muriel Spark is able to introduce these somewhat sophisticated ideas into the description of a schoolgirl's thoughts without any disturbance of tone, for we accept the description as an articulation of intuitions only partly understood by the girl herself. The advantages of this narrative method are also exemplified in an equally important passage that describes the burgeoning of religious awareness in Sandy some years later:

> Nobody in her life, at home or at school, had ever spoken of Calvinism except as a joke that had once been taken seriously. . . . All she was conscious of now was that some quality of life peculiar to Edinburgh and nowhere else had been going on unbeknown to her all the time, and however undesirable it might be, she felt deprived of it; however undesirable, she desired to know what it was, and to cease to be protected from it by enlightened people.
>
> In fact it was the religion of Calvin of which Sandy felt deprived, or rather a specified recognition of it. She desired this birthright; something definite to reject. It pervaded the place in proportion as it was unacknowledged. In some ways the most real and rooted people whom Sandy knew were Miss Gaunt and the Kerr sisters who made no evasions about their belief that God had planned for practically everybody before they were born a nasty surprise when they died. Later, when Sandy read John Calvin, she found that although popular conceptions of Calvinism were sometimes mistaken, in this particular there was no mistake, indeed it was but a mild understatement of the case, he having made it God's pleasure to implant in certain people an erroneous sense of joy and salvation, so that their surprise might be the nastier.
>
> Sandy was unable to formulate these exciting propositions; nevertheless she experienced them in the air she breathed, she sensed them in the curiously defiant way in which the people she knew broke the Sabbath, and she smelt them in the excesses of Miss Brodie in her prime. . . . In this oblique way, she began to sense what went to the makings of Miss Brodie who had elected herself to grace in so particular a way and with more exotic suicidal enchantment than if she had simply taken to drink like other spinsters who couldn't stand it any more. (108–9)

The connection between Miss Brodie and Calvinism hinted at in the earlier passage about the walk through Edinburgh is here made much more explicit. Miss Brodie, though superficially in reaction against the Calvinistic moral code, in fact lives by a personal, secularized version of it, 'electing herself to grace', but fatally ignoring the possibility that her sense of justification may be erroneous. Sandy's insight into the paradoxes of Calvinism develops *pari passu* with her insight into the paradoxes of Miss Brodie, and for both she feels a mixture of attraction and repulsion. The statement that Sandy desired to know what Calvinism was, if only as 'something definite to reject', reminds us of a conversation reported earlier, but occurring much later, when Sandy is a nun and is questioned by an admirer of her treatise:

> 'The influences of one's teens are very important,' said the man.
> 'Oh, yes,' said Sandy, 'even if they provide something to react against.'
> 'What was your biggest influence, then, Sister Helena? Was it political, personal? Was it Calvinism?'
> 'Oh, no,' said Sandy. 'But there was a Miss Jean Brodie in her prime.' (35)

Sandy's intuitive interpretation of Miss Brodie's behaviour in Calvinistic terms is directly linked to her conviction that the teacher is plotting a love affair between Rose and Mr Lloyd. The long passage just quoted continues:

> It was plain that Miss Brodie wanted Rose with her instinct to start preparing to be Teddy Lloyd's lover, and Sandy with her insight to act as informant on the affair. It was to this end that Rose and Sandy had been chosen as the crème de la crème. There was a whiff of sulphur about the idea which fascinated Sandy in her present mind. After all, it was only an idea. And there was no pressing hurry in the matter, for Miss Brodie liked to take her leisure over the unfolding of her plans, most of the joy deriving from the preparation. . . . (109)

Sandy is prepared to collaborate with Miss Brodie, acting as her spy, as long as the 'idea' she has detected remains a hypothesis. But eventually the hypothesis is confirmed, and Sandy instantly clinches the religious analogy we have been tracing:

> 'I am his [i.e. Lloyd's] Muse,' said Miss Brodie. 'But I have renounced his love in order to dedicate my prime to the young girls in my care. I am his Muse but Rose shall take my place.'
> She thinks she is Providence, thought Sandy, she thinks she is the God of Calvin, she sees the beginning and the end. And Sandy thought, too, the woman is an unconscious Lesbian. And many

theories from the books of psychology categorized Miss Brodie, but failed to obliterate her image from the canvases of one-armed Teddy Lloyd. (120)

The way this passage immediately follows the religious diagnosis with references to other, naturalistic diagnoses is characteristic of the author, who always provides a 'cover' for her most serious utterances, and never offers the reader the comfort of a single explanation of events. To the Lesbian theory, we may add the theory that Miss Brodie must be going through the menopause during the time of the main action, though it is only belatedly and indirectly that we discover that she must have been forty when the girls first met her, because she is fifty-six at her death in 1946 (56). Miss Brodie's 'Prime' may be a euphemism for, or a sublimation of, the experience of the menopause, which would be particularly traumatic for a spinster, and would explain many of the vagaries of her behaviour. More than once Miss Brodie's Prime is contrasted casually, but significantly, with normal, fertile sexuality. At Sandy's birthday tea, for instance, Jenny says:

'They say, make the most of your schooldays, because you never know what lies ahead of you.'
'Miss Brodie says prime is best,' Sandy said.
'Yes, but she never got married like our mothers and fathers.'
'They don't have primes,' said Sandy.
'They have sexual intercourse,' Jenny said. (16)

There is, then, plenty of evidence for a clinical psychological explanation of Miss Brodie's conduct, but Sandy's religious interpretation has the most force. Miss Brodie, she realizes, has created her own secular religion of which she is simultaneously the God, Redeemer and minister to the elect. She tries to create the girls in her own image, and to direct their destinies according to her own divine plan. Like Christ she is betrayed by one of her own disciples, but unlike Christ she does not know she is going to be betrayed, and never discovers for certain the identity of her Judas. In fact, because she is a pseudo-Christ she cannot be betrayed: that at least is Sandy's self-defence. 'If you did not betray us, it is impossible that you should have been betrayed,' Sandy writes to Miss Brodie after the latter's dismissal (126); and later she says to Monica,

'It's only possible to betray where loyalty is due.'
'Well, wasn't it due to Miss Brodie?'
'Only up to a point.' (127)

For Sandy, Miss Brodie's delusion of holding omnipotent sway over other people's destinies is well beyond that point. When Sandy realizes that Miss Brodie 'thinks she is the God of Calvin, she sees the beginning and the end', she goes out of her way to have an affair with Teddy Lloyd, thus deliberately falsifying Miss Brodie's prediction that Rose will be the favoured one.

> Miss Brodie came to the point: 'Rose tells me you have become his lover.'
> 'Yes, does it matter which one of us it is?'
> 'Whatever possessed you?' said Miss Brodie, in a very Scottish way, as if Sandy had given away a pound of marmalade to an English duke.
> 'He interests me,' said Sandy.
> 'Interests you, forsooth,' said Miss Brodie. 'A girl with a mind, a girl with insight. He is a Roman Catholic and I don't see how you can have to do with a man who can't think for himself. Rose was suitable. Rose has instinct, but no insight.' (123)

This is just after Miss Brodie's return from Germany in 1938. In the film, Sandy does not tell Miss Brodie about her affair with Teddy Lloyd until *after* betraying her, and it is strongly suggested that she sought the experience out of pique at Miss Brodie's depreciation of her (Sandy's) sexual attractiveness. In this way an important point is lost. For what Sandy is doing here is (to borrow terms from Frank Kermode's discussion of apocalyptic thought in *The Sense of an Ending*) disconfirming a naïve prediction, exercising 'clerkly scepticism' in action. But Miss Brodie does not take the hint. Like members of millennial sects who are not seriously discomfited when their predictions of the end of the world fail to come true, but turn quickly to making new calculations and looking for new 'consonances', so Miss Brodie's egotism is not seriously shaken by Sandy's reversal of her expectations, and she goes on blithely planning other people's lives, with disastrous consequences for Joyce Emily. Then Sandy decides that she must put a stop to Miss Brodie.

That Miss Brodie is punished for pretending to 'see the beginning and the end' in a novel that freely exploits the convention of authorial omniscience, may seem to be an instance of what Christopher Ricks chiefly complains of in Muriel Spark—that she commits as novelist the sins she condemns in her characters.[8] Muriel Spark had, of course, worried at precisely this paradox in *The Comforters*, and Caroline's defiance of the 'artificial plot' of the hallucinatory novelist is clearly comparable to Sandy's defiance of Miss Brodie's allocation of roles to herself and Rose. The conclusion Mrs Spark seems to have drawn from that highly experimental first novel, however, is that since playing at being God is inherent in the business of making fictions (cf. Fielding's 'allusion and metaphor') one might as well make the most of it. Furthermore, there is all the difference in the world between pretending to omniscience in fiction and pretending to it in real life, and Miss Brodie is dangerous precisely because she confuses the two. It is useful to invoke Kermode again, here:

> We have to distinguish between myths and fictions. Fictions can degenerate into myths whenever they are not consciously held to be fictive. In this sense anti-Semitism is a degenerate fiction, a myth; *Lear* is a fiction. Myth operates within diagrams of ritual, which presupposes total and adequate explanations of things as they are and were; it is a sequence of radically unchangeable gestures. Fictions are for finding things out, and they change as the needs of sense-making change. Myths are the agents of stability, fictions the agents of change. Myths call for absolute, fictions for conditional assent . . . literary fictions belong to Vaihinger's category of the consciously false. They are not subject, like hypotheses, to proof or disconfirmation, only, if they come to lose their operational effectiveness, to neglect.[9]

When Miss Brodie tries to push Rose into the arms of Teddy Lloyd she misapplies a private fiction about the character of Rose and her own relationship to Teddy Lloyd, tries to put it to experimental proof, and thus turns it into a myth; just as the dictator she admires misapplied the fictions of Wagner and Nietzsche. Everything Kermode says about myth fits Miss Brodie's insistence on fixed, absolute and unalterable attitudes: that Sandy has insight, that Rose has instinct, that Giotto is the greatest Italian painter, that she will never be betrayed, that she is in her prime—which is the inclusive myth on which her whole world is built. The novel echoes with her unqualified, declarative statements, which the girls tend to mimic in their speech, but against which the much more subtle, syntactically complex passages of authorial comment or rendering of Sandy's consciousness are clearly contrasted. For Sandy uses fictions—her adaptations of *Kidnapped* and *The Lady of Shalott*, her fantasy about the policewoman who interviews Jenny (68ff.)—correctly, 'for finding things out', neglecting them when they lose their operational effectiveness (the burial of the romance about Miss Brodie is a clear case of this). *The Prime of Miss*

Jean Brodie itself is of course a literary fiction like *Lear*, 'consciously false', and the author's pretensions to omniscience are therefore useful and not dangerous.

VI

Sandy's diagnosis of Miss Brodie's instability as a private and distorted form of Calvinism is followed by her own conversion to Roman Catholicism, the theological antithesis of Calvinism. And when Miss Brodie, a few weeks before her death learns that Sandy has become a nun, she recognizes the apostacy from her own 'Church', and for the first time contemplates the possibility that Sandy may have been her betrayer.

> 'What a waste. This is not the sort of dedication I meant. Do you think she has done this to annoy me? I begin to wonder if it was not Sandy who betrayed me.' (63)

There is an interesting passage a little later where the author speculates that Miss Brodie herself might have been saved by Catholicism, though she despised it as a Church of superstition:

> In some ways her attitude was a strange one, because she was by temperament suited only to the Roman Catholic Church; possibly it could have embraced, even while it disciplined, her soaring and diving spirit, it might even have normalized her. But perhaps this was the reason she shunned it. . . . (85)

Lest *The Prime of Miss Jean Brodie* appear under this analysis as a kind of Catholic tract, it is important to emphasize that the dogmatism which runs through it is qualified in a number of ways. The chief representative of Catholicism in the novel, Sandy, is by no means a wholly attractive character, and there is a suggestion in the way she receives her visitors at the convent that she lacks the repose of true spirituality:

> She clutched the bars of the grille as if she wanted to escape from the dim parlour beyond, for she was not composed like the other nuns who sat, when they received their rare visitors, well back in the darkness with folded hands. But Sandy always leaned forward and peered, clutching the bars with both hands, and the other sisters remarked it and said that Sister Helena had too much to bear from the world. . . . (35)

Sandy seems, not exactly guilty about having betrayed Miss Brodie, but wistfully regretful. In the theological perspective Sandy acquires from her intimacy with Teddy Lloyd (from his mind 'she extracted, among other things, his religion as a pith from a husk' (123)), Miss Brodie was not a wicked woman, but a dangerously innocent one. ' "Oh, she was quite an innocent in her way," said Sandy [to Jenny], clutching the bars of her grille' (127). It is the kind of innocence, dangerous and volatile because ignorant of real good and evil, which Graham Greene describes through his narrator in *The Quiet American*:

> Innocence always calls mutely for protection, when we would be so much wiser to guard ourselves against it: innocence is like a dumb leper who has lost his bell, wandering the world, meaning no harm.[10]

Sandy decides that Miss Brodie must be put a stop to, before she does any more harm. But Sandy has enough liking and admiration for her teacher to feel a certain regret at the necessity of this action. Like Edinburgh itself, Miss Brodie can seem touchingly attractive in certain lights:

> Sandy felt warmly towards Miss Brodie at those times when she saw how she was misled in her idea of Rose. It was then that Miss Brodie looked beautiful and fragile, just as dark, heavy Edinburgh itself could suddenly be changed into a floating city when the light was a special pearly white and fell upon one of the gracefully fashioned streets. In the same way Miss Brodie's masterful features became clear and sweet to Sandy when viewed in the curious light of the woman's folly, and she never felt more affection for her in her later years than when she thought upon Miss Brodie as silly. (111)

Frank Kermode has said of the novel that 'the dominant image is of the justified Miss Brodie presiding calmly over a lost innocence'.[11] Miss Brodie's sense of justification is illusory, and I think only the author can be said to preside calmly over the experience of the novel; but its theme is certainly the loss of primal innocence. The world of *The Prime of Miss Jean Brodie* is a fallen world in which everybody is to some extent imperfect, including members of the True Church like Sandy. The true and the good are not to be found in an absolute and pure form except in God. When Sandy is having tea with Miss Brodie at the Braid Hills Hotel, in 1946

They looked out of the wide windows at the little Braid Burn trickling through the fields and at the hills beyond, so austere from everlasting that they had never been capable of losing anything by the war. (56)

A familiar kind of contrast between the permanent forms of nature and the mutability of human life is given a religious twist here by the surprising word 'everlasting', with its Biblical associations:

'The blessings of thy father have prevailed above the blessings of my progenitors unto the utmost bound of the everlasting hills'
(Genesis 49: 26)

In a later description of the same scene we learn for the first time that Sandy was Miss Brodie's betrayer. Part of the passage has already been quoted: 'It is seven years, thought Sandy, since I betrayed this tiresome woman. What does she mean by "betray"? She was looking at the hills as if to see there the first and unbetrayable Miss Brodie, indifferent to criticism as a crag.' (60) The association of the everlasting hills of Genesis with an unbetrayable Miss Brodie expresses Sandy's nostalgia for a lost primal innocence, her regret that, the world being what it is, Miss Brodie's good qualities are so mixed with bad that she had to be betrayed.

In the Great Hall of Marcia Blaine School, we are told on the second page of the novel, laid beneath the Founder's portrait, was a Bible opened at the text, 'Oh where shall I find a virtuous woman, for her price is above rubies.' Muriel Spark's answer seems to be: not in this world.

7 The Chesterbelloc and the Jews

G. K. Chesterton (1874–1936) and Hilaire Belloc (1870–1953) have suffered a steep decline in popularity over the last three decades. Chesterton is read more and more selectively by fewer and fewer people; and Belloc is in almost total eclipse. The world-famous partnership that George Bernard Shaw dubbed 'the Chesterbelloc' has had a great fall, and few seem interested in putting it together again. There are many reasons for this. The Modern Movement in literature, which Chesterton and Belloc either opposed or ignored, has become classical for our culture, and their own work looks thin and faded in comparison. The form to which they devoted so much of their time and energy—the whimsical, ruminative essay—is dead and unmourned. Their intellectual amateurism is unfashionable. And the ideas for which they stood have largely lost their relevance.

Those ideas were always controversial, but they once commanded considerable respect, and the support of a large Christian, specifically Catholic, reading public. The Chesterbelloc's brand of Catholicism* however—triumphalist, proselytizing, theologically conservative, Europe-orientated—is hardly congenial to the mood of the Church since Pope John XXIII and the Second Vatican Council. Chesterton and Belloc were the propagandists and cheer-leaders of the Catholic ghetto, dedicated to proving that it was really the City of God. Belloc described their strategy in a revealing letter:

> Threaten we cannot, because we are nobody, all the temporal power is on the other side. But we *can* spread the mood that we are the bosses and the *chic* and that a man who does not accept the Faith writes himself down as suburban. Upon these amiable lines do I proceed.[1]

There is a certain irony in associating Chesterton and Belloc with the Catholic 'ghetto', because one of the major factors in the decline of their popularity is that they have the reputation of being antisemitic. For liberal, non-Catholics this was always an objection to

---

* Chesterton was not officially received into the Catholic Church until 1922; but he had been a Catholic in spirit long before, delaying his reception out of regard for his wife; and there is little in the writings of his Anglican period to distinguish him from a Catholic.

their work. W. H. Auden, for instance, gives as his first reason for neglecting Chesterton earlier in life, 'His reputation as an anti-semite. Though he denied the charge and did, certainly, denounce Hitler's persecution, he cannot, I fear, be completely exonerated.'[2] Contemporary Catholic readers seem to have been undismayed by this aspect of Chesterton's work, still more prominent in Belloc's. It is since the last World War, since 'Hitler's persecution' that the anti-Jewish sentiment in these two Catholic writers has become an embarrassment to their co-religionists. As Belloc's biographer, Robert Speaight, says of the repulsive Jewish financier, Mr Barnett, portrayed in Belloc's first novel, 'too much has happened to the Jews since *Emmanuel Burden* was written for Mr Barnett to make comfortable reading today'.[3]

The death of some six million European Jews under Hitler's Nazi regime was arguably the most traumatic episode in modern European history, and we have gradually come to realize that the guilt and responsibility cannot be confined to the Nazis alone. Books like Arthur D. Morse's *While Six Million Died* have exposed the culpable failure of the Western democracies to help the Jews when it was possible to do so. Scholars such as Norman Cohn (*Warrant for Genocide*) and James Parkes (*Antisemitism*) have shown that Hitler's 'final solution' was the ghastly climax to two thousand years of Christian prejudice. Prompted by studies like Gordon Zahn's *German Catholics and Hitler's Wars*, or goaded by polemics like Hochhuth's *The Representative*, Catholics have, with other Christians, acknowledged that the Church seriously failed to meet the challenge of the greatest evil of our time. And so there has been, belatedly, a real attempt in the post-Conciliar Church to redefine the Christian's attitude to the Jews, in the liturgy, in catachetics, and in theological dialogue. Chesterton and Belloc would have found it hard to adapt to these changes.

The alleged anti-semitism of these two writers is not perhaps a purely literary question; but they were not purely literary writers. The charge has undoubtedly affected the reception of their work, yet it has never, as far as I know, been properly documented by their accusers, or honestly investigated by their defenders. It seems worthwhile, therefore, to try and establish exactly what the Chesterbelloc's attitude to the Jews was, how it fitted into the total structure of the two men's ideas, and how it related to attitudes and events in society at large.

Anti-semitism is only one form of a persistent and deplorable tendency of human beings, individually and collectively, to relieve feelings of fear and frustration by projecting them on to others. There are few minorities, from so-called witches to modern hippies, who have not been made victims of this syndrome, and in certain situations, of course, Christians have suffered in this way. Unhappily, the roots of anti-semitism itself are Christian.

In the days of the Early Church, Christianity was regarded as a Jewish sect, and Christians were as concerned to dissociate themselves from the Jews as from pagans. The effect of this acrimony can be seen in St John's use of the blanket term 'the Jews', where the earlier evangelists Matthew, Mark and Luke had used the more specific terms scribes, pharisees, elders, etc., to describe the opponents of Christ. In this way the idea developed that it was not mankind that had crucified Christ, but 'the Jews', a cursed race who were punished for their deicide by the Dispersion, but unrepentantly retained a spirit of revengeful malice, like the Devil himself. The Jewish Messiah was identified with the Antichrist of Revelations. The Jews were regarded as the children of the Devil, and it was widely believed that they abused the consecrated Host and crucified Christian children, using their blood to prepare ritual food. In the Middle Ages these superstitions flourished especially at times of crisis. Thus, the Jews were widely blamed for plagues such as the Black Death; and the religious hysteria of the First Crusade found an outlet in the first pogrom.

This strain of Christian superstition in anti-semitism continued into modern times, and was far from being exclusive to professed Christians. As readers of Bernard Malamud's historical novel *The Fixer* will know, stories of Jewish ritual murders were widely believed in late nineteenth-century Europe; and in the rhetoric of Goebbels ('Those who vanquish the world-Jew will save the earth from the Devil')[4] one can hear the unmistakable echo of Medieval apocalypse. Modern anti-semitism, however, also has other origins. It seems to begin with the attempt of a few clerical writers, early in the nineteenth century, to blame the French Revolution on a Jewish-Masonic conspiracy. This preposterous theory did not really catch on, but it was significant because, as Cohn points out, the eruption of anti-semitism later in the century was especially contagious among the people who felt most threatened by the changes in society that the Revolution had ushered in: democracy, industrialization, secularization.

The Jews themselves had benefited from those changes in Western Europe. Granted full civil rights, they came out of the ghettos and began to play a full part in society, their tradition and history fitting them for success in modern urban professions such as banking, commerce, journalism and the arts. This success, however, only produced envy and fear which could be exploited by fanatics and politicians. The Dreyfus case was a classic example: conservative and patriotic Frenchmen, demoralized by defeat in the Franco-Prussian war, found a perfect scapegoat in the notion of a Jewish spy who had infiltrated the top levels of military command. In Russia, the tottering Czarist regime sought to divert the unrest and frustration of its ill-governed people against the Jewish settlements in a series of organized pogroms. And it was the Czarist secret service which forged the notorious 'Protocols of the Elders of Zion' some time in the late 1890s.

This document, which purported to be the blueprint of a secret Jewish organization's plot to dominate the world, was definitively exposed as a clumsy forgery in the London *Times* in 1921, but received enormous circulation and wide acceptance both before and after this date, and was a powerful tool in the hands of Hitler's propagandists. The syndrome of which anti-semitism is a manifestation requires that the victim be weak enough to be persecuted, but sinister enough to be feared. The Jews were everywhere a weak minority; the *Protocols* and associated literature provided the fear. Since the conspiracy was 'secret', anything of which you disapproved, from monopoly capitalism to Bolshevism, from German imperialism if you happened to be British, to British imperialism if you happened to be German, could be regarded as a 'cover' for it. The Jewish people were thus set up to be the scapegoats for all modern discontents.

Hilaire Belloc and G. K. Chesterton both denied, on many occasions, that they were anti-semites; and it is true that neither of them manifested this kind of prejudice in its most violent and extreme form. They both roundly condemned persecution and attempted extermination of Jews, and they dissociated themselves from race-hatred and the wilder fantasies about a Jewish conspiracy to dominate the world. Both were able to invoke the 'Some of my best friends . . .' argument. But they were, for various reasons, receptive to the two strains of anti-semitism summarily described above. Although they denied that there was a religious element in their feelings about the Jews, for Belloc at least the old idea of deicide was a reality, as this gruesomely arch comment in a letter reveals:

> The poor darlings, I'm awfully fond of them, and I'm awfully sorry for them, but it's their own silly fault—they ought to have left God alone.[5]

The Christianity of both men was of a romantically conservative character, yearning back to a somewhat idealized medieval Christendom —the period when the demonology of anti-semitism was fully developed. Chesterton, particularly, was emotionally and imaginatively attracted to the aggressive Christianity of the Crusades, and in a late poem, 'The Modern Magic', he contrasts the chivalrous conflict of Christian and Saracen with the cynical mercenary realities of the Jewish National Home in Palestine:

> No battle-noise and no battle news
> But shaking of shekels and laughter of Jews
> And a rattle of golden balls they toss
> High o'er the ruins of Crescent and Cross,
> And a usurer's voice in cold command,
> These are the sounds from the Holy Land.

There is, however, quite as much political and economic animus behind this verse as religious, and the word 'usurer' provides the connection. It refers specifically to Sir Herbert Samuel, an old adversary of Chesterton's, whom the British Government had appointed as its representative in Palestine; but the implications are much wider.

Both Chesterton and Belloc were intensely critical of industrial capitalism. So, perhaps, were most enlightened men of their time; but whereas the latter tended to espouse some form of socialism as the solution, Chesterton and Belloc saw this as only promising a different kind of political and economic slavery. Their own political programme of Distributism (i.e. sharing out land in small parcels among the people) cut right across the conventional political spectrum. It was a quite impracticable policy, which led both men ultimately into frustration and a flirtation with fascism; but it provided the base from which they launched their critique of capitalism, in which usury was a key concept.

Usury, or lending money for interest, was regarded as a grave sin until about the seventeenth century, after which the prohibition quietly lapsed in the face of irresistible economic developments. In medieval times Jews were licensed to provide the service forbidden to Christians. They often grew rich in the process, sowing the seeds of envy and resentment among Christians, and giving rise to the stereotype of the grasping Jewish moneylender, which Shakespeare touched with poetry and compassion in his portrait of Shylock. To Chesterton and Belloc, nineteenth-century capitalism was essentially usury, and the fact that

6

Jews (most notably the Rothschild family) were prominent in the field
of high finance was evidence that capitalism was essentially alien to
Christian culture. Much (though not all) of their 'anti-semitism' con-
sisted of identifying Jewry with the evils of modern capitalism. A
journalist summed up a talk Chesterton gave to the Jewish West End
Literary Society as 'The Poor Jews Were Nice and The Rich Were
Nasty'.[6] In a letter, Belloc described parliamentary democracy in
Europe as a sham: 'It means in practice government by a few rich men
with an absurd preponderance of financial banking and largely Jewish
power.'[7]

This kind of statement is not really falsifiable. That modern capitalism
is a Jewish invention, or monopoly, is demonstrably untrue. But who
can say whether Jews have exercised disproportionate or exceptionally
unscrupulous control over it? It seems likely that, allowing for the fact
that Jews have been channelled into commerce by their history, there
has not been a more than average number of Jewish millionaires and
Jewish swindlers; but how could you ever demonstrate this statistically?
The position adopted by Chesterton and Belloc was of the kind which
is not open to negative evidence, and for which positive evidence, in the
nature of things, must inevitably be forthcoming. This is why their
attitude sometimes appears uncomfortably like the paranoia of the
fanatical anti-semite.

Their critique of British Imperialism in its late phase was often
morally justified, but was unbalanced by their exaggeration of the part
played by Jewish finance in imperialistic adventures. They claimed that
the Boer War was engineered by Jewish millionaires with investments
in South African mines. No doubt this *was* a factor, and Belloc's
scathing 'Verses to a Lord who, in the House of Lords, said that those
who opposed the South African Adventure confused Soldiers with
Money-Grubbers' makes the point forcefully. But many other people
besides Jews had investments of either money or patriotic emotion in
the war, without which it could not have been conducted.

The Lord addressed by Belloc would have been a businessman of
Jewish extraction who had gone into politics and been rewarded with a
peerage for his services and financial contributions to one of the parties.
This was a common occurrence, and one that goaded the Chesterbelloc
to fury. In their view such men were aliens who, under assumed names,
had infiltrated the already corrupt British political system, and were
using the privileges of power to further their own interests and those
of the international Jewish business community, disregarding the interests of their adopted country. Belloc's early satirical novels were

dedicated to exposing this type, especially in the character who appears in *Emmanuel Burden* (1904) as Mr Barnett (not of course his real name) and reappears in *Mr Clutterbuck's Election* (1908), *A Change in the Cabinet* (1909) and *Pongo and the Bull* (1910), acquiring the titles of Lord Lambeth and the Duke of Battersea as he climbs the ladder of power. Barnett is the stock type of the odious Jewish financier: he is physically repulsive, with hooked nose, thick lips, gross body and greasy curls (Chesterton's illustrations to *Emmanuel Burden* enforce the point); he lacks refinement of manners, speaks with a lisp in broken syntax, and betrays his origins (the Frankfurt ghetto) with every gesture. Having survived the bankruptcy of his first shady business enterprise, he makes his fortune in foreign speculations conducted under the respectable cover of imperialist expansion, manipulating the market and public opinion through a network of contacts and hirelings in politics and journalism.

These novels tend to follow a standard formula. There is a decent but stupid British merchant who becomes the tool of a Jewish-controlled ring of politicians and financiers, which is in turn opposed by a bluff, honest Englishman. *Mr Clutterbuck's Election* is particularly interesting because of the character of the bluff honest Englishman, Mr Bailey. For Mr Bailey is an avowed anti-semite:

> He had gone mad upon the Hebrew race. He saw Jews everywhere: he not only saw them everywhere, but he saw them in conspiracy.
> ... According to him Lombroso was a Jew, Mr Roosevelt's friends and supporters the Belmonts were Jews, half the moneyed backers of Roosevelt were Jews, the famous critic Brandes was a Jew, Zola was a Jew, Nordau was a Jew, Witte was a Jew—or in some mysterious way connected with the Jews. ... The disease advanced with his advancing age; soon all the great family of Arnold were Jews; half the aristocracy had Jewish blood; for a little he would have accused the Pope of Rome or the Royal Family itself; and I need hardly say that every widespread influence, from Freemasonry to the international finance of Europe, was Israelite in his eyes. ...[8]

At first sight this looks like a caricature of the anti-semite, put in to counterbalance, for the sake of fairness, the portrait of Barnett. The list of Jews and Jewish influences (which I have much reduced) seems intentionally preposterous. The narrator of this novel, however, is unreliable, and the truth is usually the reverse of what he appears to say. According to the logic of the book's rhetoric, therefore, the prejudices recorded in this passage are well-founded, and in fact the story confirms them: Mr Bailey *does* uncover Jewish-inspired corruption and intrigue everywhere he goes. No doubt Belloc protected himself by throwing in a few patent absurdities—like the Pope and the Royal Family, but there is little doubt, on internal and external evidence, that Belloc presents Bailey as a man who erred, if he erred at all, on the side of truth.

Belloc was always the more violently anti-Jewish half of the Chester-belloc, partly because he was more of a natural hater, a hard and aggressive man compared to the genial and much-loved Chesterton; and partly because of his origins and upbringing. Belloc was born in France, of a French father, received part of his education in France and served voluntarily in the French Army. At this time—the late nineteenth century—anti-semitism flourished in France on a scale, with a violence and publicity, quite unknown in England; and as a scion of the clericalist, patriotic bourgeoisie, Belloc was fully exposed to its influence. He was inevitably a fanatical anti-Dreyfusard, to the consternation of the English Liberals with whom he chiefly associated at the time, and to the end of his life he refused to concede Dreyfus's innocence.

Before he met Belloc, Chesterton wrote a poem, 'To A Certain Nation', deploring the persecution of Dreyfus. When he reprinted it in 1905 he noted that he had changed his mind about the subject. This instance, noted by Maisie Ward, is only one of many indications that Belloc was a strong influence on Chesterton's attitude to the Jews. Another was Chesterton's brother Cecil, who was editor of the *New Witness*, formerly the *Eye Witness*—two journals with which Belloc and Chesterton were closely associated—when the Marconi scandal broke.

The Marconi affair is little remembered today, but to the Chesterton circle it was at least as important as the Dreyfus case, an exemplary instance of the political and financial corruption against which they had been campaigning for years. In his *Autobiography* (1936) Chesterton seriously predicted that 'it will be seen as one of the turning-points of the whole history of England and the world'. The details of the episode are much too complicated to attempt an exposition here, and in any case were never satisfactorily established at the time, but the basic facts were as follows. In 1911 the British Government decided to establish a chain of wireless stations throughout the Empire. In 1912 the Postmaster General, Herbert Samuels, awarded the contract to the then languishing Marconi company, of which the managing director was Godfrey Isaacs. Godfrey's brother Rufus was Attorney General in the Government. Before the contract was publicly announced or ratified by the House of Commons, Godfrey went to the United States and bought a large number of shares in the *American* Marconi company. This was independent of the British company, but stood to gain prestige from the recent success of the British company. Godfrey returned to England and sold some of his shares to another brother, Harry, who sold them to Rufus, who sold some to Lloyd George (later to be Prime Minister); and all this was done before the shares were officially on the market. Cecil Chesterton, who had been gunning for the Isaacs brothers for some time, raised a hue and cry; there were angry scenes in the Houses of Parliament; long, inconclusive investigations were initiated; Godfrey Isaacs sued Cecil Chesterton; Chesterton lost the case but was lightly fined; and both sides claimed victory. The Ministers concerned were eventually cleared of charges of misconduct, but Belloc and the Chestertons were not the only ones to feel that the whole affair had a nasty smell about it which lingered. Belloc indeed might have been forgiven for thinking that life had imitated the art of his own novels. Chesterton's attitude to the Jews was irrevocably hardened by the episode. Consider, for example, the barely-controlled indignation of his open letter of 1918 to Rufus Isaacs, by that time Lord Reading and Lord Chief Justice of England, when he was selected to accompany Lloyd George to the Versailles Peace Conference:

Have you ever considered, in a moment of meditation, how curiously valuable you would really have to be, that Englishmen should in comparison be careless of all the things you have corrupted, and indifferent to all the things that you may yet destroy? Are we to lose the War which we have already won? That and nothing else is involved in losing the full satisfaction of the national claim of Poland. Is there any man who doubts that the Jewish International is unsympathetic with that full national demand? And is there any man who doubts that you will be sympathetic with the Jewish International? . . . Do you seriously imagine that those who know, that those who care, are so idolatrously infatuated with Rufus Daniel Isaacs as to tolerate such risk, let alone such ruin? Are we to set up as the standing representative of England a man who is a standing joke against England? That and nothing else is involved in setting up the chief Marconi Minister as our Foreign Minister.[9]

Chesterton had a valid point here—the Versailles conference was a disaster from almost every point of view—and he was understandably moved when he wrote this piece by the recent death of his brother Cecil, one of the last casualties of the Great War. But one checks on the phrase 'Jewish International'. No doubt there was organized Jewish opinion and sentiment that cut across the national frontiers of Europe, just as there was organized Catholic opinion and sentiment. But 'Jewish International' has the ring of the *Protocols*. And that is the disturbing thing about the Chesterbelloc's attitude to the Jews: though both men were too humane and too intelligent to indulge in the hateful and irrational kind of anti-semitism which prepared the way for Hitler's policy of genocide, they often seem to be either unconsciously or irresponsibly flirting with it.

A crucial document here is Belloc's book, *The Jews* (1922). In the course of it, he exposes the contradictions of extreme anti-semitism, and declares (he was of course writing after *The Times*'s exposure of the *Protocols*), 'the conception of a vast, age-long plot culminating in the contemporary Russian affair will not hold water' (p. 168). But he does say that 'the Anti-Semitic movement is essentially a reaction against the abnormal growth in Jewish power, and the new strength of Anti-Semitism is largely due to the Jews themselves' (p. 159). He does say that 'the Bolshevist Movement was *a* Jewish Movement' (p. 55). He does say that 'the Jew has *collectively* a power today, in the white world, altogether excessive' (p. 19). Again and again in this book, his most serious and responsible statement on the subject, Belloc uses the existence of anti-semitism as evidence that a 'problem' exists, never perceiving that anti-semitism itself might be the problem.

'It is the thesis of this book', Belloc begins, 'that the continued presence of the Jewish nation intermixed with other nations alien to it presents a permanent problem of the gravest character' (p. 3). Once you begin talking about 'problems' (it was Hitler's favourite diplomatic ploy), you imply the need for a solution, and the only solution in this case was Hitler's 'Final Solution'. Belloc claimed that there was an alternative—not 'elimination' but 'segregation' or, as he preferred to term it, 'recognition'. Considering the length of the book, Belloc is suspiciously vague about what this would entail, but it seems to mean some surrender of civil rights by the Jews in exchange for certain privileges—a return in fact to something like the medieval ghetto. Chesterton was evidently thinking along the same lines when he wrote in *The New Jerusalem* (1920):

I would leave as few Jews as possible in other established nations [i.e. other than Zionist settlements] and to these I would give a special position best described as privilege; some sort of self-governing enclave with special laws and exemptions; for instance I would certainly excuse them from conscription, which I think a gross injustice in their case. Of course the privileged exile would also lose the rights of a native (p. 299).

Belloc said that 'recognition' should be mutually agreed, but added darkly that if the Jew refused to co-operate, 'then the community will be compelled to legislate in spite of him' (p. 304). This all has an ominously prophetic note in view of the Nazis' initial legislative persecution of the Jews in the 'thirties. And when Chesterton whimsically suggests that the Jewish problem in England could be solved simply by requiring every Jew to dress like an Arab, so that 'we should know where we are; and he would know where he is, which is in a foreign land' (p. 272), one cannot help thinking forward to the yellow stars stitched to the sleeves of Hitler's victims.

Is it fair to read such statements in the light of tragic later events? Certainly it is important to recognize that the kind of prejudice Chesterton and Belloc displayed was by no means uncommon in their time. When Belloc visited the United States in 1923, he was almost embarrassed by the violence of the anti-semitism he encountered. 'The Jew Question is a frightful bore here,' he wrote in a letter. 'People talk of it morning, noon and night. Those who know I have written a book on it take it for granted that I am in approval of a general massacre.'[10]

The clichés of anti-Jewish prejudice litter the pages of twentieth-century literature up to the last War. T. S. Eliot and Ezra Pound are notorious in this respect. Their right-wing politics and (in Eliot's case) militant Christian orthodoxy made them sympathetic to the proto-fascist *Action Française* group led by Charles Maurras, which was a hot-bed of anti-semitism. But writers of every ideological shade and level of brow were apt to exploit the stock response in portraying Jews. Wells and Arnold Bennett were guilty on occasion. 'An hotel full of Jews of the wrong, rich sort', sounds like a line from John Buchan, but is in fact from a story by D. H. Lawrence ('The Captain's Doll').

In an essay on John Buchan, Gertrude Himmelfarb has argued that:

this kind of anti-semitism, indulged in at that time and place, was both too common and too passive to be scandalous. Men were normally anti-semitic, unless by some quirk of temperament or ideology they happened to be philo-semitic. So long as the world itself was normal, this was of no great consequence. It was only later, when social impediments became fatal disabilities, when anti-semitism ceased to be the prerogative of English gentlemen and became the affair of politicians and demagogues, that sensitive men were shamed into silence.[11]

But perhaps this is to be too indulgent. Anti-semitism was a tool of politicians and demagogues before Hitler, and any contribution to it was an encouragement of evil. Take, for example, this passage from one of Chesterton's best books, *Heretics* (1905):

> The idea that there is something English in the repression of one's feelings is one of those ideas which Englishmen had never heard of until England began to be governed exclusively by Scotsmen, Americans and Jews (p. 209).

Omit the word 'Jews', and you have a quite inoffensive joke, which would be readily enjoyed by Scotsmen and Americans. But in its original form it has a slightly sour note, and I don't think one could expect Jews to find it funny, and for the following reason: the proposition that Americans and Scots have taken over England is consciously false, a huge exaggeration of the facts, and that is why it is a joke. But the idea that England has been taken over by the Jews is a falsehood of a quite different order: it was widely believed. The first kind of statement relieves aggression, the second kind fosters it. Chesterton and Belloc often rejected this kind of distinction as a sentimental discrimination in favour of the Jews, but in so doing they ignored social and historical realities. They were playing with fire; fire that (though the possibility never crossed their minds and would have shocked and horrified them had it done so) eventually burned in the ovens of Auschwitz.

Basically, theirs was a failure of imagination. Celebrated for wit, humour, irony and paradox, they never seem to have turned these liberating modes of perception upon their own assumptions and prejudices. Belloc simply does not see that when (in *The Jews*) he solemnly states with the air of uncovering a sinister secret, that Matthew Arnold, Charles Kingsley, 'General' Moss-Booth (founder of the Salvation Army) and Robert Browning had Jewish blood, he is making nonsense of his own argument that Jews are not assimilable into other societies—for it would be difficult to choose a more quintessentially English quartet of Eminent Victorians. He does not see that his own sense of nationality, so clearly divided between France and England, was precisely parallel to the dual nationality with which he taxed European Jews. Most glaringly of all, neither Chesterton nor Belloc perceived how vulnerable they were as members of the Catholic Church in a Protestant-secular state, to the criticisms they themselves made of the Jews. As Robert Speaight observes: 'Here, too, was a society highly, though less secretly organized, and in a measure set apart; conscious of its superiority, alien to some extent to all that stood outside it; international and in certain matters of moral consequence challenging civic authority; persecuted and perpetually resurgent.'[12] In fact anti-Catholic prejudice tends to follow much the same pattern as anti-semitism, and Jesuits have, in their time, been accused of the same crimes, from poisoning wells to global conspiracy, as Rabbis.

'Fancy a Jew an Irishman!' Belloc exclaims in *The Jews*, as if the absurdity of such a conception is enough to scuttle all nonsense about assimilation. There is a nice irony in the fact that in the very same year, 1922, in which Belloc wrote these words the greatest of all modern novels appeared, with an Irish Jew as its hero.

—Persecution, says he, all the history of the world is full of it.
Perpetuating national hatred among nations.
—But do you know what a nation means? says John Wyse.
—Yes, says Bloom.
—What is it? says John Wyse.
—A nation? says Bloom. A nation is the same people living in the same place.
—By God, then says Ned laughing, if that's so I'm a nation for I'm living in the same place for the past five years.
So of course everyone had a laugh at Bloom and says he, trying to muck out of it:
—Or also living in different places.
—That covers my case, says Joe.
—What is your nation if I may ask, says the citizen.
—Ireland, says Bloom. I was born here. Ireland.[13]

Leopold Bloom is indisputably Irish, and indisputably Jewish. Above all he is indisputably human; and for that reason *Ulysses* is the perfect antidote to anti-semitism. Probably no character in the history of fiction has been portrayed in more humiliating and ignoble postures than Leopold Bloom, yet the reader's heart and mind are drawn irresistibly towards him. In this respect, and most others, James Joyce,

6*

the renegade Catholic, put the recognized literary spokesmen of his Church to shame. Let us, by way of conclusion, pick up again that conversation in Barney Kiernan's pub:

—But it's no use, says he. Force, hatred, history, all that. That's no life for men and women, insult and hatred. And everybody knows that it's the very opposite of that that is really life.
—What? says Alf.
—Love, says Bloom. I mean the opposite of hatred.

Part IV Fiction and Modernism

I

Have we come to handle the *avant-garde* too gently? From the *Lyrical Ballads* to *Ulysses* our literary history is very much a chronicle of revolutionary works hooted and reviled by the literary establishments of their times, appreciated by a small élite of initiates, and belatedly elevated to classic status by succeeding literary establishments. Since the 1920s, however, the time lag between the publication and the public recognition of such works has got shorter and shorter, until now we are, perhaps, more in danger of mistaking than neglecting masterpieces. Part of the reason is the radical change which has overtaken academic criticism in this period: the groves of academe, that were once enclaves of conservative literary taste, are now only too eager to welcome what is new. Another, and perhaps more important reason is that through the development of the mass media and what one might call the boom in the culture market, the 'small élite of initiates' which in the past constituted the only audience for experimental art, good and bad, is now able to bring its influence to bear very swiftly and powerfully on the larger public.

Nothing illustrates this latter process more strikingly than the way the reputation of William Burroughs has grown since Mary McCarthy praised *The Naked Lunch* at the Edinburgh Writers' Conference of 1962. (Miss McCarthy has since complained that her words on that occasion were distorted and exaggerated by the press; but it could be argued that writers who participate in such events, which are peculiar to our own cultural era, must expect and accept such treatment.) What is noteworthy about Burroughs's reputation is not so much the encomiums his work has received from such confrères as Miss McCarthy, Norman Mailer ('I think that William Burroughs is the only American novelist living today who may conceivably be possessed of genius') and Jack Kerouac ('Burroughs is the greatest satirical writer since Jonathan Swift'), as the way in which this body of opinion has acted on the public mind so as to secure the smooth acceptance and accommodation of such books as *The Naked Lunch* and *Nova Express*. It seems to illustrate very well what Lionel Trilling has described as the institutionalization of the 'adversary culture' of modernism; and like him, I do not see this process as a symptom of cultural health.

The Naked Lunch, whatever else it may be, is a very indecent book, and *Nova Express*, whatever else it may be, is a very tedious book. These novels' pretensions to serious literary significance which, if realized, would justify the indecency and the tedium (or rather force us to redefine these qualities) need to be examined rather more rigorously than our present literary climate generally encourages. Before doing so, it may be advisable to attempt a description of these books. I say 'attempt' because they both resist any conventional summary of character and action.

II

The Naked Lunch begins with the first-person narrative of a drug addict who, pursued by the New York police, travels across America with a companion to Mexico; his account of the journey is mingled with reminiscences of various characters from the drugs underworld. In the second chapter the novel parts with actuality and takes on the quality of dream. The action shifts abruptly from place to place, sometimes between mythical states called Freeland, Annexia and Interzone, which bear a parodic relationship to the actual world. There is no plot, but a general impression of intrigue and pursuit, sometimes on a cops-and-robbers level, sometimes on a political level. The narrative mode shifts from first person to third person to dramatic dialogue. Many of the scenes have a hallucinatory, surrealistic quality reminiscent of the Circe episode in *Ulysses*. The images of the book are primarily of violence, squalor and sexual perversion. There is a notorious orgiastic sequence in which orgasm is achieved by hanging and finally eating the sexual partner. We seem to be sharing the dream, or nightmare, of an addict—perhaps, as Miss McCarthy has suggested, one who is taking a cure and suffering the agonies of 'withdrawal'.

In *Nova Express* the dislocation of narrative and logical continuity is much more radical, for here Burroughs has used what he describes as a 'cut-up' or 'fold-in' technique—that is, a montage of fragments of his own and other people's writings, achieved, for instance, by over-lapping two pages of text and reading straight across. Basically the book is a science fiction fantasy based on the premise that the earth has been invaded by extraterrestrial gangsters, the 'Nova Mob', whose mission is to infiltrate human institutions and encourage all forms of evil in order to accelerate this planet's progress on the path to destruction. They are pursued by the 'Nova Police', who also work invisibly through human agencies, causing, it would seem, almost as much havoc. Only such fantastic suppositions, it is implied, will account for the political lunacy and moral decay of the modern world. That the fantasy is more real than what we take to be actuality is emphasized by such conceits as that life is a 'biological movie' created and manipulated in a 'reality Studio' for the control of which Nova factions are competing.

III

Burroughs has, principally, two claims on the attention of serious readers: as a moralist, and as an innovator. On both counts, it seems to me, he cannot be considered as more than a minor, eccentric figure. Undoubtedly he has a certain literary talent, particularly for comedy and the grotesque, but in both precept and practice he is deeply confused and ultimately unsatisfying. *The Naked Lunch* seems to offer an appropriate epitaph on his work: 'Confusion hath fuck his masterpiece.'

To begin with, there is a deep confusion, not only in Burroughs but in his admirers too, on the subject of narcotics. Much of Burroughs's notoriety derives from the fact that he is a morphine addict, who has been cured, but who still writes very much out of the experience of addiction. He tells us in the Introduction to *The Naked Lunch* that it is based on notes taken during the sickness and delirium of addiction. He is our modern De Quincey; and undoubtedly this accounts for his adoption by the hipster wing of the American literary scene. Herbert Gold has called *The Naked Lunch* 'the definitive hip book' and Burroughs tells us that the title was donated by the arch-hipster Jack Kerouac. 'I did not understand what the title meant until my recovery. The title means exactly what the words say: NAKED lunch—a frozen moment when everyone sees what is on the end of every fork.' These words clearly imply that the drugged state gives access to a special vision of truth—that the junkie, like Conrad's Kurtz, is an inverted hero of the spirit who truly sees 'the horror, the horror' that ordinary, conforming humanity refuses to face. But in other places Burroughs undercuts this argument, which alone could justify his distressingly explicit (so much more explicit than Conrad's) descriptions of the horror. In an interview published in the *Paris Review* (XXXV, Autumn 1965) he agreed that 'The visions of drugs and the visions of art don't mix'; and both novels contain a great deal of obtrusive propaganda against the use of narcotics and on behalf of the apomorphine treatment by which Burroughs himself was cured. The interviewer challenged him on this point—'You regard addiction as an illness, but also a central human fact, a drama?'—and Burroughs's reply is revealing:

> Both, absolutely. It's as simple as the way in which anyone happens to become an alcoholic. . . . The idea that addiction is somehow a psychological illness is, I think, totally ridiculous. It's as psychological as malaria. It's a matter of exposure. . . . There are also all forms of spiritual addiction. . . . Many policemen and narcotics agents are precisely addicted to power, to exercising a certain nasty kind of power over people who are helpless. The nasty sort of power: white junk I call it—rightness. . . .

It will be noted how Burroughs slides here from a literal, clinical view of addiction to a figurative or symbolic one. Both views are at odds with the assumption behind *The Naked Lunch* that the junkie's delirium yields truth; and they are also at odds with each other. In the first view addiction is seen as a preventable sickness, in the second it is seen as a metaphor for authoritarianism. On the one hand it is not 'psychological', on the other hand it can be 'spiritual'. In the first place the junkie is a sick man in need of society's protection, in the second place he is a victim of society.

This kind of equivocation is particularly evident in Burroughs's treatment of the police. In *The Naked Lunch* a certain sympathy is generated for the junkies on the run from the police, yet it is difficult to see how the exposure of the individual to drugs, which according to Burroughs is the cause of addiction, could be prevented without the police. In *Nova Express* the Nova Police seem to be the 'goodies' as the Nova Mob are the 'baddies', but Burroughs, in the interview already cited, says, 'They're like police anywhere. . . . Once you get them in there, by God, they begin acting like any police. They're always an ambivalent agency.' In this case, how are we to read the following passage about the Nova Police:

> The difference between this department and the parasitic excrescence that often travels under the name 'Police' can be expressed in metabolic terms: The distinction between morphine and apomorphine. . . . The Nova Police can be compared to apomorphine, a regulating instance that need not continue and has no intention of continuing after its work is done.

The confusion that surrounds these two novels of Burroughs can, I think, be partly explained by the fact that they are very different works which Burroughs is trying to present as in some sense continuous, two stages in a coherent programme. *The Naked Lunch* is essentially a nihilistic work and as such it must be granted a certain horrible power; but it is prefaced by an Introduction which seeks to justify it on orthodox moral grounds, and to present its hero as a brand snatched from the burning.

> Since *The Naked Lunch* treats this health problem [addiction], it is necessarily brutal, obscene and disgusting. Sickness has often repulsive details not for weak stomachs.
>
> Certain passages in the book that have been called pornographic were written as a tract against Capital Punishment in the manner of Jonathan Swift's *Modest Proposal*. These sections are intended to reveal capital punishment as the obscene, barbaric and disgusting anachronism that it is.

How literature can deal with evil without morally compromising itself is of course a perennial and perhaps insoluble problem, but Burroughs's defence is either naïve or disingenuous. The analogy with Swift won't stand up. Whereas in *A Modest Proposal* Swift maintains a constant logical connection between his fable (the monstrous 'proposal') and his facts (the miseries of the Irish people), so that in revolting from the former we are compelled to revolt from the latter, it is doubtful whether the uninformed reader would see any connection at all between the Orgasm Death Gimmick and Capital Punishment. It may be that the disgust Mr Burroughs feels for Capital Punishment has been transferred to the antics of his sexual perverts, but the reverse process which should occur for the reader is by no means to be relied upon. The power of Swift's piece inheres very largely in the tone of calm reasonableness with which the proposal is put forward, so that we feel obliged to supply the emotion which is missing. In *The Naked Lunch*, instead of this subtly controlled irony we have a kinetic narrative style which suspends rather than activates the reader's moral sense, and incites him to an imaginative collaboration in the orgy. Since I do not propose to quote from this particular scene here, I shall illustrate my point with a rather less offensive passage:

> Rock and Roll adolescent hoodlums storm the streets of all nations. They rush into the Louvre and throw acid in the Mona Lisa's face. They open zoos, insane asylums, prisons, burst water mains with air hammers, chop the floor out of passenger plane lavatories, shoot out light-houses, file elevator cables to

one thin wire, turn sewers into the water supply, throw sharks
and sting rays, electric eels and candiru into swimming pools . . .
in nautical costumes ram the *Queen Mary* full speed into New
York Harbor, play chicken with passenger planes and busses,
rush into hospitals in white coats carrying saws and axes and
scalpels three feet long. . . .

This is vivid, inventive writing, but it is scarcely satire. There is a
note of celebration here, a hilarious anarchism which relishes the
mindless destruction it describes; and it extends to the most successfully drawn characters in the book, the brutal surgeon Benway and
the inspired practical joker A. J. There *are* patches of effective satire in
The Naked Lunch (notably a parody of conversation between some
'good old boys' of the Deep South—'These city fellers come down here
and burn a nigger and don't even settle up for the gasoline'), but the
tone and structure of the whole will not support the serious moral
significance that is claimed for it. Indeed, the account of the Nova
Mob's subversive activities in *Nova Express* seems damagingly
appropriate to *The Naked Lunch*: 'We need a peg to hang evil full
length. By God show them how ugly the ugliest pictures in the dark
room can be'. . . . 'Take orgasm noises sir and cut them in with
torture and accident groans and screams sir and operating-room jokes
sir and flicker sex and torture film right with it sir'. Burroughs's
reference to himself as an undercover agent of the Nova Police who
wrote 'a so-called pornographic novel' as a bait to lure the Nova Mob
into the open seems an arch evasion of responsibility.

Nova Express itself is a much more 'responsible' book, much more
consistent with the avowed moral intentions of its author—and also
much more boring. I find Burroughs more impressive (if no more
congenial) as a nihilist than as a moralist, and the sick fantasies of the
junkie more interesting than the portentous salvationism of the
reclaimed addict. While it is good to know that Mr Burroughs has
been cured of addiction, his attempt to load this private experience
with universal significance, equating morphine with evil and apomorphine with redemption, becomes tiresome. But what most makes
for boredom in this novel is its technical experiment.

IV

First, an example, taken from a chapter vulnerably entitled 'Are
These Experiments Necessary?':

Saturday March 17th, 1962, Present Time of Knowledge—
Scio is knowing and open food in The Homicide Act—Logos
you got it?—Dia through noose—England spent the weekend
with a bargain before release certificate is issued—Dogs must be
carried reluctant to the center—It's a grand feeling—There's a
lot ended—This condition is best expressed queen walks serenely
down dollar process known as overwhelming—What we want is
Watney's Woodbines and the Garden of Delights—And what
could you have?—What would you?—State of news?—Inquire
on hospitals? what?

This seems to be a 'cut-up' of English newspapers, advertisements, public notices, etc. One can identify the likely contexts from which the fragments were taken. But does their juxtaposition create any significant new meaning? I think not.

The comparisons which have been canvassed by Burroughs and his admirers between his method and the methods of Eliot and Joyce (Burroughs has described *The Waste Land* as 'the first great cut-up collage', and a reviewer in the *New York Herald-Tribune* has likened *Nova Express* to *Finnegans Wake*) will not bear scrutiny. Compare:

There I saw one I knew, and stopped him, crying: 'Stetson!
You who were with me in the ships at Mylae!
That corpse you planted last year in your garden,
Has it begun to sprout? Will it bloom this year?
Or has the sudden frost disturbed its bed?
Oh keep the Dog far hence, that's friend to men,
Or with his nails he'll dig it up again!
You! hypocrite lecteur!—mon semblable—mon frère!'

riverrun, past Eve and Adam's, from swerve of shore to bend of
bay, brings us by a commodius vicus of recirculation back to
Howth Castle and Environs.

What these passages have in common, and what is signally lacking in the Burroughs passage, is continuity. In the Eliot passage it is a thematic and dramatic continuity: the lines, incongruous, anachronistic and inconsequential as they are, nevertheless all relate to the idea of the 'Burial of the Dead' and communicate a very lively sense of the speaker's complex mood of surprise, impudence, admonition and complicity. In the Joyce passage it is a narrative or descriptive continuity: we hold on tight to the lightning tour of Dublin's topography, while being dimly aware that it is also a tour of human history from Adam and Eve onwards according to the cyclic theories of Vico. The more you read each passage the more you get out of it, and everything you get out of it thickens and confirms the sense of continuity and hence of meaning (for in the verbal medium meaning *is* continuity: discrete particulars are meaningless).

Burroughs has much less in common, both in precept and practice, with these modern classics, than with the art which Frank Kermode has dubbed 'neo-modernism' ('Modernisms Again: Objects, Jokes and Art', *Encounter*, XXVI (1966), pp. 65–74). Extreme examples of neo-modernism are the tins of Campbell's soup which Andy Warhol signs and sells as *objets d'art*, or the piano piece *4′ 33″* by composer John Cage, in which the performer sits before a closed piano in total silence and immobility for the prescribed time while the audience, in theory, becomes aesthetically aware of the noises around them, inside and outside the auditorium. Behind all these experiments is the principle of chance. Chance is allowed to determine the aesthetic product and the aesthetic experience; the artist confines himself to providing an aesthetic occasion within which the random particulars of our environment may be perceived with a new depth of awareness. As Kermode points out, 'Artists have always known that there was an element of luck in good work ("grace" if you like) and that they rarely knew what they meant till they'd seen what they said'; but neo-modernism trusts, or tries to trust, completely to luck. Kermode's conclusion seems to me the right one; that neo-modernism, apart from its merely humorous intent and value, is involved in a logical contradiction, for when it succeeds it does so by creating an order of the kind which it seeks to deny. 'Research into form is the true means of discovery, even when form is denied existence. So it becomes a real question whether it helps to introduce indeterminacy into the research.'

This seems very relevant to Burroughs's experiments, about which he is characteristically equivocal. The cut-up or fold-in technique is clearly designed to introduce a radical element of chance into literary composition. You run two pages of text into one another and allow chance to produce new units of sense (or nonsense). Burroughs defends such experiments (in the *Paris Review* interview) by an appeal to experience. Thus, he describes how he was struck, during a train journey to St Louis, by the congruence of his thoughts and what he saw outside the window:

For example, a friend of mine has a loft apartment in New York. He said, 'Every time we go out of the house and come back, if we leave the bathroom door open, there's a rat in the house.' I look out of the window, there's Able Pest Control.

'Cut-ups', says Burroughs, 'make explicit a psycho-sensory process that is going on all the time anyway.' Precisely: that is why they are so uninteresting. We can all produce our own coincidences—we go to art for something more. One might guess that Joyce's discovery of a Vico Road in Dublin was a lucky break for him, a coincidence like Burroughs's observation of Able Pest Control (which reappears, incidentally, in a piece of imaginative writing, *St Louis Return*, published in the same issue of the *Paris Review*). But in the case of Joyce we are not aware of it *as* coincidence because it is incorporated into a verbal structure in which innumerable effects of a similar kind are created by means that are palpably not due to luck but to art. I do not mean to imply that we value works of literature solely in proportion to the conscious artifice we are able to impute to the process of composition (though this consideration always has some weight). Rather, that in the experience of successful literature we feel compelled to credit all its excitement and interest, whether this was produced by luck or not, to the creating mind behind it.

There is an essay by Paul Valéry, 'The Course in Poetics: the First Lesson' (reprinted in *The Creative Process*, ed. Brewster Ghiselin, 1955), which deals very profoundly with the difficult problem of indeterminacy in artistic creation. Valéry admits, indeed insists, that 'every act of mind is always somehow accompanied by a certain more or less perceptible atmosphere of indetermination'. But he goes on to point out that the finished art-work 'is the outcome of a succession of inner changes which are as disordered as you please but which must necessarily be reconciled at the moment when the hand moves to write under one unique command, whether happy or not'. As a romantic-symbolist, Valéry is prepared to grant the indeterminate a great deal of play—'the dispersion always threatening the mind contributes almost as importantly to the production of the work as concentration itself'—but the dispersion is a threat, concentration is essential. The cut-up method, by which the writer selects from random collocations of ready-made units of discourse, seems a lazy short-cut, a way of evading the difficult and demanding task of reducing to order the personally felt experience of disorder.

Fortunately Burroughs does not always practise what he preaches.

Kermode remarks: 'Admirers of William Burroughs's *Nova Express* admit that the randomness of the composition pays off only when the text looks as if it had been composed straightforwardly, with calculated inspiration.' I would wager that the following passage *was* composed straightforwardly:

> 'The Subliminal Kid' moved in and took over bars and
> cafés and juke boxes of the world cities and installed radio
> transmitters and microphones in each bar so that the music and
> talk of any bar could be heard in all his bars and he had tape
> recorders in each bar that played and recorded at arbitrary
> intervals and his agents moved back and fourth with portable
> tape recorders and brought back street sound and talk and music
> and poured it into his recorder array so he set waves and eddies
> and tornadoes of sound down all your streets and by the river
> of all language—Word dust drifted streets of broken music
> car horns and air hammers—The Word broken pounded
> twisted exploded in smoke—

Here it does not seem inappropriate to invoke Eliot and Joyce. There is continuity here—narrative, logical, syntactical and thematic. The language is disordered to imitate disorder, but it is orderly enough to form a complex, unified impression. It is worth noting, too, that the meaning of the passage is a conservative and traditional one—a criticism of those forces in modern civilization that are mutilating and destroying words and The Word, and the values they embody and preserve. The passage thus contradicts Burroughs's protestations (see the *Paris Review* interview) that his experiments are designed to break down our 'superstitious reverence for the word'.

V

The function of the *avant-garde* is to win new freedom, new expressive possibilities, for the arts. But these things have to be *won*, have to be fought for; and the struggle is not merely with external canons of taste, but within the artist himself. To bend the existing conventions without breaking them—this is the strenuous and heroic calling of the experimental artist. To break them is too easy.

I believe this principle can be extended to cover not only formal conventions, but also the social conventions that governs the content of public discourse. From the Romantics onwards the revolutionary works have commonly affronted not only their audience's aesthetic standards, but also their moral standards. *Madame Bovary* and *Ulysses*, for example, shocked and dismayed the publics of their respective periods by mentioning the unmentionable. But these works gradually won acceptance because discriminating readers appreciated that their breaches of existing decorums were not lightly or irresponsibly made, and that their authors had substituted for received disciplines and controls, disciplines and controls of their own even more austere and demanding. Much of the work of today's *avant-garde*, including that of Burroughs, carries no such internal guarantee of integrity. Its freedom is stolen, not earned. The end product is hence startling and exciting on the first impression, but ultimately boring.

Finnegans Wake deliberately violates the conventions of language: it seeks to overthrow the law that we can only think and communicate lineally, one thing at a time. Most of us can manage the same trick—we can throw off a Joycean pun once in a while (I offer one free of charge to Mr Burroughs: 'fission chips'). But to produce hundreds and thousands of such puns, as Joyce does, and to weld them all into a complex whole—this is to create not destroy convention, and is a task of staggering difficulty. Similarly, most of us can compose a good obscene joke on occasion, or produce a powerful emotive effect by the use of obscene words; but to give these things authority as public discourse we have to ensure that they will survive the passing of the initial shock—we have not merely to violate, but to recreate the public sensibility, a task requiring precise imaginative control. One can't avoid the conclusion that a lot of Burroughs's most immediately effective writing (e.g. 'A. J. the notorious Merchant of Sex, who scandalized international society when he appeared at the Duc du Ventre's ball as a walking penis covered by a huge condom emblazoned with the A.J. motto "They Shall Not Pass"') has the short-lived appeal of a witty obscenity; or, in its more grotesque and horrific forms ('Two Lesbian Agents with glazed faces of grafted penis flesh sat sipping spinal fluid through alabaster straws') amounts to a reckless and self-defeating squandering of the powerful emotive forces that great literature handles with jealous care and economy.

9 Samuel Beckett:
Some Ping Understood

The enigma of Samuel Beckett's *Ping* (*Encounter*, February 1967) derives a special interest from the context of debate, initiated in the same journal by Frank Kermode (March-April 1966) and carried on by Ihab Hassan (January 1967) and Bernard Bergonzi (May 1967) concerning the contemporary *avant-garde*. Whether fortuitously or not, *Ping* seems a timely illustrative or testing 'case' for such critical speculation.

The speculation is, I take it, concerned basically with such questions as: is contemporary *avant-garde* literature, in common with experimental art in other media, making a much more radical break with 'tradition' than did the literature and art of what Kermode calls 'paleomodernism'? Is it, in effect, seeking the extinction of literary culture by denying from within the epistemological function of the literary medium itself (i.e. language)? Is it, not literature at all, but 'anti-literature'? Is it immune to conventional criticism; and if so, does this demonstrate criticism's impotence, or its own?

Of the three critics mentioned above, the one who answers these questions in a spirit most sympathetic to radical discontinuity with tradition is Ihab Hassan. The essential argument of his article 'The Literature of Silence' is that today, 'Literature, turning against itself, aspires to silence, leaving us with uneasy intimations of outrage and apocalypse. If there is an *avant-garde* in our time, it is probably bent on discovery through suicide.' Beckett is one of Hassan's chief examples:

> Writing for Beckett is absurd play. In a certain sense, all his works may be thought of as a parody of Wittgenstein's notion that language is a set of games, akin to the arithmetic of primitive tribes. Beckett's parodies, which are full of self-spite, designate a general tendency in anti-literature. Hugh Kenner brilliantly describes this tendency when he states: 'The dominant intellectual analogy of the present age is drawn not from biology, not from psychology . . . but from general number theory.' Art in a closed field thus becomes an absurd game of permutations, like Molloy sucking stones at the beach; and 'the retreat from the word' (the phrase is George Steiner's) reduces language to pure ratio.

> Beckett . . . comes close to reducing literature to a mathe-
> matical tautology. The syllogism of Beckett assumes that
> history has spent itself; we are merely playing an end game. . . .
> Language has become void; therefore words can only
> demonstrate their emptiness. . . . Thus literature becomes the
> inaudible game of a solipsist.

Professor Hassan must have been gratified by the appearance of *Ping* in the very next issue of *Encounter*, for one of its key-words is *silence*, and in other ways it appears to confirm his description of Beckett's art. 'Permutation', for instance, seems an appropriate description of the way language is used in *Ping*: that is, an unusually limited number of words are repeated to an unusual extent in various combinations. (By 'unusual' I mean unusual for a piece of literary prose of this length.) There are only a few words that occur only once in *Ping*: *brief, hair, nails, scars, torn, henceforth, unlustrous.* Other words are used at least twice, and most words are used more than twice. The word *white*, which seems to be the most frequently recurring word, is used more than ninety times. Many phrases or word groups are repeated, but rarely an entire sentence. Thus, if the first sentence is divided up into the following word groups:

> All known/all white/bare white body fixed/one yard/legs joined
> like sewn.

each word group recurs later in the piece, but never with all the others in the same order in a single sentence—always with some modification or addition. Typical variations are:

> Bare white body fixed one yard ping fixed elsewhere. (15)*
> Bare white body fixed one yard ping fixed elsewhere white on
> white invisible heart breath no sound. (40/42)
> Bare white one yard fixed ping fixed elsewhere no sound legs
> joined like sewn heels together right angle hands hanging palms
> front. (66/68)

It is this kind of repetition with variation that makes *Ping* so difficult to read, and the label 'anti-literature' a plausible one. Repetition is often a key to meaning in literary discourse, but repetition on this scale tends to defeat the pursuit of meaning. That is, a familiar critical strategy in dealing with narrative prose is to look for

---

* Line references are to the text printed in *Encounter* (February, 1967), pp. 25–6, reprinted at the end of this essay.

some significant pattern of repetition hidden in the variegated texture of the discourse: the variegated texture, by which 'solidity of specification' is achieved, is woven in a logical, temporal progression, while the pattern of repetition holds the work together in a kind of spatial order and suggests the nature of the overall theme. But in *Ping* this relationship is inverted: the repetition is far from hidden—it overwhelms the reader in its profusion and disrupts the sense of specificity and of logical, temporal progression. It is extraordinarily difficult to read through the entire piece, short as it is, with sustained concentration. After about forty or fifty lines the words begin to slide and blur before the eyes, and to echo bewilderingly in the ear. This is caused not merely by the elaborate repetition, but also by the meagreness of explicit syntax, the drastic reduction of such aids to communication as punctuation, finite verbs, conjunctions, articles, prepositions and subordination.

All this, then, goes to confirm Hassan's comments; and as a general account of what Beckett is up to they are no doubt fair enough. But I must confess to finding something unsatisfactory about this kind of critical response. I don't see, for instance, how it could help us to distinguish between one piece by Beckett and another, except as progressive—or regressive—steps towards silence. If the sole object of the game is to expose the limitations of language by a bewildering permutation of words, it wouldn't matter what particular words were used, or what their referential content was. But I think that the more closely acquainted we become with *Ping* the more certain we become that it does matter what words are used, and that they refer to something more specific than the futility of life or the futility of art. Beckett is telling us 'about' something; and if the telling is extraordinarily difficult to follow this is not simply because all experience is difficult to communicate (though this is true) but because this experience is difficult to communicate in *this* particular way.

It would be dishonest to make this assertion without going on to suggest what *Ping* is about. What follows doesn't pretend to be a definitive or exclusive reading, but its tentativeness differs only in degree from the tentativeness imposed on the critic by any complex literary work.

I suggest that *Ping* is the rendering of the consciousness of a person confined in a small, bare, white room, a person who is evidently under extreme duress, and probably at the last gasp of life. He has no freedom of movement: his body is 'fixed', the legs are joined together, the heels turning at right angles, the hands hanging palms front; the 'heart breath' makes 'no sound' (43). 'Only the eyes only just . . .'— can we say, *move?* (4). There are parts of the room he cannot see, and he evidently can't move his head to see them, though he thinks there is 'perhaps a way out' there (25 and 50).

The first words of the piece are 'all known', and this phrase recurs (11, 21, 30/1 etc.). But the 'all' that is 'known' is severely limited and yields 'no meaning' (7/8 and *passim*) though the narrator is reluctant to admit this: 'perhaps a meaning' (32). *Ping* seems to record the struggles of an expiring consciousness to find some meaning in a situation which offers no purchase to the mind or to sensation. The consciousness makes repeated, feeble efforts to assert the possibility of colour, movement, sound, memory, another person's presence, only to fall back hopelessly into the recognition of colourlessness, paralysis, silence, oblivion, solitude. This rhythm of tentative assertion and collapse is marked by the frequently recurring collocation 'only just almost never' (11 and *passim*).

By colourlessness I mean the predominance of white, which is no colour, or at least the 'last colour' (74). The shining white planes of walls, floor and ceiling, the whiteness of his own body, make it difficult for the person to see more than 'traces, blurs, signs' (7 and *passim*). The attempt to assert colour—black, rose, light blue, light grey— nearly always fades into an admission that it is really 'almost white', 'white on white', is 'invisible', has 'no meaning':

Traces blurs light grey almost white on white. (4/5)
Traces blurs signs no meaning light grey almost white. (7/8)
Traces alone unover given black light grey almost white on white. (13/14)
Traces alone unover given black grey blurs signs no meaning light grey almost white always the same. (51/53)

Aural experience is equally meagre. There is 'silence within' (10). These words are followed by 'Brief murmurs'; but the murmurs are immediately qualified by 'only just almost never' (10/11). However, the next 'murmur' is associated with the speculation 'perhaps not alone' (19). A little later there is another *perhaps*-phrase, again associated with 'murmur':

Ping murmur perhaps a nature one second almost never that much memory almost never. (28/29)

This is a particularly interesting and tantalizing sentence. What does 'a nature' mean? A human nature? His own, or another's? It seems to be associated with memory, anyway, and memory with meaning, for a few lines later we get: 'Ping murmur only just almost never one second perhaps a meaning that much memory almost never' (31/34).

Towards the close of the piece I think there are more definite indications that the character's search for meaning and grasp on life are connected with some effort of memory, some effort to recall a human image, and thus break out of total impotence and solitude:

> Ping perhaps not alone one second with image same time a
> little less dim eye black and white half closed long lashes
> imploring that much memory almost never. (70/72)

'Long lashes imploring' is the most human touch, the most emotive phrase, in the entire piece. It deviates sharply from the linguistic norms which have been set up, and which project a generally de-humanized version of experience. It therefore has a strong impact, and this is reinforced by other features of the sentence. The 'image' is 'a little less dim'. We have met the phrase 'a little less' before (e.g. 54 and 63), but not with 'dim'—it is as if only now can the consciousness complete the phrase it has been struggling to formulate. The eye is 'black and white'—it is not black fading into light grey, into almost white, into white on white.

This sentence, then, seems to mark the apex of the character's effort at memory. It is 'Afar flash of time', but short-lived: almost immediately it is swamped by the despairing sequence:

> all white all over all of old ping flash white walls shining
> white no trace eyes holes light blue almost white last colour
> ping white over. (72/74)

The next two sentences also end with the word *over*, as does the whole piece. *Over*, which makes its first appearance in line 56, seems to echo the curious nonce-word *unover* (13, 18, 37, 43, etc.) which presumably means 'not over', and is invariably preceded by the word *alone*, for example: 'Traces alone unover given black light grey almost white on white' (13/14). Such sentences, which occur mainly in the first half of the text, seem to define the very limited sense in which experience is on-going, 'not over'; but after the vision or image of the eye with 'long lashes imploring' the emphasis shifts to the idea that experience is finished, over. The formula 'that much memory almost never' is changed to 'that much memory *henceforth* never' in line 82. The image of the eye recurs unexpectedly in the last two lines of the piece, with the addition of the word *unlustrous*—a word rather striking in itself, and notable for occurring only this once in *Ping*, thus giving a further specificity to the 'eye black and white half-closed long lashes imploring'. But this seems to be the last effort of the consciousness— the sentence continues and ends, 'ping silence ping over'. The image or vision is over, consciousness is over, the story is over.

I have implied that the black and white eye (singular) is not one of the character's own eyes, which are, I think, the ones referred to throughout the passage (in the plural) as being light blue or grey, tending to the overall condition of whiteness. This black eye with the lashes is, I suggest, someone else's eye, part of some emotional and human connection which the character is struggling to recall through memory. The effort to do so is only successful to a very limited extent, and exhausts him, perhaps kills him: 'ping silence ping over'.

I can't offer any confident explanation of the word *ping* itself. On the referential level it might denote the noise emitted by some piece of apparatus, perhaps marking the passage of time (there are repeated references to 'one second', though the *pings* do not occur at regular intervals). On the level of connotation, *ping* is a feeble, pathetic, unresonant, irritating, even maddening sound, making it an appropriate enough title for this piece, which it punctuates like the striking of a triangle at intervals in the course of a complicated fugue.

The above commentary is based on some introductory remarks made by the present writer to a discussion of *Ping* by some members of the English Department at Birmingham University.* My remarks were followed by the independently prepared comments of a linguist, whose descriptive analysis of the structure of the piece was in general accord with my own (though it corrected some rash assertions I had made). I shall try to do justice to the main points of this linguistic commentary in a general account of the discussion as a whole.

In this discussion there was inevitably a good deal of conflict, but on the whole the measure of agreement was more striking. A minority of the participants were inclined to think that *Ping* was indeed a language game, a verbal construct cunningly devised to yield an infinite

* The other participants were: Miss Vera Adamson, K. M. Green, T. P. Matheson, Mrs Joan Rees, I. A. Shapiro, T. A. Shippey, G. T. Shepherd, J. M. Sinclair, H. A. Smith, S. W. Wells and M. Wilding. This article is published with their kind permission, but it does not pretend to give a full or faithful record of their contributions to the discussion. It is highly selective and based on imperfect memory, and for this reason I have not attributed opinions to individuals.

number of interpretations—and therefore, in effect, resistant to interpretation. It could be about a man having a bath or a shower or a man under rifle fire or a man being tortured; *ping* might be the sound of a bullet ricocheting, or the sound of water dripping or the sound of a bell, and the bell might be a bicycle bell or a sanctus bell or a typewriter bell (perhaps the writer's own typewriter bell). But the majority were disposed to find *Ping* more specifically meaningful, to see it as the rendering of a certain kind of experience, and as having a perceptible design. While it might not be possible to agree on a formulation of the experience more precise than the effort of a consciousness to assert its identity in the teeth of the void, the verbal medium was operating selectively to induce a much more finely discriminated range of effects than that formulation suggested. Considered as a whole, in isolation, the piece satisfied the traditional aesthetic criteria of *integritas, consonantia,* and *claritas.* At the same time it had an obvious continuity with the rest of Beckett's work, and to consider it in relation to his whole *œuvre* would be the next logical step in interpretation.

The two main points of dispute, and the ones where I feel my own reading of *Ping* to have been most inadequate, concerned the possibility of some allusion to Christ, and the significance of the word *ping* itself.

As to the first, it was pointed out that there are a number of words and phrases reminiscent of the passion and death of Christ: 'legs joined like sewn', 'hands hanging palms front' are vaguely evocative of the Crucifixion; 'seam like sewn invisible' suggests the cloak without a seam. More striking is this passage:

Given rose only just nails fallen white over. Long hair fallen white invisible over. White scars invisible same white as flesh torn of old given rose only just. (55/57)

The words *nails, hair, scars, flesh, torn,* belong to that (in *Ping*) rare class that occur only once, and their clustering together here might well be designed to alert us to an interpretative clue. For a dizzy moment we entertained the possibility that the whole piece might be a bleakly anti-metaphysical rendering of the consciousness of the dying Christ—Christ in the tomb rather than Christ on the Cross (hence the cramped, cell-like room)—in short, Beckett's version of *The Man Who Died.* But this reading seemed not only to leave much unexplained, but to be impoverishing; for the piece doesn't read like a riddle to which there is a single answer. However, the possibility of some allusion to Christ cannot, I think, be discounted.

Discussion about the significance of the word *ping* polarized around those who, like myself, regarded it as a noise external to the discourse, which it punctuated at arbitrary intervals, a noise so meaningless as not to enter into the murmur/silence dichotomy, the most meaningless item, in fact, in the character's field of perception; and on the other hand those who regarded it as part of the discourse, as having some conceptual content or as being an ironic, or movingly pathetic, substitute or code-word for some concept that cannot be fully and openly entertained, such as God (cf. 'Godot'). Thus the sentence 'Ping elsewhere always there only known not' (36/37) becomes almost lucid if you replace *Ping* with *God*; and it is interesting to note that this is one of the rare sentences that recur in exactly the same form (69).

Strengthening this case that *ping* is part of the discourse, or stream of consciousness, rather than an arbitrary intrusion from outside, is the fact that it is associated with a selective number of other words and phrases. Thus, going through the piece and noting the words which immediately follow the word *ping*, we get the following pattern:

ping fixed elsewhere
ping fixed elsewhere
ping fixed elsewhere
Ping murmur
ping murmur
ping silence
Ping murmur
Ping murmur
ping elsewhere
Ping elsewhere
ping murmur
ping fixed elsewhere
Ping murmurs
Ping perhaps a nature
ping perhaps way out
ping silence
Ping perhaps not alone
ping silence
Ping image
Ping a nature

ping a meaning
ping silence
ping fixed elsewhere
Ping elsewhere
Ping perhaps not alone
ping flash
ping white over
Ping fixed last elsewhere
ping of old
Ping of old
ping last murmur
ping silence
ping over.

This doesn't look like random occurrence. *Ping* tends to be followed by words or phrases which suggest the possibility of some other presence or place: *fixed elsewhere, murmur, image, perhaps a nature, perhaps a way out, perhaps not alone*, etc. It is natural, I think, to look first at the words and phrases which follow *ping*, for if it has a quasi-grammatical status it would appear to be that of a subject—it is, for instance, often the first word of a sentence. If we look at the words and phrases which immediately precede *ping* we get, in fact, a sequence which is no less patterned, but it is interesting that these words and phrases are mostly of a quite different order; they tend to stress the bleak limitations of the character's situation and field of perceptions: *bare white body fixed, invisible, never seen, almost never*, are among the most frequently recurring. We might suggest that *ping* marks the intervals between the oscillating movements of the character's consciousness from dull despair to tentative hope; though this leaves open the question of whether it is part of the discourse, or an intrusion from outside which stimulates thought in a mechanical and arbitrary way.

I should note, finally, the ingenious suggestion that *ping* alludes to the parlour game 'Ping Pong' which assumes that all words and concepts can be placed in one of two great categories, 'Ping' and 'Pong'. Thus, for example, *white* is Ping and *black* is Pong; and Beckett's piece is the account of a man inhabiting a Ping world, struggling feebly to reach out to or recover a Pong world.

The above discussion, needless to say, leaves much unexplained or in doubt (a phrase which particularly puzzles me is 'blue and white in the wind' 49, 58, 64, 81). But it does suggest, I think, that *Ping* is not, as it appears at first sight, totally impenetrable and meaningless. The important point was made in the course of our discussion that the piece *has* got a syntax: it is rudimentary, but it does control the possible range of meaning. It would be perverse, for instance, to read the first sentence grouping the words in this way:

All/known all white bare/white body fixed one/yard legs/joined like/sewn.

The piece draws on the principles of a shared language, especially the principle of word order. ('Ping' itself is the most ambiguous word in the text precisely because it is the one least defined by any referential or structural function in ordinary usage.) Though these principles are drastically modified, they are never abandoned. A good deal of logical organization persists, as can be demonstrated by reading the text backwards and measuring the loss of sense.

If Beckett were really writing anti-literature, it wouldn't matter whether we read the text backwards or forwards, from left to right or from right to left. Of course, terms like 'anti-literature' and 'literature of silence' are rhetorical paradoxes aimed to suggest a radical degree of innovation: they are not to be taken literally. But they can have the effect of deterring us from engaging closely with a text like *Ping*. To confirm Professor Hassan's comments on Beckett, it is not necessary to give *Ping* more than a quick, superficial glance. If the object of the exercise is merely to baffle our intelligences and cheat our conventional expectations, why should we bother to do more? But if we do bother to do more, the rewards are surprisingly great. *Ping* proves, after all, not to be totally resistant to methods of critical reading derived from conventional literature. Its language is not void; its words do not merely demonstrate their emptiness. It is, like any literary artefact, a marriage of form and meaning.

Ping

All known all white bare white body fixed one yard legs joined like sewn. Light heat white floor one square yard never seen. White walls one yard by two white ceiling one square yard never seen. Bare white body fixed only the eyes only just. Traces blurs light
5 grey almost white on white. Hands hanging palms front white feet heels together right angle. Light heat white planes shining white bare white body fixed ping fixed elsewhere. Traces blurs signs no

7

meaning light grey almost white. Bare white body fixed white on
white invisible. Only the eyes only just light blue almost white.
10 Head haught eyes light blue almost white silence within. Brief
murmurs only just almost never all known. Traces blurs signs no
meaning light grey almost white. Legs joined like sewn heels
together right angle. Traces alone unover given black light grey
almost white on white. Light heat white walls shining white one
15 yard by two. Bare white body fixed one yard ping fixed elsewhere.
Traces blurs signs no meaning light grey almost white. White feet
toes joined like sewn heels together right angle invisible. Eyes
alone unover given blue light blue almost white. Murmur only just
almost never one second perhaps not alone. Given rose only just
20 bare white body fixed one yard white on white invisible. All white
all known murmurs only just almost never always the same all
known. Light heat hands hanging palms front white on white
invisible. Bare white body fixed ping fixed elsewhere. Only the
eyes only just light blue almost white fixed front. Ping murmur
25 only just almost never one second perhaps a way out. Head haught
eyes light blue almost white fixed front ping murmur ping silence.
Eyes holes light blue almost white mouth white seam like sewn
invisible. Ping murmur perhaps a nature one second almost never
that much memory almost never. White walls each its trace grey
30 blur signs no meaning light grey almost white. Light heat all
known all white planes meeting invisible. Ping murmur only just
almost never one second perhaps a meaning that much memory
almost never. White feet toes joining like sewn heels together
right angle ping elsewhere no sound. Hands hanging palms front
35 legs joined like sewn. Head haught eyes holes light blue almost
white fixed front silence within. Ping elsewhere always there only
known not. Eyes holes light blue alone unover given blue light
blue almost white only colour fixed front. All white all known
white planes shining white ping murmur only just almost never
40 one second light time that much memory almost never. Bare white
body fixed one yard ping fixed elsewhere white on white invisible
heart breath no sound. Only the eyes given blue light blue almost
white fixed front only colour alone unover. Planes meeting
invisible only one shining white infinitely only known not. Nose
45 ears white holes mouth white seam like sewn invisible. Ping
murmurs only just almost never one second always the same all
known. Given rose only just bare white body fixed one yard invisible all known without within. Ping perhaps a nature one second

with image same time a little less blue and white in the wind. White
50 ceiling shining white one square yard never seen ping perhaps way
out there one second ping silence. Traces alone unover given black
grey blurs signs no meaning light grey almost white always the
same. Ping perhaps not alone one second with image always the
same same time a little less that much memory almost never ping
55 silence. Given rose only just nails fallen white over. Long hair
fallen white invisible over. White scars invisible same white as
flesh torn of old given rose only just. Ping image only just almost
never one second light time blue and white in the wind. Head
haught nose ears white holes mouth white seam like sewn invisible
60 over. Only the eyes given blue fixed front light blue almost white
only colour alone unover. Light heat white planes shining white
on only shining white infinite only known not. Ping a nature only
just almost never one second with image same time a little less blue
and white in the wind. Traces blurs light grey eyes holes light
65 blue almost white fixed front ping a meaning only just almost never
ping silence. Bare white one yard fixed ping fixed elsewhere no
sound legs joined like sewn heels together right angle hands hanging
palms front. Head haught eyes holes light blue almost white fixed
front silence within. Ping elsewhere always there only known not.
70 Ping perhaps not alone one second with image same time a little
less dim eye black and white half closed long lashes imploring that
much memory almost never. Afar flash of time all white all over all
of old ping flash white walls shining white no trace eyes holes light
blue almost white last colour ping white over. Ping fixed last else-
75 where legs joined like sewn heels together right angle hands
hanging palms front head haught eyes white invisible fixed front
over. Given rose only just one yard invisible bare white all known
without within over. White ceiling never seen ping of old only
just almost never one second light time white floor never seen
80 ping of old perhaps there. Ping of old only just perhaps a meaning
a nature one second almost never blue and white in the wind that
much memory henceforth never. White planes no trace shining
white one only shining white infinite only known not. Light heat
all known all white heart breath no sound. Head haught eyes white
85 fixed front old ping last murmur one second perhaps not only eye
unlustrous black and white half closed long lashes imploring ping
silence ping over.

Translated from the French by the author

10   Hemingway's Clean, Well-lighted, Puzzling Place

I

'A Clean, Well-lighted Place' is one of Ernest Hemingway's best-known and most often reprinted short stories; yet until very recently its text contained a curious anomaly: curious, especially, in that it for so long apparently escaped the attention both of Hemingway himself and of his readers. For this crux is not a minor, incidental matter, but one that vitally affects one's reading of the whole story. In fact, the text which appeared in *Scribner's Magazine* in March 1933, and was reprinted in all editions up until 1966 (and which is still appearing in textbooks and anthologies[1]) simply doesn't make sense.

I first discovered this for myself a few years ago in the 1963 Scribner's paperback edition of *The Snows of Kilimanjaro and Other Stories.* Enquiries revealed that a number of articles had appeared on the problem, beginning in 1959, and that Scribner's had emended the text in their 1967 edition of *The Short Stories of Ernest Hemingway*, adopting a solution proposed by John V. Hagopian.[2] This solution seems to me the right one; and I discuss the problem here, not in order to suggest an alternative solution, but as a starting-point for an analysis of the story as a whole.

The original, unemended text which obtained up until 1966, is as follows:

A Clean, Well-lighted Place

It was late and every one had left the café except an old man who sat in the shadow the leaves of the tree made against the electric light. In the day time the street was dusty, but at night the dew settled the dust and the old man liked to sit late because he was
5 deaf and now at night it was quiet and he felt the difference. The two waiters inside the café knew that the old man was a little drunk, and while he was a good client they knew that if he became too drunk he would leave without paying, so they kept watch on him.
10 'Last week he tried to commit suicide,' one waiter said.
      'Why?'

'He was in despair.'

'What about?'

'Nothing.'

15 'How do you know it was nothing?'

'He has plenty of money.'

They sat together at a table that was close against the wall near the door of the café and looked at the terrace where the tables were all empty except where the old man sat in the shadow
20 of the leaves of the tree that moved slightly in the wind. A girl and a soldier went by in the street. The street light shone on the brass number on his collar. The girl wore no head covering and hurried beside him.

'The guard will pick him up,' one waiter said.

25 'What does it matter if he gets what he's after?'

'He had better get off the street now. The guard will get him. They went by five minutes ago.'

The old man sitting in the shadow rapped on his saucer with his glass. The younger waiter went over to him.

30 'What do you want?'

The old man looked at him. 'Another brandy,' he said.

'You'll be drunk,' the waiter said. The old man looked at him. The waiter went away.

'He'll stay all night,' he said to his colleague. 'I'm sleepy now.
35 I never get into bed before three o'clock. He should have killed himself last week.'

The waiter took the brandy bottle and another saucer from the counter inside the café and marched out to the old man's table. He put down the saucer and poured the glass full of brandy.

40 'You should have killed yourself last week,' he said to the deaf man. The old man motioned with his finger. 'A little more,' he said. The waiter poured on into the glass so that the brandy slopped over and ran down the stem into the top saucer of the pile. 'Thank you,' the old man said. The waiter took the bottle back
45 inside the café. He sat down at the table with his colleague again.

'He's drunk now,' he said.

'He's drunk every night.'

'What did he want to kill himself for?'

'How should I know.'

50 'How did he do it?'

'He hung himself with a rope.'

'Who cut him down?'

'His niece.'

'Why did they do it?'

55 'Fear for his soul.'

'How much money has he got?'

'He's got plenty.'

'He must be eighty years old.'

'Anyway I should say he was eighty.'

60 'I wish he would go home. I never get to bed before three o'clock. What kind of hour is that to go to bed?'

'He stays up because he likes it.'

'He's lonely. I'm not lonely. I have a wife waiting in bed for me.'

65 'He had a wife once too.'

'A wife would be no good to him now.'

'You can't tell. He might be better with a wife.'

'His niece looks after him.'

'I know. You said she cut him down.'

70 'I wouldn't want to be that old. An old man is a nasty thing.'

'Not always. This old man is clean. He drinks without spilling. Even now, drunk. Look at him.'

'I don't want to look at him. I wish he would go home. He has no regard for those who must work.'

75 The old man looked from his glass across the square, then over at the waiters.

'Another brandy,' he said, pointing to his glass. The waiter who was in a hurry came over.

'Finished,' he said, speaking with that omission of syntax stupid 80 people employ when talking to drunken people or foreigners. 'No more tonight. Close now.'

'Another,' said the old man.

'No. Finished.' The waiter wiped the edge of the table with a towel and shook his head.

85 The old man stood up, slowly counted the saucers, took a leather coin purse from his pocket and paid for the drinks, leaving half a peseta tip.

The waiter watched him go down the street, a very old man walking unsteadily but with dignity.

90 'Why didn't you let him stay and drink?' the unhurried waiter asked. They were putting up the shutters. 'It is not half-past two.'

'I want to go home to bed.'

'What is an hour?'

'More to me than to him.'

95 'An hour is the same.'

'You talk like an old man yourself. He can buy a bottle and drink at home.'

'It's not the same.'

'No, it is not,' agreed the waiter with a wife. He did not wish
100 to be unjust. He was only in a hurry.

'And you? You have no fear of going home before your usual hour?'

'Are you trying to insult me?'

'No, hombre, only to make a joke.'

105 'No,' the waiter who was in a hurry said, rising from pulling down the metal shutters. 'I have confidence. I am all confidence.'

'You have youth, confidence, and a job,' the older waiter said. 'You have everything.'

'And what do you lack?'

110 'Everything but work.'

'You have everything I have.'

'No. I have never had confidence and I am not young.'

'Come on. Stop talking nonsense and lock up.'

'I am of those who like to stay late at the café,' the older waiter
115 said. 'With all those who do not want to go to bed. With all those who need a light for the night.'

'I want to go home and into bed.'

'We are of two different kinds,' the older waiter said. He was now dressed to go home. 'It is not only a question of youth and
120 confidence although those things are very beautiful. Each night I am reluctant to close up because there may be someone who needs the café.'

'Hombre, there are bodegas open all night long.'

'You do not understand. This is a clean and pleasant café. It is
125 well lighted. The light is very good and also, now, there are shadows of the leaves.'

'Good night,' said the younger waiter.

'Good night,' the other said. Turning off the electric light he continued the conversation with himself. It is the light of course
130 but it is necessary that the place be clean and pleasant. You do not want music. Certainly you do not want music. Nor can you stand before a bar with dignity although that is all that is provided for these hours. What did he fear? It was not fear or dread. It was a nothing that he knew too well. It was all a nothing and

135   a man was nothing too. It was only that and light was all it needed
and a certain cleanness and order. Some lived in it and never felt
it but he knew it all was nada y pues nada y nada y pues nada.
Our nada who art in nada, nada be thy name thy kingdom nada
thy will be nada in nada as it is in nada. Give us this nada our
140   daily nada and nada us our nada as we nada our nadas and nada
us not into nada but deliver us from nada; pues nada. Hail nothing
full of nothing, nothing is with thee. He smiled and stood before
a bar with a shining steam pressure coffee machine.
'What's yours?' asked the barman.
145   'Nada.'
'Otro loco mas,' said the barman and turned away.
'A little cup,' said the waiter.
The barman poured it for him.
'The light is very bright and pleasant but the bar is unpolished,'
150   the waiter said.
The barman looked at him but did not answer. It was too late
at night for conversation.
'You want another copita?' the barman asked.
'No, thank you,' said the waiter and went out. He disliked bars
155   and bodegas. A clean, well-lighted café was a very different thing.
Now, without thinking further, he would go home to his room.
He would lie in the bed and finally, with daylight, he would go
to sleep. After all, he said to himself, it is probably only insomnia.
Many must have it.

The attentive reader will have observed a logical inconsistency at line
69, in the long dialogue between the two waiters beginning line 46.
It is clear that it is the 'younger waiter' who is serving the old man
(see line 29). It is therefore the younger waiter who (lines 44–7) rejoins
the older waiter at the table and reopens the conversation:

> The waiter took the bottle back inside the café. He sat down at the
> table with his colleague again.
> 'He's drunk now,' he [the younger waiter]* said.

Taking this as a key to the attribution of dialogue, it is clear that it is
the younger waiter who is asking the questions about the old man's

---

* The same identification can be made by working backwards from line 63, 'I have
a wife waiting in bed for me', which must be spoken by the younger waiter.

suicide attempt, and the older waiter who is answering them. The young waiter asks, 'Who cut him down?' The older waiter replies, 'His niece' (52–3). But when the younger waiter seeks to dismiss the old man's lack of a wife by saying, 'His niece looks after him', the older waiter says: 'I know. *You* said she cut him down' (68–9. My italics.) Two short articles by F. P. Kroeger and William E. Colburn, printed side by side in *College English* (1959),[3] first drew attention to this contradiction. Mr Kroeger implied that the story had been carelessly written and/or edited. Mr Colburn castigated Hemingway's critics for overlooking or evading the problem. Both writers recognized that the crux affected the attribution of the first dialogue between the two waiters (10–16). For the long third dialogue, beginning line 46, is the only *logical* guide to the correct attribution of the first dialogue. If in the long dialogue it is the younger waiter who is asking all the questions about the suicide attempt, and the older waiter who is answering them, then it is logical to attribute the opening exchange as follows:

Older Waiter:	Last week he tried to commit suicide.
Younger Waiter:	Why?
O.W.:	He was in despair.
Y.W.:	What about?
O.W.:	Nothing.
Y.W.:	How do you know it was nothing?
O.W.:	He has plenty of money.

In this case the older waiter is being consciously ironic at the younger waiter's expense. By 'Nothing', the older waiter refers privately to the sense of 'nada' which, as we later discover, he himself shares, and which is quite enough to drive a man to suicide. His younger colleague, however, as we also discover later, has no perception of 'nada', and no sympathy for those who are afflicted by it, so 'Nothing' will also serve to mean that, in common-sense terms, the old man had no reason to despair. 'How do you know it was nothing?' indicates that the younger waiter does indeed interpret the word in this sense; and the older waiter underlines the impossibility of explaining the suicide attempt in the rational, materialistic terms the younger waiter would understand, by saying, 'He has plenty of money.'

If, however, we ignore the logical key provided by the opening of the long, third dialogue (which is itself, in our original text, logically confused) it is possible to attribute the lines of the opening dialogue in reverse order, as, for instance, Carlos Baker does:[4]

7*

> Young Waiter: Last week he tried to commit suicide.
> Old Waiter: Why?
> Y.W.:   He was in despair.
> O.W.:   What about?
> Y.W.:   Nothing.
> O.W.:   How do you know it was nothing?
> Y.W.:   He has plenty of money.

n this case the younger waiter reveals his unimaginative materialism by 'Nothing' (in its ordinary colloquial sense) and 'He has plenty of money'; while the older waiter anticipates his later development of the meaning of 'nothing' by his question, 'How do you know it was nothing?'. As regards the overall meaning of the story there is little to choose between these two, opposite attributions, since both can be interpreted as making the same distinction between the two waiters— one through the older waiter's concealed, conscious irony, and the other through an ironical, but unconscious self-betrayal by the younger waiter. Superficially, the lines 'Nothing' and 'He has plenty of money' seem entirely appropriate to the coarser sensibility of the younger waiter as it is later displayed in the story.

Otto Reinert placed so much weight on this last point that, in the next published contribution to the discussion[5] he made it the keystone of his argument. His premise was that it is the younger waiter who says 'He's got plenty of money' and therefore it is he who knows all about the suicide attempt of the old man. To reconcile this reading with the third dialogue, beginning line 46, he suggested that here Hemingway violated the usual convention that in a printed dialogue a new, indented line implies a new speaker, 'in order to suggest a reflective pause between two sentences'. He suggested that the younger waiter says *both* 'He's drunk now' *and* 'He's drunk every night' (46–7); and that the older waiter says *both* 'He must be eighty years old' *and* 'Anyway I should say he was eighty' (58–9). This, of course, has the effect of making the older waiter ask all the questions, and the younger waiter answer them, so that there is then no inconsistency about line 69.

It is true that 'He's drunk every night' and 'Anyway I should say he was eighty' *could* be afterthoughts by the speakers of the previous lines, and would be accepted as such without question if they had been printed continuously. Reinert also argues, with some plausibility, that 'Anyway I should say he was eighty' seems more natural as an amplification of the preceding remark than as a response by the other speaker. However, on this last point, Edward Stone has observed that 'Anyway' here is an attempt to render a phrase in colloquial Spanish indicating agreement or confirmation.[6] The main objection to Reinert's theory, as John Hagopian later pointed out,[7] is the implausibility of Hemingway's having deliberately violated a well-established typographical convention in a way for which there is no precedent elsewhere in his work (nor, one might add, anywhere else), for a purpose that could easily have been accomplished by other means. Had Reinert suggested that the placing of the 'afterthoughts' on a new, indented line was a printer's error, his case would have been more plausible. For, contrary to Hagopian's assertion, the idea that it is the younger waiter who knows about the suicide attempt is quite compatible with the idea that 'it is the old waiter who is obsessed with the awareness of nada and who recognizes and sympathizes with a fellow sufferer in the old man at the café', because, as we have seen in the opening dialogue, so many lines are capable of being read in two, opposite ways. One can only say that it is slightly more fitting, in emotional and aesthetic terms, that the older waiter should be acquainted with the old man's history and background; and that if he is being ironical in the opening dialogue (as we *must* suppose if he is the first speaker) then this is consonant with his more overt irony at the younger waiter's expense later in the story. The superior merit of Hagopian's solution is that it is simpler, inherently more plausible, and deals directly with line 69, the justification of which is the only logical support for Reinert's hypothesis.

Between Reinert and Hagopian, however, came Joseph F. Gabriel, ingeniously but perversely arguing that the text of the story was sound, and that the 'inconsistency in the dialogue is deliberate, an integral part of the pattern of meaning actualized in the story. . . . In so far as the dialogue fails to conform to the norms of logic, the reader himself is, like the older waiter, plunged into the existential predicament and made to confront the absurd.'[8] Gabriel's article was the longest, and in many ways the most critically perceptive of those that had so far appeared. He was the first commentator to point out that the dialogue in the first two exchanges could be attributed in different ways without affecting the qualitative contrast between the two waiters, and that this ambiguity was probably deliberate. It is not, however, legitimate to assimilate the inconsistency of line 69 into the concept of literary ambiguity. The *ambiguities* which Gabriel rightly observes in the text, are all, in the end, capable of resolution or, if left open, do not affect the authority of the story. This cannot be said of the *inconsistency* in line 69, and it is its uniqueness in this respect which makes it a problem. A logical inconsistency of this kind, if deliberate, can only have the effect in narrative of radically undermining the authority of either the narrator or the characters or both; but this will always entail the sense of some authorial mind behind both narrator and characters who *is* reliable, to the extent that we can infer that he has some literary purpose in exploiting inconsistency. This purpose could be to expose the deceptiveness of fictions; or, in this case, it could be to reveal that neither of the two waiters really knows anything for certain about the old man—that they are making up a story about him for their own psychological purposes, and forget their respective roles in the process, as sometimes happens in the theatre of the absurd. The situation from which 'A Clean, Well-lighted Place' starts, *might* have been explored in this way. Unfortunately for Mr Gabriel's argument, it wasn't. There are no other equivalent inconsistencies which would confirm the radical unreliability of the narrator. And, so far from the two waiters being ironically distanced and presented as equally confused (as would happen if we believed neither of them knew what they were talking about), the story turns on a discrimination between them, and a resolution of the story's ambiguities by a change of presentation—the shift into the older waiter's consciousness. That the facts about the old man are 'true', and that the older waiter is a reliable character, are essential preconditions if the latter's interior monologue is to be at all moving or persuasive. The story works by packing meanings under its realistic surface, not by undermining that surface so that it collapses.

Hagopian's solution is simply to emend the text by moving the words, 'You said she cut him down' to the preceding line, thus:

Young Waiter: A wife would be no good to him now.
Old Waiter: You can't tell. He might be better with a wife.
Y.W.:   His niece looks after him. You said she cut him down.
O.W.:   I know.
Y.W.:   I wouldn't want to be that old. . . .

Gloss: the younger waiter discounts the older waiter's suggestion that the old man might be better if he had a wife by saying that the only use he would have, at his age, for a woman, i.e. someone to look after him, is already supplied by his niece—a fact he has deduced from the information given earlier that the niece cut him down. The older waiter's 'I know' is a conventional phrase of agreement, but, like some of his previous remarks, carries an ironical implication: what you say is true but it doesn't take my point, which I'm not going to try and explain to you because you wouldn't understand it. With this emendation, the whole dialogue, beginning line 46, becomes quite coherent and consistent, and provides a reliable basis for deciding that it is the older waiter who knows the facts about the old man and who opens the first dialogue at line 10.

Hagopian does not speculate as to how, when or by whom the words 'You said she cut him down' were misplaced, and unless and until the original manuscript is available for scrutiny, it is impossible to answer these questions—or even to know for certain that he is right. But his solution is clearly the best one of those that have been proposed. Everything we know about Hemingway's working habits—the immense concentration and care that he brought to the act of composition—suggests that it is highly unlikely that he himself was careless or confused about which of the two waiters had the information about the old man. It is odd that he did not pick up the error in proof or print. But it is even odder that none of his readers and critics commented publicly on the inconsistency in line 69 until twenty-five years after the story first appeared. Clearly, the inconsistency remained unnoticed for so long because so much of the dialogue in the first half of the story is presented dramatically, with no specific indication of who is speaking. Is this just an irritating mannerism, creating unnecessary confusion? It seems to me more reasonable to regard it as a deliberate rhetorical device. As we begin reading the story for the first time, we probably form the expectation that the story is going to be 'about' the old man; but as we read on, we discover that it is about the difference between the two waiters. The ambiguity concerning which of the two waiters is speaking at any one time, therefore, keeps the reader's attention partly preoccupied with distinguishing between them, even though the main focus of the narrative is initially upon the old man, and thus prepares the reader for its subsequent development. Moreover, as I will try to show in the third part of this essay, Hemingway deliberately encourages the reader to make initially an incorrect discrimination between the two waiters which, when discovered and corrected, amounts to a kind of peripeteia. Hemingway, in short, is making things deliberately difficult for his readers in this story. Ironically, he succeeded so well that a quite gratuitous and non-functional difficulty has passed unnoticed by most of them.

II

There are four well-established categories in the critical discussion of Hemingway's fiction—particularly his earlier fiction, and particularly the short stories: the Hemingway universe, the Hemingway code, the Hemingway hero and, embracing and articulating these three, the Hemingway style. The Hemingway universe is the metaphysically vacant wasteland of much modern literature, but with a special emphasis on meaningless suffering.

'What have we done to have that happen to us?' complains the woman in 'The Snows of Kilimanjaro', referring to Harry's fatal infection. Harry replies with deliberate literalism, 'I suppose what I did was to forget to put iodine on it when I first scratched it. Then I didn't pay any attention to it because I never infect. Then, later, when it got bad, it was probably using that weak carbolic solution when the other antiseptics ran out that paralyzed the minute blood vessels and started the gangrene.' He looked at her. 'What else?' Harry's reply is determinedly positivist, ruling out any attempt to explain suffering by reference to a moral or metaphysical scheme. Suffering and death are essentially arbitrary, part of the order—or, rather, the disorder—of things. Hence the emphasis in Hemingway's work is not upon seeking explanations or solutions for the problems of existence, but upon the question of how to live with them.

The answer, in part, is the Hemingway code: the cultivation of the masculine virtues of courage, dignity and stoic endurance. These qualities are represented by such characters as the gambler in 'The Gambler, the Nun and the Radio', and the Major in 'In Another Country'. There is no suggestion that the code can reduce suffering—the gambler tells Mr Fraser that only consideration for his fellow patients prevented him from screaming aloud in his pain. Still less can the code *avert* suffering: the Major has schooled himself to accept his mutilation without illusions of being cured, but is then struck from behind by the cruel and totally unpredictable death of his wife, whom he had carefully abstained from marrying until he was out of the war. His words to the narrator—'A man must not marry. . . . He should not place himself in a position to lose. He should find things he cannot lose'—is not intended as practical advice, but implies that it is a necessary condition of our being human that we lay ourselves open to the pain of loss.

As Philip Young, from whom I take these concepts of the code and the hero, has perceptively shown,[9] the Hemingway *hero* is not defined by the simple terms of the Hemingway code. The hero is a man who admires the code, and aspires to it, often by seeking to harden himself in the direct experience of violence and suffering. But whether such experience has been willed (as in the case of war) or involuntary (as in childhood) the hero is never entirely able to reconcile himself to it. It leaves him with wounds both physical and psychological, which never entirely heal, and whose pain he tries to assuage in a number of ways: by attaching himself to those who live by the code, by private rituals such as hunting, fishing, drinking or playing the radio, by writing, or by the process, akin to writing, of recovering and ordering the past by concentrated efforts of memory.

This brings us to the Hemingway style. Out of the commentaries of various critics[10] we can draw its profile fairly sharply. It is characterized by extreme grammatical and lexical simplicity: short, simple sentences, often linked together by conjunctions, especially *and*, to form compound sentences; precise, plain, colloquial diction, in which only the occasional foreign or technical word causes any difficulty of understanding; a heavy reliance on basic verbs, particularly the verb *to be*, and on the most ordinary adjectives, *big*, *fine*, *nice*, etc., thus putting maximum emphasis on nouns. Such a description, however, might apply equally well to the style of Defoe, from whom Hemingway is far removed, not only temporally and culturally, but in terms of literary effect. How are these linguistic features combined and exploited to create the special quality of Hemingway's style? We might begin by saying that it is a style almost easier to define by what it avoids than by what it does—avoiding complex or periodic syntactical structures, elegant variation, consciously 'literary' language of any kind. *Avoids* is the operative word, for Hemingway's style, unlike Defoe's, communicates a sense of the austere poetics on which it is based: we are always aware of the easy, decorative or evasive formulations which have been scrupulously rejected. This is partly a historical matter, for without the foil of English (and American) narrative prose as it developed through the eighteenth and nineteenth centuries, Hemingway's stark simplicity would lose much of its effectiveness. Superficially naïve, his style is highly sophisticated and demands a sophisticated reader for full appreciation of its effects.

By its scrupulous avoidance of what is usually thought of as rhetoric, Hemingway's style itself functions as a powerful rhetoric of sincerity, bearing horrified, or traumatized, witness to the ugliness of life and death. At the same time, this style, particularly in its avoidance of syntactical subordination—the linguistic tool with which we arrange the items of our knowledge to show priorities or relationships of cause and effect—carries a large philosophical implication; the denial of metaphysics and the suggestion that life is ultimately meaningless.

III

Nowhere in Hemingway's work is this view of life more bleakly presented than 'A Clean, Well-lighted Place'. The key-word of the story is certainly 'nothing' or 'nada', and the way it invades the prayers, the 'Hail Mary' and the 'Our Father', at the end makes explicit the rejection of any metaphysical explanation or consolation. God is very dead in this story. The only positive values it endorses are the very limited ones of light and cleanliness. The richer dimensions of the physical life, for example sexuality, mentioned in connection with the soldier and the younger waiter, are implicitly devalued as vain or transient or vulnerable.

The Hemingway code, as defined above, is not fully embodied in this story. The code is something to which both the old man and the older waiter aspire, but incompletely, unconfidently. The old man's unsuccessful suicide attempt is an index of his failure, but though he is a broken man he still preserves certain features of the code, which are remarked approvingly by the waiter or the narrator:

'This old man is clean. He drinks without spilling. Even now, drunk' (71-2).

(In contrast the younger waiter pours the brandy so that it 'slopped over and ran down the stem into the top saucer of the pile' (42-3).
'. . . a very old man walking unsteadily but with dignity' (88-9).

'Nor can you stand before a bar with dignity' the older waiter reflects later, 'though that is all that is provided for these hours' (131-3). The clean, well-lighted café is, therefore, valued because it enables a very limited practice of the code.

The hero of the story, again in the sense defined above, is clearly the older waiter. This only gradually becomes evident, as the difference between the two waiters becomes more perceptible, and as the point of view from which the story is told shifts from an impersonal authorial mode to that of the older waiter's consciousness. These two processes—the shift in point-of-view, and the gradual discrimination between the two waiters—are the basic rhetorical strategies of the story.

We begin with the spectacle of the old man, described by the impersonal narrator, sitting alone at the café in the small hours. The second sentence is interesting for the way in which its appearance of logical explanation dissolves under scrutiny. It seems to be saying that the old man likes to sit in the café late at night because by then the dust has settled, but then a different physical reason is produced—the quietness of the street at night, which is also a little unexpected because he is deaf and therefore, one might have supposed, less sensitive to noise. The statement appears to be a privileged authorial comment on the old man's behaviour, but the haziness of the logic suggests that it is, if not an unreliable, at least an inadequate explanation; and this is confirmed by the later development of the story. The old man's behaviour is a puzzle, an enigma, a provocation, and this is reflected in the conversation about him between the two waiters. He is, for the purpose of the story, an image of the Human Condition. To use such a portentous abstraction is to fall into the dishonest habits of language Hemingway's art implicitly criticizes, but he has taken steps to stress the representative nature of his three characters. None of them is named, nor are they distinguished by any descriptive particularity of dress, personal appearance, etc., such as we normally expect from realistic fiction. We don't even know where the story is set until line 104, where the word *hombre* indicates that the setting is Spain. This singular anonymity, as well as stressing the representative or symbolic significance of the characters, means that the very limited terms of reference in which they *are* distinguished carry enormous weight. The old man is just that —the old man. He is referred to once as 'the deaf man' (40–1) to explain the waiter's callous remark, 'You should have killed yourself last week', but otherwise he is referred to as 'the old man' or 'a very old man' (88). It is highly significant, therefore, that the first time one waiter is explicitly distinguished from the other is by the word 'younger' in line 29: 'The younger waiter went over to him.' In other words, the primary distinction made between the two waiters belongs to the same category as that used to describe their customer: age. Thematically, this is obviously important. It is strongly suggested in the story that hope (or 'confidence') can only be entertained by the young (see lines 107–12), and that since youth is transient, hope is a vain illusion.[11] Going back to line 29, we now know that one waiter is younger than the other, and it follows that the other waiter is older; but this formula, 'the older waiter' is not in fact introduced for another eighty lines. In fact no *explicit* distinction is made between the two waiters between line 29 and lines 77–8 ('The waiter who was in a hurry', followed by 'the unhurried waiter' 90). As we have seen, the reader must attend very carefully to attribute the dialogue correctly in this part of the story, and before line 29 he has no means at all of keeping the two waiters distinct in his mind.

The last sentence of the first paragraph presents the two waiters as a single unit of consciousness:

> The two waiters inside the café knew that the old man was a little
> drunk, and while he was a good client they knew that if he became
> too drunk he would leave without paying, so they kept watch on him.

This authorial comment, like the preceding sentence, is somewhat
misleading—deliberately so. It presents the two waiters as being in
complete accord and agreement, professionally allied against the old
man. The story goes on to reveal an ever-increasing gap between the
sensibilities of the two waiters, and to suggest a spiritual alliance between the older waiter and the old man against the younger waiter. It
is some time before this becomes clear, however, because the reader
has difficulty in distinguishing between the two waiters.

The first exchange of remarks between them (10–16) reveals a difference in the information each possesses about the old man, but not,
at this stage, a definable difference of attitude towards him. The next
piece of dialogue (24–7) reveals a difference of attitude—but not towards the old man (this should perhaps alert us to the possibility that
the story is not going to be 'about' the old man, but about the
difference between the two waiters—otherwise the introduction of the
soldier and his girl will seem an irrelevant distraction). It is therefore
impossible to match, with any confidence, the lines of the second
dialogue with those of the first. When we come to the first explicit
distinction between the two waiters with 'the younger waiter' in
line 29, our instinct may be to refer back to the two passages of
dialogue to see if we can now identify which lines were spoken by the
younger waiter, but we still cannot do so. As the story proceeds,
however, the character of the younger waiter is sharply defined by his
callous attitude towards the old man, especially his remark to the older
waiter, 'He should have killed himself last week' (35–6), repeated to the
old man himself at line 40. If, with this clearer picture of the younger
waiter, we refer back once more to the opening dialogue, we shall
probably decide that the line, 'He has plenty of money' has a callous
cynicism that fits the character of the younger waiter, and that it is
therefore he who opens the dialogue at line 10. We may then find the
same callous cynicism in the line 'What does it matter if he gets what
he's after?' in the second dialogue, and assign this line also to the
younger waiter. The remarks of the other waiter in this dialogue, about
the guard, will then, by contrast, appear to express a humane solicitude,
and we may find a similar quality in the question 'How do you know
it was nothing?', which we have assigned to him in the first dialogue.
It all seems to be fitting together.

But when we come to the long dialogue beginning line 46 this hypothesis crumbles. For reasons given above, it is clearly the younger waiter who opens this dialogue, and goes on to ask questions about the old man's suicide attempt. It must therefore have been the older waiter who opened the first dialogue at line 10 by saying 'Last week he tried to commit suicide.' As the long dialogue continues it becomes more and more evident that the older waiter is compassionate towards the old man, so that we have to revise our interpretation of the lines 'Nothing' and 'He has plenty of money' in the first dialogue. To do this we have to read further into the story. That 'He has plenty of money' was ironic is supported by the older waiter's obviously ironic references to 'job' and 'work' in lines 107 and 110. The real import of the first 'Nothing' (14) does not become evident until we reach the older waiter's long meditation on nothing, beginning: 'It was a nothing that he knew too well' (134). Then a kind of electric spark travels back to the earlier occurrence of 'Nothing', and we realize that when the older waiter said the old man was in despair about nothing, he didn't mean that the old man had no reason to despair, but that it was an awareness of nothingness, nada, the meaninglessness of existence, that caused his despair; and that in this respect he, the older waiter, feels an affinity with the old man. (With this enhanced understanding of the characters of the two waiters, we can agree fairly confidently with Hagopian's attribution of the second dialogue, as follows:

Young Waiter: The guard will pick him up.
Old Waiter: What does it matter if he gets what he's after?
Young Waiter: He had better get off the street now. The guard will get him. They went by five minutes ago.

Hagopian takes the younger waiter's remarks as an expression of malicious pleasure in another's impending misfortune and of his preoccupation with the lateness of the hour. The older waiter's remark is 'consistent with his indifference to the usual social norms, with his nihilism, and with his awareness of the value of youth and confidence'.)

This affinity has already been established by increasing emphasis on the difference between the two waiters. In the middle of the story we are helped to discriminate between the two waiters by more distinguishing phrases than before:

the waiter who was in a hurry (77–8, 105)
the unhurried waiter (90)
the waiter with a wife (99)
the older waiter (107, 114, 118)

At line 96, the younger waiter says to the older waiter, 'You talk like an old man yourself.' The older waiter says to him, 'We are of two different kinds' (118).

The 'two kinds' are, on the one hand, those who, like the younger waiter 'lived in it and never felt it' (136–7) and on the other, those like the old man and the older waiter who live in it and *do* feel it. What is 'it'? The story asserts the impossibility of defining 'it' any more precisely than 'nothing' or 'nada'. It is worth noting how often, and how ambiguously, the word 'it' is used in lines 133–7. When the older waiter actually names 'it' as 'insomnia' in the last line of the story—'After all, he said to himself, it is probably only insomnia. Many must have it'—the naming is plainly meant to be ironically inadequate to the experience presented. The symptoms are those of insomnia, but the clinical diagnosis is irrelevant. The darkness of night (a recurrent archetypal motif in Hemingway's work) heightens the sense of *nada* and makes sleep impossible—hence the importance of erecting some defence against it for 'these hours'. Here it is the refuge of the café, the clean, well-lighted place, its light and order opposed to the darkness and disorder of existence. 'I am of those who like to stay late at the café,' the older waiter says (114), 'With all those who do not want to go to bed. With all those who need a light for the night.'

With this speech the theme of the story—the idea of some community or brotherhood of those who are oppressed by nada—becomes explicit. The effect of resonant emphasis is imparted mainly by the parallelism of rhythm and structure in the three sentences. For there is nothing particularly striking about the diction of this speech—there is no word in it which has not already occurred several times in the story. *Stay, late, café, bed, light, night*: these are staple words in the remarkably limited vocabulary of the story, especially *night* and *light*, which occur twelve times and nine times respectively in this very short text, but never in such close juxtaposition as here: 'a light for the night'.

This is a characteristic example of Hemingway's very artful use of repetition. I call it artful because it manages to generate a kind of verbal intensity of the kind that we associate with lyric poetry, while maintaining a surface of realistic illusion, an impression of straight, objective reporting. The high degree of repetition, which we cannot be unaware of, seems, on one level, to be merely a function of the austerely exact, simple, unpretentious narrative tone, that reports every action and speech without selection, compression or elegant variation. But the words that are repeated define experience in a very basic way: we have a sense of life pared down to its bare essentials. *Clean, light, late, café, old man, shadow, leaves, tree, street, night, waiter, drunk, brandy, money, table, saucer, bottle, glass, bed, wife, kill, home, lonely, hurry, fear, confidence, bar, nothing*—these are the basic terms in which experience is presented in the story—these are the words which occur and recur in the flat, neutral descriptions of the impersonal narrator, or in the rambling realistically redundant conversation of the two waiters. It only needs a slight adjustment—a shift into a slightly artificial rhythm or syntactical structure—to transfigure the apparently banal particulars of the story and to invest them with moving significance. The effect is closely comparable with Joyce's stories in *Dubliners*, where the 'epiphany' is usually marked by the lifting of the language from its normative 'scrupulous meanness' (as Joyce described it) to a more poetically heightened mode—for example, at the end of 'Araby':

> Gazing up into the darkness I saw myself as a creature driven and derided by vanity; and my eyes burned with anguish and anger.

Hemingway's most extravagant use of repetition and incantatory rhythm is in the long 'nada' passage, where it is licensed by two factors; firstly, that it is parodying prayers which are themselves rhythmically and rhetorically patterned, and secondly that the story has now shifted its centre from the impersonal narrator to the point of view of the older waiter. One might also note here that considerable literary advantages accrue from the fact that the story is set in Spain. To some readers the prayer-parodies will always seem contrived, but clearly they would arise most naturally in a mind conditioned by a Catholic religious culture. All the speech, both in dialogue and in interior monologue, is by implication a rendering of Spanish, so that the sceptical reader cannot test its authenticity with any confidence. The sprinkling of Spanish words in the text follows a familiar narrative convention for giving 'local colour', but it has other more subtle effects. The word *nada*, for instance, is obviously far more resonant, mysterious and sinister as a foreign word appearing in an English language context than it would be in a wholly Spanish context.

The shift in point of view is managed so discreetly that we are scarcely aware of it. The impersonal narrator withdraws with the forgiving remark *à propos* the younger waiter, 'He did not wish to be unjust. He was only in a hurry' (99–100). But this withdrawal is covered by the ongoing dialogue, and the movement into the older waiter's consciousness is presented as a continuation of the dialogue: 'Turning off the electric light he continued the conversation with himself' (128–9). This device doesn't seem unnatural because it has already been established that communication between the two waiters has broken down. It was always tenuous—as we have seen, many of the older waiter's remarks have a private meaning unperceived by the younger waiter, and when he tries obliquely to communicate what oppresses him, the younger waiter says 'Stop talking nonsense' (113). (This moment is re-enacted later, in a more extreme form, when the older waiter orders 'nada' in the bodega, and the barman dismisses him as a madman (lines 144–6).) Thus, when the older waiter says, 'I am of those who like to stay late at the café,' he is already in a sense talking to himself rather than to the younger waiter, he is embarked on an effort of self-definition, a declaration of faith, or rather of scepticism, the slightly incantatory rhythm of that declaration 'of those . . . with all those . . . with all those' preparing for the prayer-parody that is to come.

The parody of the Lord's Prayer rises to a kind of climax as the word *nada* replaces more and more of the meaningful words of the prayer, so that at the beginning the words, *who art, name, kingdom*, etc., are retained, but towards the end of the parody all the nouns and verbs are replaced by 'nada'—'and nada us our nada as we nada our nadas and nada us not into nada,'—and then comes a significant reversion to the actual prayer: 'but *deliver* us from nada' (141, my italics). 'A Clean, Well-lighted Place' implies very strongly that there is no deliverance from nada.

Part V Fiction and Utopia

The centenary in 1966 of the birth of H. G. Wells found the literary and intellectual world still divided and perplexed as to how to assess his importance. He is not, of course, in any sense a 'fashionable' figure. He was never in fashion, perhaps, after the 1914–18 War. One of the many ironies of his career was that the Armageddon which he fore-shadowed in such fantasies as *The War of the Worlds* (1898) and *The War in the Air* (1908) caused a radical shift in sensibility to which he was not able to attune himself. Wells, who could be an acute critic of himself, was quick to appreciate the fact. 'My boom is over,' he said to Arnold Bennett in 1917. 'I've had my boom. I'm yesterday.'

The trouble was, he had then another thirty-nine years to live, and none passed without at least one book from Wells. These were not all failures by any means—*The Outline of History* was an international best-seller—but he no longer influenced the readers and writers who mattered. Virginia Woolf's well-known essay 'Modern Fiction' (1919) and D. H. Lawrence's review of *The World of William Clissold* (1926) in the *Calendar of Modern Letters* marked his rejection by the literary avant-garde of the 'twenties. Orwell's references to Wells in *The Road to Wigan Pier* (1937) and Christopher Caudwell's chapter in *Studies in a Dying Culture* (1938), show that his kind of Utopian radicalism evoked no responsive chords in the 'thirties. As he grew older he was something of an embarrassment on the literary scene: a writer who had long outlived his creative life, but obstinately went on writing.

It was Wells's painful experience to see the title of one of his books, *The War That Will End War* (1914) become the ironic catch-phrase of a whole generation's disillusionment, and the adjective formed from his name become synonymous with facile and materialistic optimism. As recently as 1962, Dr Leavis evidently felt it was sufficient to discredit Lord Snow's idea of a scientific culture by dubbing it 'Wellsian'. Wells's last published work, *Mind at the End of its Tether* (1945) was far from Wellsian. But that short, bitterly pessimistic pamphlet was generally taken as a confession, expressed with an extravagance that was attributed to his ailing mind and body, that his life's work and thought had been misdirected. At his death in 1946, Wells was a discredited thinker; as a novelist he was allowed the doubtful honour of having fathered 'science fiction', but was remembered chiefly as the creator of engaging but light-weight sub-Dickensian comedies of lower middle-class manners.

In recent years, however, there has been something of a revival of interest in and respect for Wells. Two main tendencies are discernible, which are to some extent mutually opposed: on the one hand, a redefinition of Wells's imaginative identity and achievement in terms more congenial to the modern literary mind; and on the other hand, an attempt to do justice to his role as a 'thinker' and transmitter of important political, social and scientific ideas in the twentieth century.

The first of these attempts at redefinition started, perhaps, with Anthony West's thoughtful essay, 'H. G. Wells', published in *Encounter* in 1957. West suggested that the pessimism of his father's last years was not a repudiation of everything he had stood for, but a reversion to

> his original profoundly-felt beliefs about the realities of the
> human situation. He was by nature a pessimist, and he was doing
> violence to his intuitions and his rational perceptions alike when
> he asserted in his middle period that mankind could make a better
> world for itself by an effort of will.

West documented his theory particularly by reference to the early scientific romances, such as *The Time Machine* (1895), *The Island of Dr. Moreau* (1896), and *The First Men in the Moon* (1901) which, as he pointed out, draw the gloomiest conclusions about the likely results of the scientific and technological progress for which Wells was later to become such an enthusiastic propagandist. In *The Early H. G. Wells* (1961) Bernard Bergonzi came to the same conclusion, and also made a persuasive case for a high literary estimate of the early scientific romances. Skilfully applying the techniques of modern criticism, Bergonzi interpreted these works as symbolic or mythopoeic explorations of such late Victorian preoccupations as evolution and the class war, written with a powerful imaginative energy, and owing more to the literary atmosphere of the Decadence than to Wells's education at the Normal School of Science.

Ironically enough, in the very same year that part, at least, of Wells's *œuvre* was thus triumphantly reclaimed by academic criticism, the American historian W. Warren Wagar was declaring:

> The heyday of the symbol-mongers and the literary technicians
> cannot last much longer; it is time again for Wells.

By which he meant Wells the journalist, the prophet, the tireless worker for a World State, too urgently concerned to save the world from destruction to take care over the form of his books. Mr Wagar's *H. G. Wells and the World State* might have been called *All for Man; or Parnassus Well Lost*. It is a useful and intelligent guide to Wells's ideas and their roots in intellectual history, even if it does not always sound convinced of its own case.

The interest of Wells's position in the English world of letters at the turn of the century has been highlighted recently by the splendidly edited volumes of correspondence emanating from the Wells archives at the University of Illinois: *Henry James and H. G. Wells* (1958), *Arnold Bennett and H. G. Wells* (1960) and *George Gissing and H. G. Wells* (1961). The General Editor of the Wells papers, Professor Gordon N. Ray, is working on a definitive biography. Meanwhile the centenary year was marked by the publication in Britain of three more books by or about Wells: a new edition of his *Experiment in Autobiography*,* *H. G. Wells: Journalism and Prophecy 1893–1946*, an anthology compiled by W. Warren Wagar,† and *The Life and Thought of H. G. Wells* by a Soviet scholar, J. Kagarlitski.‡

Mr Kagarlitski's book is not without its incidental insights, but these insights are invariably destructive, pointing out the confusions and inconsistencies in Wells's thought, while the general tone of the book is one of vague reverence. Mr Kagarlitski concludes by saying, 'Now we have the right to call [Wells] a great writer,' but there is little in the book to substantiate this claim. Not surprisingly, because although Mr Kagarlitski is not a doctrinaire Marxist, he necessarily judges Wells within the framework of Marxian orthodoxy, and is thus prevented from endorsing either Bergonzi's Wells or Wagar's Wells. After describing *The Time Machine*'s picture of human decadence in the year 802701, Mr Kagarlitski comments, 'In spite of the obviously scientific basis for this judgment, the picture is, of course, quite false.' In fact the basis of Wells's prophecy is not scientific at all, but intuitive and imaginative. Its power is a rhetorical power, its truth a literary truth; and to appreciate this power and this truth we must suspend our ideological preferences.

This is something Mr Kagarlitski cannot do. 'Progress cannot cease', he says, 'for the properties of matter are inexhaustible and

---

* Re-issued by Gollancz and Cresset Press (1966) (2 vols., illus. by the author).
† Bodley Head.
‡ Tr. Moura Budberg (Sidgwick & Jackson).

however long mankind exists, each milestone passed will simply lead to the next.' Mr Kagarlitski rightly points out that Wells adopts this very position in the later Utopian novel, *Men Like Gods* (1923). But the later, optimistic Wells is no more congenial to Mr Kagarlitski than the early pessimistic Wells.

> Wells is unable to draw a picture of ideal communal life, for basically his Utopian ideas stem from a bourgeois outlook and are limited by the mediocre possibilities such an outlook can offer.

This echoes Marxist comment on Wells from Lenin onwards. 'What a bourgeois he is! He is a Philistine,' exclaimed Lenin after their meeting in 1920. Wells never denied it. 'Lenin was a sound observer,' he wrote in the *Autobiography*. 'I was middle-class,—"petty bourgeois" as the Marxists have it.'

Mr Wagar claims no great originality for Wells as a political thinker: 'His was a middle-class socialism somewhere between the visions of Auguste Comte and the British Fabians.' Rather, he sees Wells as a twentieth-century *philosophe*, a journalist and popularizer who ranged over a wide area of human knowledge, putting into general currency a host of revolutionary new ideas. He was 'the most popular of the serious writers and the most serious of the popular.' Mr Wagar's anthology, drawn largely from Wells's occasional writings, provides a useful basis for attempting a non-literary assessment of his importance.

The first part of the anthology is mainly concerned with Wells as a commentator on social and political trends in his lifetime and as a prophet of long and short-term developments in human civilization. The liveliest passages in the latter mode are from *Anticipations* (1902), the book which established Wells as an intellectual force to be reckoned with, but which West and Bergonzi see as marking the betrayal of his own imagination. In fact the book is far from infatuated with the technological developments it predicts. The undertone of glee derives more from the imputed destruction of the existing order than from faith in the new. It is the Decadent game of *épater les bourgeois* transposed into a scientific key.

Wells was undoubtedly an acute prophet, though often wrong in his dating. He did not anticipate the arrival of the aeroplane before 1950. He foretold the development of large-scale motor traffic, but he was over-optimistic in predicting that the segregation of traffic and pedestrians would start in the first decade of the twentieth century. (With characteristic insight into the British character, however, he predicted that we would lag behind Germany and America in this respect.) He foretold the decentralization of business, the growth of suburbia, the disappearance of servants and their replacement by labour-saving appliances. He predicted the development of aerial warfare, the obsolescence of the idea of 'non-combatants' and, in a resonant phrase, 'the imminence of unanticipated death' as characterizing the experience of war in the future. In *The World Set Free* (1914) he prophesied the holocaust of atomic warfare.

As a commentator on politics, Wells often made major misjudgments but, never afraid of contradicting himself, he usually recovered his step and adopted a position which may be described as enlightened. Thus, he dismayed his friends of the pacifist Left by his vulgar and blood-thirsty jingoism at the outbreak of the First World War; but by 1916 he saw its likely outcome as 'the exhaustion in varying degrees of all the combatants and the succumbing of the most exhausted'. He was one of the first propagandists for a League of Nations and one of the first to see that it was emasculated at birth. He saw clearly the evil of the Versailles Treaty, but he continued to underestimate the power of Hitler's Germany even after he had, in 1938, adopted the Churchillian position about appeasement. But, writing in the summer of 1939, Wells did not indulge the hope he had expressed in 1914 that the impending war would provide the impetus for the creation of a new world order. 'It will be another war for the alteration or preservation of frontiers,' he prophesied gloomily. The Second World War must have seemed like history's sneer at everything Wells had hoped and worked for. Orwell rubbed it in, in his essay 'Wells, Hitler and the World State' (1941):

> For Hitler's sake a great nation has been willing to overwork itself for six years and then to fight for two years more, whereas for the commonsense, essentially hedonistic world-view which Mr Wells puts forward, hardly a human creature is willing to shed a pint of blood.

Wells is hardly unique among idealistic thinkers in this respect, but his failure to capture enthusiasm for his idea of a world state, humanity united under the aegis of an enlightened technocracy, deserves some scrutiny, for he invested most of the energies of his mature life in this effort. The second part of Mr Wagar's anthology, 'Portraits', reminds one of how eagerly Wells seized his opportunities to meet world leaders—opportunities probably unique for a writer in the twentieth century. Wells had interviews with both Roosevelts and with Lenin and Stalin. It was flattering, no doubt, that both Theodore Roosevelt and Lenin discussed Wells's own work, but significant that they both confined themselves to *The Time Machine*, scarcely the most propitious text for settling the world's problems.

Recording the interview with Roosevelt, Wells referred deprecatingly to *The Time Machine* as 'a little book of mine, an early book full of the deliberate pessimism of youth'; and, following Anthony West, we may suggest that part of the reason for Wells's failure as a propagandist for a new world order was that this role committed him to a denial of his own most powerful insights, and therefore of his most powerful rhetoric. His favourite Utopian image of man standing on the earth as on a footstool, and reaching out amid the stars, seems pale and sentimental against the Swiftian emblems of man's bestiality in *The Island of Dr. Moreau*.

'Wells in effect preached a biological doctrine of original sin, which turned Christianity inside out but amounted to much the same thing,' Mr Wagar has acutely observed. The original sin was man's essential animality; the hope of redemption was man's intelligence, which would lead him to peaceful co-operation in the cause of progress. (For a short period, spanned by *God, the Invisible King* (1917) and *The Undying Fire* (1919), which he later recalled with embarrassment, Wells even tried to present this redemption in religious terms.) The theory of evolution itself gave no certain indication of man's future; his survival might be attributed to his innate adaptability or to a run of luck which could end at any moment. In 1939 Wells wrote:

> Either the human imagination and the human will to live, rises
> to the plain necessity of our case, and a renascent *Homo Sapiens*
> struggles on to a new, harder and happier world dominion, or he
> blunders down the slopes of failure through a series of unhappy
> phases, in the wake of all the monster reptiles and beasts that have
> lorded it over the earth before him, to his ultimate extinction.

Here the future is presented as a matter of choice; but from his youth Wells was haunted by the possibility that evolution did not permit of choice. In *The War of the Worlds*, for instance, humanity is shown helpless and panic-stricken before the invasion of creatures who had a start of several millennia on our race in the evolutionary process. Throughout the novel there is an insistent strain of zoological imagery and allusion through which the Martians' ruthless treatment of man is compared to man's treatment of the animal world: bison, dodos, ants, frogs, bees, rabbits, and even the infusoria in water. The

effect is of the Lord of Nature getting his well-deserved come-
uppance. Man survives the Martian invasion, but he is saved 'after all
man's devices had failed, by the humblest things that God, in his
wisdom, has put upon the earth'—bacteria, to which the Martians
are not immune.

It is not only in Wells's early work that an anti-humanist moral is
drawn from the idea of evolution. Take, for example, *Mr. Blettsworthy
on Rampole Island* (1928). I have read this on the recommendation of
Mr Kagarlitski, who sees it as redeeming Wells's generally poor
performance as a novelist between the wars: 'an integral, forceful,
deep book, filled with civic passion, wit, bitterness, fantasy—in a word
the kind of novel that, it had seemed, Wells had forgotten how to
write.' It is not quite as good as that, and not, I think, good for the
reasons Mr Kagarlitski gives. But it is certainly an interesting novel,
and worth resurrecting.

It falls into three parts. In the first part the hero-narrator describes
his upbringing under the bracing influence of a Broad Churchman who
was able cheerfully to reconcile Evolution and Muscular Christianity.
After serio-comic defeats in love and commerce, treated in a pale
imitation of Wells's prewar novels, the hero goes to sea, quarrels
with his captain, and is abandoned on a storm-wrecked ship somewhere off the coast of South America. Delirious and half dead, he
drifts to Rampole Island, where he lives on sufferance, regarded as a
quasi-divine lunatic, with a tribe of cannibals. It is essentially the
Gulliver situation again. The Islanders live squalid, degraded lives,
prevented by various meaningless taboos from utilizing the full
resources of their habitat. In particular, they live in superstitious fear
of the Megatheria, or giant sloths, that inhabit the Island. The
narrator exploits his privileged position to try and rouse the Islanders
to improve the quality of their lives, painting glowing but dishonest
pictures of modern Western society. One of the savages tells him:
'You are a dreamer. . . . The real world is about you here and now,
the only real world. See it for what it is.' In life on Rampole Island
we see a kind of allegory of the real world: thus the war with a
neighbouring tribe caricatures the military inefficiency and emotional
hysteria of the Great War. In fact, in the third Book, it is revealed that
Blettsworthy's life on Rampole Island has been not an allegory but a
delirious distortion of the real world. He was rescued from the ship
in a state of nervous collapse and taken back to New York for treatment, during which time the War has broken out. Restored to sanity,

the hero returns to Europe and enlists, but his experiences at the Front suggest that Rampole Island was more of an idyll than a nightmare. 'Rampole Island', said I, 'was sanity to this.'

Picking up a casual reference, towards the end of the novel, to the Sacco and Vanzetti trial, Mr Kagarlitski sees it as a searing indictment 'of a world in which such a trial could take place'. The myth of Rampole Island, however, like the myth of *Lord of the Flies* (and Golding, despite the ironic epigraph from the *Outline of History* to *The Inheritors*, is very much a literary descendant of Wells) is memorable not for its topical allusiveness, but for its general implications about the nature of man. In this part of the novel Wells returns to pessimistic speculation about evolution, and in the treatment of the Megatheria he does so with the startling imaginative concreteness of his best early work. The repulsive sloths are described with tremendous verve:

> Its skin is a disagreeable pink, but mostly hidden by long coarse hairs that are almost quills, the colour of old thatch and infested not only with a diverse creeping population, including the largest black ticks I have ever beheld, but with a slimy growth of greenish algae and lichens that form pendant masses over the flanks and tail. Over the rump and tail there is real soil; I have seen weeds, and even a little white flower, actually growing there.

The Megatheria have exterminated all other animal life on the Island, and they are gradually nibbling away its vegetation. They are immensely old and no longer procreate. For Blettsworthy they represent a daunting denial of optimistic theories of evolution:

> The struggle for life can terminate in the triumph of types unfit to live, types merely successfully most noxious. . . . So that far from Evolution being necessarily a strenuous upward progress to more and more life, it might become, it could and did evidently in this case become, a graceless drift towards a dead end.

Blettsworthy consoles himself with the thought that 'Man . . . is not an animal, the analogy is false.' He falls asleep dreaming of Utopia, only to be woken and ignominiously chased by one of the sloths.

Whenever Wells's imagination catches fire in this novel it leads him to a pessimistic vision of man and nature. Yet at the end of the book we are treated to a typically 'Wellsian' upbeat sermon from an improbably reformed character who swindled the hero in Book One:

'You do not know the mighty adventures that are close at hand for mankind. . . . Take my word for it—it is your Rampole Island that will pass away and I who will come true.'

The conflict in Wells between optimism and pessimism is by no means unique: it is more or less the natural condition of the modern intellectual. As Lionel Trilling has often observed, most of us lead double lives: liberal, humane, civic-minded citizens in practical matters, we nevertheless seem to prefer artists and thinkers who cry havoc on the civilization we are constructing. It is a kind of inverted hypocrisy by which we pretend to be worse than we evidently are; and it provides a shaky position from which to accuse Wells of inconsistency and contradiction. After all, it might be argued, we are in no position to sneer at Wells's idea of a World State. The United Nations may not stir us to great enthusiasm, but it is our main hope for preserving peace in the world, and even General de Gaulle, one suspects, would not really have wished to abolish it. The United Nations is, of course, a long way from Wells's World State, but it is a tottering step in that direction, and indirectly Wells contributed to its constitution by his part in the Sankey Declaration of Human Rights.

There is a temptation, then, to see Wells as a kind of hero of the spirit who tried to resolve the contradiction described above by deliberately suppressing his pessimistic intuitions and willing his imagination into more constructive channels, even at the expense of weakening its power. But this image of Wells isn't quite convincing, and it never quite convinced Wells himself. He is an almost unique example of a writer who, to use Stephen Spender's terminology,[1] started as a 'modern' and turned himself into a 'contemporary'. In the process he lost his place in the literary Pantheon of our time. This would not matter, perhaps, if we could say confidently that he achieved anything substantial outside the sphere of literary creation. To be sure, he 'influenced' the public mind—Orwell doubted whether 'anyone who was writing books between 1900 and 1920 . . . influenced the young so much'—but it was in a way peculiarly difficult to define and evaluate. Ultimately, perhaps, we can only measure such influence by its depth and duration or by its practical results. Wells's influence, if Orwell is representative, was short-lived in those who experienced it; and it is difficult to point to any aspect of our lives that has been affected specifically by Wells.

As, in the inter-war period, Wells applied his energies more and more to popularization and propaganda, the failure of his ideas to take root became more evident. It would seem that in a complex,

pluralist and specialized culture like ours, 'to be the most popular of
the serious writers and the most serious of the popular' is to forsake
real seriousness and with it real influence. As Aldous Huxley pointed
out (in *The Olive Tree*) Wells's audience was immense, but he failed
to reach the right people. Considering that Wells's own plans for
reforming the world, most explicitly developed in *The Open Conspiracy* (1928), were distinctly élitist, his failure to convert the élite
of his own cultural community is all the more ironic.

Whatever influence Wells exerted on his age he was able to exert
by virtue of his reputation as an imaginative writer, and his influence
declined as that reputation declined. It seems to me that (*pace* Mr
Wagar) it is as an imaginative writer that he will be best remembered,
and that any assessment of him must centre on his restless, ambivalent
and inconclusive dealings with the art of fiction.

Wells remarks in his *Autobiography*, 'I find before me a considerable
accumulation of material, first assembled together in a folder labelled,
"Whether I am a Novelist".' It was a question that exercised many
besides himself. It exercised Henry James, and in that same section of
the *Autobiography*, entitled 'Digression about Novels', Wells says:
'I find myself worrying round various talks and discussions I had with
Henry James a third of a century ago.'

The relationship between James and Wells, as documented by Leon
Edel and Gordon N. Ray,[2] is one of the most fascinating episodes in
modern literary history. But it was unfortunate that their debate came
to its head at a time when Wells was not writing his best work. Few
readers would now quarrel with James's strictures, in his 1914 essay
'The Younger Generation', on *The New Machiavelli*, *The Passionate
Friends* and *Marriage*; and later Wells himself was to concede their
cogency. (Of *Marriage*, for instance, Wells says in the *Autobiography*,
'Indisputably the writing is scamped in places. It could have been just
as light and better done.') The point that Wells was arguing with
Henry James, 'that the novel of completely consistent characterization
arranged beautifully in a strong and rounded story, and painted deep
and round' did not exhaust the possibilities of the form, was a valid
one, but could have been better illustrated by an appeal to Wells's
scientific romances, or to *Tono-Bungay*. There is little allusion to these
works in the Wells-James correspondence, and by the time their
debate came into the open Wells was following and seeking to justify
a much less original kind of undertaking—the discussion-novel-of-
ideas, which though he denied it, was a throwback to Victorian forms.

(The best of these novels, *Boon* (1915), is an acknowledged imitation of Mallock's *The New Republic*.)

Wells's peculiar gift as a writer of fiction lay in his ability to invest speculations about changes in life and society in general with a startling and imaginatively persuasive concreteness. He is the most *descriptive* of writers. Description in Wells's fiction bears the weight of significance reserved, in conventional fiction, for individual human actions and individual consciousness. In stories like *The Time Machine* and *The War of the Worlds*, the narrator-heroes are deliberately and appropriately characterless: their function is to be reliable reporters of spectacular changes in the environment around them. 'The Star' has no characters at all; it is all description, and description of a power and eloquence that makes nonsense of Wells's frequent disclaimers of a concern for the niceties of prose style.*

In fact, Wells was always attracted as well as repelled by the 'aesthetic' approach to the writing of fiction. As a reviewer of novels for the *Saturday Review* in the late 'nineties, he applied strict standards of formal analysis, to the detriment of popular favourites of the period, such as Hall Caine and Marie Corelli, and to the advantage of such novelists as Stephen Crane, Conrad, Gissing, Hardy, Kipling, Meredith, George Moore and Turgenev.[3] Wells befriended several of these writers and engaged in discussions of the art of fiction with them. Reminiscing about this period of his life, Wells later liked to see himself as a barbarian, irked and rebellious in the company of the aesthetes. In 1930 he wrote pugnaciously:

> Save for an incidental lapse or so . . . I have never taken any
> great pains about writing. I am outside the hierarchy of conscious
> and deliberate writers altogether. I am the absolute antithesis
> of Mr James Joyce.

Yet according to Arnold Bennett, Wells's 'praise of *A Portrait of the Artist* had very considerable influence . . . he commanded me to read it and to admire it extremely'. And there was to be a place for 'the high mystery of the Novel, as it was understood by Henry James' in his plan for a World Encyclopaedia outlined in 1932 (and reprinted by Mr Wagar).

* According to the Norwegian scholar Ingvald Raknem, this story is largely cribbed from a French work, *La Fin du Monde* (1893) by Camille Flammarion, but is much superior to it. As Wells follows the sequence of events in his source very closely, the superiority must lie in Wells's rhetoric. See I. Raknem, *H. G. Wells and his Critics* (1963), a formidably exhaustive compilation of obscure information and comment about Wells's fiction.

To return to Wells's earlier career, it is evident that he was competing with the better novelists of his time more keenly than he later liked to admit. His first conscious bid for literary distinction, over which he took great pains, was *Love and Mr. Lewisham* (1900), and his comments on this book at the time show a curious misjudgment of his own talent. To justify this attempt at a conventional realistic novel he felt obliged to belittle his scientific romances. Writing to Arnold Bennett, who had evidently made a different comparison, he said:

> I am doomed to write 'scientific romances' and short stories for
> you creatures of the mob, and my novels must be my private
> dissipation.

Wells was not to enjoy the luxury of neglected merit for long, for *Love and Mr. Lewisham* led to *Kipps* (1905) and *The History of Mr. Polly* (1910), both resounding successes. *Mr. Polly* is indeed a highly entertaining novel, and within its limits a successful one; but taken together, the three novels suggest that the realistic novel of lower-middle-class manners was not really Wells's *métier*. (*Tono-Bungay* (1909), which is often grouped with these novels, is in fact a very different and much superior kind of work, as I have argued elsewhere:[4] a Condition of England novel in which Wells's peculiar strengths as a descriptive and speculative writer are given full play, and his limitations in the presentation of individual character and action scarcely felt.) It is impossible to accept Professor Ray's comparison of Wells's portrayal of Mr Lewisham as a student at South Kensington with Joyce's portrayal of Stephen at University College, Dublin. The setting is observed realistically enough, but Wells interposes a thick wadding—half-patronizing, half-sentimental—of authorial 'manner' between us and Lewisham's experience, e.g.:

> Lewisham ingloriously headed the second class, and Miss
> Heydinger's name did not appear. . . . So the student pays for the
> finer emotions. And in the spacious solitude of the Museum
> gallery devoted to the Raphael cartoons sat Lewisham, plunged
> in gloomy meditation. A negligent hand pulled thoughtfully
> at the indisputable moustache, with particular attention to such
> portions as were long enough to gnaw.

When he attempts 'realism', Wells falls back on Victorian mannerisms. Thus in *Kipps*, dialogue and indirect speech are littered with capitalized words and phrases with which the characters seek to articulate their *petit bourgeois* values and aspirations: 'At first Kipps hesitated whether he should confide an equal desire for Benevolent activities or for further Depravity. . . . He rather affected the pose of the Good Intentioned Dog.' The trick is a Dickensian one. But whereas Dickens's characters create or appropriate such phrases and invest them with an individual significance, Wells's characters seem to be groping hopelessly about in a heap of tawdry, second-hand diction for some feeble sense of identity. The effect is diminishing, and gives a curiously hollow note to the comedy—a note which finally asserts itself in the authorial outburst towards the conclusion of the novel—'The stupid little tragedies of these clipped and limited lives'—and thus makes nonsense of its 'happy ending'.

The History of Mr. Polly is a much more satisfactory novel, and it is worth noting that here Kipps's enslavement to capitalized cliché is replaced by Mr Polly's garbled but creative literary idiom. Crying, 'Whoa, my friskacious palfrey!' to an unstable windsor chair, Mr Polly articulates his unskilled determination to embrace a richer kind of existence. He obtains it in the end, by committing arson and by waging unscrupulous war against the bully who threatens his enjoyment of the idyllic country pub. The problem of the frustrated *petit bourgeois* is at last resolved, but at the expense of endorsing an essentially anti-social hero. Perhaps this is why Wells wrote no more novels in the vein of *Mr. Polly*. If so, it may offer a clue to the apparently perverse twists and turns of Wells's literary career.

That career was, initially, a literary and social success-story of the first order. H. G. Wells, the son of a gardener and a lady's maid, never quite got over it. There is a revealing passage from the preface to a Russian edition of one of Wells's books in 1909, where he explains that a successful literary career in England is

> one of the modern forms of adventure. . . . One is lifted out of
> one's narrow circumstances into familiar and unrestrained
> intercourse with a great variety of people. One sees the world.
> One meets philosophers, scientific men, soldiers, artists, pro-
> fessional men, politicians of all sorts, the rich, the great, and one
> may make such use of them as one can. One finds oneself no
> longer reading in books and papers but hearing and touching
> at first hand the big discussions that sway men, the initiatives
> that shape human affairs.

There is an uncomfortable similarity between this description of the successful literary man, and Wells's account of the successful commercial adventures in *Tono-Bungay*, published in the same year. It is not entirely fanciful, I think, to suppose that Wells himself felt uncomfortable on this score. Certainly he could be betrayed into blatantly insincere writing on the subject. In an early *Saturday Review* article, 'Excelsior' (1895), he wrote:

> Better a little grocery, a life of sordid anxiety, love and a tumult of children, than this Dead Sea fruit of success. It is fun to struggle, but tragedy to win.

Quoting this passage in the *Autobiography*, Wells commented, 'To which betrayal of a mood I add thirty-nine years later only one word: "Nonsense." ' But the mood had infected several of his novels with its sentimentality: *Kipps*, for instance, where, at the end, the 'little grocery' is transformed into a 'little bookshop', conveniently cushioned against financial failure by a second, fortuitous source of income; or *Love and Mr. Lewisham*, which concludes with the hero unconvincingly reconciled to the ruination of his scientific career and the acceptance of humdrum domestic responsibilities.

At the most critical period of his own life, Wells was in almost exactly the same situation as Lewisham. Each young man won a scholarship to the Normal School of Science, started promisingly, then neglected his studies and lost his opportunity, having fallen passionately in love with an unsuitable young woman, whom he subsequently married. Each young man found himself in early manhood working as an unqualified teacher, without prospects and with growing family responsibilities. Fortunately for Wells, literature and the second Mrs Wells provided an escape route. Mr Lewisham was not so lucky. In novel after novel Wells worried at the same situation: the hero whose personal self-fulfilment, usually located in the disinterested pursuit of knowledge, is threatened or destroyed by a combination of imprudent marriage, socio-economic pressures and personal weakness. You find it in *Mr. Lewisham*; you find it in *Tono-Bungay*; you find it in *Marriage*; you even find it in 'A Story of the Days to Come'.

Wells's most pressing motive for commencing a literary career was his need for money, and it persisted throughout his early career. The first part of the *Autobiography* vividly communicates his excitement at seeing his income rise. This didn't matter as long as, under the pressure of this ambition, or this insecurity, he produced works of the calibre of *The Time Machine* or *Dr. Moreau*. But the pattern of such novels as *Tono-Bungay* and *Marriage*, in which the heroes abandon science and their ideals to make a cynical fortune in commerce, suggests that Wells to some extent saw his own failure in scientific studies and his desperate, spectacularly successful switch to writing, in a similar light.* Furthermore, as a radical he may have felt compromised by the fact that the work which was bringing him success and all the good things of life was distinctly pessimistic, particularly about the prospects of a more equitable distribution of these good things in the near or distant future.

About the turn of the century he begins to force optimistic meanings out of his prophetic novels, with some damage to their imaginative life. Then he endeavours to confront the problem of the private pursuit of happiness in 'realistic' social novels. But either the happiness is falsely contrived (as in *Kipps*) or it is falsely identified (as in *Mr. Lewisham*). What comes across most powerfully is Wells's felt sense of the confusion of values in society as a whole, and the consequent impoverishment of the individual lives within it, but only in *Tono-Bungay* is the style and structure of the novel designed to carry such a meaning. With *Mr. Polly* Wells found a solution, but it was an individualistic solution, not a collective one, and conveyed not 'realistically', but through a kind of idyll of violence. Wells was back to the point he had reached in the scientific romances, Mr Polly's arson being a private enactment of the earlier visions of global destruction. Again Wells sets off in a new direction—the novel of ideas—in pursuit of a literary mode that would be more than literary, that would offer some constructive solution to the problems it posed, and thus justify Wells to himself.

Wells's radicalism was based on personal experience and keen observation of the inefficiency and injustices of the British social system. To him that system was essentially irresponsible. I am suggesting that he secretly, perhaps subconsciously, felt his own success had been contingent on that irresponsibility, and that his later career was one long, misguided effort to vindicate himself. This is necessarily speculation. But it would explain why he tended to disparage his early imaginative writing, and to dissociate himself, with excessive vehemence, from any pretensions to 'pure' literary achievement. He refused to acknowledge the truth his own best work illustrates: that the artist's primary responsibility is to realize the

---

* In this context it is worth recalling (as C. P. Snow has in his recent memoir) that Wells always coveted a Fellowship of the Royal Society. He took enormous satisfaction in successfully submitting, at the age of seventy-eight, a scientific thesis for the degree of Ph.D. at London University.

maximum expressive possibilities of his own experience and his own intuitions—one which may cut across conventional public concepts of responsibility. In his honourable concern for the latter, Wells increasingly neglected the former.

An interesting piece, written in 1927, has been reprinted by Mr Wagar, in which Wells goes over this ground in weighing the relative merits of the man of science and the man of letters, represented by Pavlov and Shaw. Intellectually, his loyalties are all on the side of the former. But he is teased by the paradox that, 'To the future Shaw will have contributed nothing, and yet he may be harder to forget'. The irony and pathos of the piece is that Wells is weighing two alternatives on both of which he had, by 1927, turned his back. But he had left behind him several imaginative works which will be hard to forget. That they all came in the earlier part of his long career was more his misfortune than ours.

12   Utopia and Criticism:
The Radical Longing for Paradise

Although Professor Armytage describes his book, *Yesterday's To-morrows*,* as a survey, it would be more accurately described as a collection. He has read a great many works, classical and modern, which describe future societies, but he seems uncertain what to do with them, apart from merely displaying them. The collection is arranged in little groups, but the grouping is seldom helpful. There is, for instance, a section entitled 'The Barchester of 1980; Early Clerical Science Fiction' which includes only two books: the Rev W. Tuckwell's *The New Utopia; or Europe in 1985* (1885) and Anthony Trollope's *A Fixed Period* (1882). Neither is about Barchester, and Trollope was not a clergyman nor, in this case, writing about the clergy. The invention of pseudo-categories could scarcely be taken further. There might have been some point in comparing Tuckwell's book with the Catholic prophetic novels of R. H. Benson, *Lord of the World* (1907) and *The Dawn of All* (1911), and with Corvo's *Hadrian the Seventh* (1904); but Professor Armytage makes no mention of these works.

It is not, however, Professor Armytage's omissions that one feels obliged to protest about (given the enormous scope of the subject, such lacunae are inevitable), but his failure to organize meaningfully the material he *has* accumulated. There are repetitions—the same descriptions of the same texts recurring without any cross-reference or further information. Often the titles of the works discussed have to be hunted down in the notes at the back of the book, and sometimes they are not even to be found there. There are almost incomprehensible synopses of novels like this:

> In *The City* (1952) men have passed away from the earth leaving it to dogs and robots. Round the hearth fires, dogs ask, 'What is man? What is a city? What is war?' The Websters, who have produced intelligent talking-dogs, go with mankind to Jupiter in order to live longer. After centuries the last of the Websters revisits earth and finds the world controlled by dogs and robots.

* *Yesterday's Tomorrows: A Historical Survey of Future Societies*, W. H. G. Armytage, Routledge & Kegan Paul, 1968.

8*

Whether the Websters are dogs or humans, or something in between, is far from clear. Neither is it clear whether the first sentence describes the situation with which the story starts or (as the last sentence implies) ends. Least of all is it clear what the point of the fable is. But we are given no further information. Most of Professor Armytage's titles flash past in this kind of blur, like stations in the night on a journey with no ascertainable destination.

There is one clue to Professor Armytage's purpose, and it is very revealing. It comes in the Preface, where he refers, with lip-smacking jargon ('normative-relevance-tree-techniques') to the application of computer-science to prediction:

> The rise of these 'conflict models' of prediction out of what might
> otherwise be regarded as a welter of futuristic fantasies is the
> theme of this book. It tries to show how, out of the long process
> of preparatory day-dreams, imagined encounters, wish-fulfilments,
> and compensatory projections, a constructive debate about
> tomorrow is emerging, providing us with operational models
> of what tomorrow could, or should, be.

The first thing that must be said is that this 'theme' is not 'shown' at all, in the sense of being held before us by a continuity of argument and illustration. Computer-based prediction is not shown to 'rise out of' the literary Utopian tradition, but merely to come after it. (This may be a more accurate account of the matter, but scarcely constitutes a 'theme'.) Secondly, the last part of the book does not deal either fully or exclusively with 'operational' prediction, but, also in a hasty and erratic fashion, with a wide assortment of discursive prophets, including Norman O. Brown, and Teilhard de Chardin (though it inexplicably ignores two contemporary utopists of at least equivalent importance, Herbert Marcuse and Marshall McLuhan). Thirdly, the prefatory remark quoted carries the astonishing implication that only in the light of modern scientifically-based prediction does the literary utopian tradition appear more than a 'welter of futuristic fantasies'. Which is to say that Plato's *Republic*, More's *Utopia*, *Gulliver's Travels*, *Erewhon*, *The Time Machine*, *Brave New World* and *1984* (to name just a few examples) only become of serious interest by courtesy of the Rand Corporation.

This prefatory remark confirms what one may deduce from Professor Armytage's somewhat clumsy way of describing and summarizing fictions and his avoidance of comparative value judgments; namely, that he has embarked on a study of largely literary materials without having (on the evidence of this book) any real feeling for literature or any idea of how to read a literary text. And this disqualification fatally vitiates the otherwise admirably broad range of intellectual interests he possesses. Because the texts in question are, in many cases, obscure and forgotten, even an inadequate account is better than nothing, and there are certainly some fascinating facts and quotations to be found in *Yesterday's Tomorrows* by the persevering reader. But even as a reference work it has the great disadvantage of not having an index of titles.

The Future as Nightmare,★ which covers some of the same ground as *Yesterday's Tomorrows*, is not exactly a scintillating piece of work, but at least it has a thesis and gives a reasonably clear account of the texts with which it is concerned. The trouble is that the thesis is too simple, or too simple-minded, to allow an adequate exploration of the texts.

Mr Hillegas begins by saying what has already been said by Anthony West, Bernard Bergonzi and others, namely, that although H. G. Wells is commonly regarded as the creator of optimistic utopias, his own early scientific romances were charged with a deeply pessimistic imagination and were anti-utopian in spirit. From this Mr Hillegas goes on to argue that the anti-utopian tradition that developed later in the century, partly in conscious reaction to the later Wells, was deeply influenced by the early Wells—that Wells left his mark, one way or the other, on every subsequent imaginative exploration of the future.

This is an interesting paradox of literary history which has a certain important element of truth. Huxley's *Brave New World* (1932), for instance, which began as a conscious parody of Wells's *Men Like Gods* (1923), has certain features which can be plausibly traced back to Wells's *The First Men in the Moon* (1901), where creatures are artificially bred and conditioned to perform specific functions. George Orwell witheringly dismissed Wells's utopias as 'the paradise of little fat men', but his *1984* has many features in common with Wells's *When the Sleeper Wakes* (1899) and 'A Story of the Days to Come' (1900), which Orwell had read and admired. For example, in the latter story the love between the hero and heroine is threatened by the tyranny of a soulless super-state; the couple escape from the huge megapolis of the twenty-second century into the deserted country-side where, like Orwell's Winston and Julia, they are wakened by the

★ *The Future as Nightmare: H. G. Wells and the Anti-Utopians*, Mark R. Hillegas, Oxford, 1967.

delightful novelty of a thrush's song. The same basic pattern—the opposition between two lovers and a repressive State—is to be found in Zamyatin's *We* (1925), which certainly influenced Orwell. But Zamyatin had also read and admired the early Wells (indeed, wrote a book about him). It is difficult to distinguish between the details transmitted directly by Wells to Orwell and those transmitted *via* Zamyatin; but either way, Wells remains seminal.

Mr Hillegas has collected a great deal of evidence of this kind, sometimes from other critics, and it adds up to an impressive testimony to Wells's influence and importance. Without wishing to diminish the latter, however, one may still question Mr Hillegas's apparent determination to trace *everything* in the modern utopian or anti-utopian tradition back to Wells. He underestimates on the one hand the extent to which Wells was himself influenced by an existing tradition, and, on the other, the extent to which actual historical events conditioned subsequent developments of the utopian imagination.

Mr Hillegas does do justice to one major influence on Wells, but it is a non-fictional one—that of his teacher T. H. Huxley. From Huxley, Wells derived that pessimistic reading of the theory of evolution which permeates his work from *The Time Machine* onwards. In his celebrated Romanes Lecture 'Evolution and Ethics' (1893) Huxley maintained that 'cosmic nature is . . . the enemy of ethical nature' and that 'retrogressive change is just as possible and practicable as progressive'. If, as science suggests, the earth is slowly cooling,

> then the time will come when evolution will mean an
> adaptation to a universal winter, and all forms of life will die
> out, except such low and simple organisms as the Diatom of the
> arctic and antarctic ice and the Protococcus of red snow.

This plainly foreshadows the closing section of *The Time Machine*. Mr Hillegas tells us that 'occasionally Huxley became so pessimistic about the evolutionary process that he would have almost welcomed "some kindly comet" to sweep the whole affair away'. It would be tempting to see this as the source of Wells's story 'The Star' if it had not been established by Ingvald Raknem that this story was virtually plagiarized from the French writer Camille Flammarion. Flammarion is not mentioned by Mr Hillegas. Neither is George Griffiths's story of the twenty-first century, *Olga Romanoff*, summarized thus by Professor Armytage:

In this the Aërians, thanks to their aeroplanes and vril, are able to renounce their control of the world, now connected by monorails and possessing a cheap power from atomised carbon and petroleum. Communication has been established with Mars. Indeed everything looks peaceful until a descendant of the last Czar (from whom the book takes its name) kidnaps the son of the President of Aëria, obtains the secret of the Aërian strength and builds an invasion fleet at Mount Terror near the South Pole. She is well on her way to overthrowing world government when the earth is burnt to a cinder by a comet. Everyone is killed except the Aërians who have taken refuge under a granite mountain, from which they emerge to repopulate the world.

There is an abundance of 'Wellsian' motifs and properties even in this bare summary, yet *Olga Romanoff* (1894) appeared a year before the publication of Wells's first scientific romance. Many other fore-runners could be found. These ideas were 'in the air' at the time, as Bernard Bergonzi has shown so well in *The Early H. G. Wells*. Mr Hillegas justly claims that when Wells borrowed from other writers, he transformed his borrowings; but he seems reluctant to accord the same freedom to the writers who subsequently borrowed from Wells —they are presented as inevitably confined to playing on a pitch marked out by him.

This brings me to the second objection to Mr Hillegas's thesis, that he minimizes the extent to which post-Wellsian utopists have assimilated into their fictions experience which was either not available to him or which he failed to cope with imaginatively. When all the debts of Orwell to the early Wells have been totted up, the fact remains that *1984* derives most of its power and authenticity from Orwell's imaginative exploitation of facts, emotions, and iconography specifically associated with Stalinist Russia, Nazi Germany and World-War-II-devastated Europe. 'Even Newspeak, I think, at least suggests Wells,' says Mr Hillegas, anxious to claim every crumb for Wells, and blithely ignoring Orwell's life-long critique of political jargon. He generously concedes that 'the post-catastrophe story is not solely Wellsian in its origins' but pleads, 'surely it is the pictures of world-collapse given by Wells that have most influenced the develop-ment of this kind of story in the twentieth century?' The influence of Hiroshima is mentioned in a casual aside.

The chief disappointment of *The Future as Nightmare*, however, is that it does not examine the obvious question that is raised by its *datum.* Wells wrote anti-utopias before he wrote utopias, and the question is: why did he change, *in this direction?* Mr Hillegas evidently does not find this surprising or puzzling (at least he never comments on it) but surely it is. The reverse shift is not so uncommon. Anti-utopias like *We, Brave New World,* and *1984* have been described as products of the 'disillusioned left'.[1] Wells, however, seems to have started off disillusioned and later embraced optimistic 'illusions' (though they were not socialist ones). The scientific progress and evolutionary process, whose end results are so gloomily predicted in the early stories, are held forth as the bases for desirable brave new worlds in *A New Utopia* and *Men Like Gods.*

The explanation for this shift is probably best sought in biographical and psychological investigation. But the literary critic can try to trace the literary symptoms of this change; and this Mr Hillegas has signally failed to do. He observes, for instance, the co-existence of two 'messages' in *The First Men in the Moon*—firstly, that the Selenites' 'scientific' civilization is inhumane, and secondly, that it is superior to ours—but does not see that they are incompatible. Cavor, the scientist-explorer in that story, is shocked when he comes upon young Selenites 'confined in jars from which only the fore-limbs protruded, who were being compressed to become machine-minders of a special sort', yet wonders if it is not 'really in the end a more humane proceeding than our earthly method of leaving children to grow into human beings, and then making machines of them'. Wells is trying to have it both ways here, but the horrific image of the bottled Selenites inevitably undercuts the (in itself) perfectly valid criticism of actual socio-economic injustice. Clearly even slavery is more 'humane' than the Selenite system; and the way is thus open to anti-utopians like Aldous Huxley to defend man's right to be miserable but human. *The First Men in the Moon* seems to mark the point at which Wells's 'progressive' ideas began to pull damagingly against his pessimistic intuitions, thus bringing to a close his remarkable first period of work. Henceforward, he gave his progressive critique of contemporary society more consistency by offering utopian models that were much more humane than the Selenite civilization, but unfortunately much less imaginatively stirring.

This next stage in Wells's career is well represented by *A Modern Utopia* (1905), now reissued by the University of Nebraska Press with an introduction by Mr Hillegas that for the most part duplicates the relevant sections of his book. The confidence in 'science' is now almost unqualified: 'Science stands, a too competent servant behind her wrangling, underbred masters, holding out resources, devices and remedies they are too stupid to use.' Wells supposes a planet that is a replica of ours, but in which the resources of Science have been rationally applied. The result is a World Welfare State of decorum and efficiency, governed by a dedicated managerial élite called (with an odd touch of swashbuckling atavism) Samurai. Wells was subsequently to expend much time and energy on propaganda for this concept of a world élite, proving, if proof were needed, that he had no fondness for socialism in the classical sense, or even for democracy.

Time has been cruel to *A Modern Utopia*. It would be difficult to arouse any enthusiasm for this vision of the good life today. Most of the things against which the current wave of youthful protest is directed in the Western world are to be found hopefully foreshadowed in Wells's Utopia: an examination-selected meritocracy, a mixed economy, paternalistic state welfare, bureaucratic control over personal freedom, privilege based on productivity but controlled by fiscal means, minority participation in government, academic monopoly over culture, and a generally low-keyed, rather conformist contentment regarded as the desirable norm in behaviour. Wells's Utopia is a class society in which the classes are distinguished not by breeding or by cash, but by intelligence and vocational aptitude, with a decent middle-class standard of living available to all. In a sense it was a generous attempt on Wells's part to imagine a social structure which would make available to everyone the kind of success and happiness he had personally achieved in the teeth of great disadvantages. Or, more cynically, you could call it the paradise of little fat men.

A Modern Utopia is, however, more engaging than it sounds in summary. Wells disarms many criticisms by anticipating them—even Orwell's jibe. The narrator is a thinly-disguised self-portrait, 'a whitish plump man, a little under the middle-size and age.... His front is convex. He droops at times like most of us, but for the most part he bears himself as valiantly as a sparrow.' This persona and his rather philistine companion, a botanist, are transported to Utopia, by a kind of illusionist's trick, in the middle of a mountain ramble in Switzerland. But the persona is not merely the usual heuristic narrator who describes his adventures, but also the authorial voice, emphasizing the purely speculative nature of the discourse, treating Utopia as a game, and justifying the rules according to which he is playing it. There is thus no attempt to create an illusion of reality, or even to obtain a willing suspension of disbelief—merely an invitation to participate in a 'constructive debate about tomorrow', and, by implication, about today. It is all very skilfully managed, and reminds one of what a fluent and poised writer Wells was in his prime. There are many characteristic flashes of the shrewdness that for the most part preserved him from cant, e.g.: 'no men are quite wise enough, good enough and cheap enough to staff jails as jails should be staffed.'

The nineteenth-century obsession with eugenics leaves its mark on Wells in his insistence on compulsory birth-control, and if necessary, sterilization, for non-productive members of the community ('the almost criminally poor') thus gradually and humanely legislating them out of existence. But there is a long chapter on Race which is remarkably enlightened for its time, and still relevant in ours—indeed Wells correctly prophesies that

> race prejudices . . . are shaping policies and modifying laws, and they will certainly be responsible for a large proportion of the wars, hardships and cruelties the immediate future holds in store for our earth.

Mr Hillegas curiously omits any reference to this chapter, which is in many ways the most impressive of all. Professor Armytage devotes only four lines of comment to the entire book.

After these strictures on *Yesterday's Tomorrows* and *The Future as Nightmare*, it seems only sporting to try and suggest what would be an adequate critical approach to the kind of writing we call 'utopian' or 'science fiction' (the two categories are not synonymous, but there is a good deal of overlap)—writing which takes such a wide variety of forms, from the almost purely discursive to the almost purely fantastic, and which is written with such a bewildering variety of motives. Admittedly it is a formidable problem, and requires a pluralistic solution.

The first requisite, of course, is that these works be approached as literature, with the methods and skills of literary criticism. All utopias are fictions not only in the wide sense propounded by Vaihinger and lately developed by Frank Kermode in *The Sense of an Ending* (1967), according to which all mental constructs are 'fictions', but in the older, more ordinary sense of the word which has made 'fiction' synonymous with imaginative literature: i.e. all utopias, by definition, deal not with the actual, but with the possible. They differ from conventional literary fictions by enlarging the concept of the possible to include what is, in common-sense terms, impossible, usually by positing some radical change in the conditions of life. But this only makes the break with actuality the more distinct. However discursive a utopia may be, however minimal, or even non-existent, its narrative content may be, however closely it resembles a description of actuality, it plainly cannot be such a description; it must be a fiction.

In theory, events could convert a utopian fiction into fact, by fulfilling every prediction made in it; but this would convert the utopia into a document of divine or occult revelation. (In the same way discredited prophecy can be converted into utopian fiction, as many people now regard the Bible.) In practice, even fortune-tellers do not live entirely by the accuracy of their predictions, and it would be a naïve and low-minded reader who judged a utopia by such criteria. Orwell's reputation does not hang on the state of the world in 1984. Utopias, like other literary fictions, are not to be verified or falsified by a straightforward appeal to history. This does not mean that they can always ignore history, any more than novels can. It depends on the literary conventions chosen by the utopist, the level on which he invites our assent.

The critic of this kind of work therefore must first of all know how to read, must be sensitive to language, alive to the varieties of narrative tone and method, analytically responsive to what Wayne Booth calls the 'rhetoric of fiction', and possessed of some theory of narrative genres and their historical development. Such a theory has been admirably expounded recently by Robert Scholes and Robert Kellogg in their *The Nature of Narrative* (1966). They suggest that the realistic novel which has dominated narrative literature for the last two hundred and fifty years was a new synthesis of four narrative modes—history, realistic imitation, romance, and allegory—which were originally held together in the oral epic, but split off and developed separately in the late classical and medieval periods; and that the new synthesis is now showing signs of disintegration. Clearly, the utopian tradition (in its widest sense) provided an outlet for narrative writers with a bent towards allegory and romance (e.g. Mary Shelley, Edgar Allan Poe, Hawthorne, Lytton, Lewis Carroll) during the long reign of the realistic novel, and is being heavily drawn on by *avant-garde* novelists now leading a break-away from realism (e.g. William Burroughs's *Nova Express*, John Barth's *Giles Goat-boy*, and Lawrence Durrell's *Tunc*). But the realistic novel had a profound effect on the utopian tradition, and many of the most important modern utopists have worked within its conventions. 'For the writer of fantastic stories to help the reader to play the game properly', said Wells, 'he must help him in every unobtrusive way to domesticate the impossible hypothesis.' It was the tradition of the realistic novel, which began by domesticating the improbable, that provided Wells with the necessary technical devices.

The influence goes deeper. For the orthodox realist novelist the creation of a plausible 'world', densely specified and historically consistent, is usually the frame within which he explores imaginary characters and actions that are the main focus of interest. It only needs a small adjustment to make the frame imaginary and the main focus of interest, and the characters and actions of importance mainly as filling out and authenticating the frame. This is what happens in most modern utopian and science fiction. The conventions of the realistic novel can thus invest the imaginary frame with an astonishing pseudo-historical verisimilitude, so that Orwell's London of 1984, for instance, seems just as 'real' as Dickens's London or Zola's Paris. We experience it from within. The future is enacted before us in the continuous present of the narrative past tense.

There would seem to be plenty of scope in the utopian tradition for critical enquiry into basic myths and archetypes, as practised, for instance, by Northrop Frye. It seems likely that the dominant myth or archetype behind modern utopian and anti-utopian literature is that of Paradise and the Fall.* Without discounting the importance of classical philosophers and the pagan oracles, it can be legitimately argued that long-range speculation about the future is particularly congenial to the Judeo-Christian world-view which sees history as linear, with a beginning, middle and end, rather than as cyclical. The Bible, as I have suggested, can be read as utopian fiction; and the Apocalyptic tradition, which Frank Kermode takes as a model for all fictions, is clearly a major theme in utopian literature, particularly of the 'science fiction' variety, so often concerned with the end or near-end of the world. Ends, however, imply beginnings, and it is no coincidence that writers of futurist fiction also often write stories about early man—either like Wells, to dramatize the story of evolution, or, like Golding, to identify the 'aboriginal calamity', 'the point from which we went astray'.†

* Since writing this, I have read George Kateb's excellent study *Utopia and its Enemies* (Free Press, New York, 1963), which makes this connection very forcefully. Kateb defines modern utopianism as 'the desire to renew creation, restore the faded glory, cancel the Adamic curse, make the earth heaven. . . .'

† The first phrase is John Henry Newman's; the second, Graham Greene's, quoting Newman in *Journey without Maps*. Greene has written a moving post-catastrophe story, *A Discovery in the Woods* (1963). Also of interest in this

Original Sin is a central issue in the utopian tradition, as Mary McCarthy recognized when she took the title and epigraph for her wise and witty satirical novel about a utopian experiment from this remark of Rousseau: 'it must be confessed that, both in this world and the next, the wicked are always a source of considerable embarrassment.'[2] Optimistic utopists are almost bound to be Pelagians. St Thomas More, I believe, was regarded as not entirely free from this heresy. Teilhard de Chardin was deeply suspect in orthodox eyes. In the more liberal theological climate now obtaining in the Church of Rome, the American Jesuit, Walter Ong, is able happily to weld together evolutionary theory, redemption history, and the technological prophecies of his fellow-Catholic Marshall McLuhan into a highly optimistic Christian utopianism.[3] But Chesterton's often-quoted objection to Utopias is more representative of the orthodox Christian position:

> The weakness of all Utopias is this, that they take the greatest
> difficulty of man (i.e. original sin) and assume it to be overcome, and
> then give an elaborate account of the overcoming of the smaller
> ones. They first assume that no man will want more than his share,
> and then are very ingenious in explaining whether his share will
> be delivered by motor car or balloon.

It was therefore entirely logical of Wells to insist in *A Modern Utopia* that 'the leading principle of the Utopian religion is the repudiation of the doctrine of original sin'.

The archetypes, however, are apt to enter by the back door. At the beginning of *The War of the Worlds*, we are told that, unknown to man, 'across the gulf of space, minds that are to our minds as ours are to those of the beasts that perish, intellects vast and cool and unsympathetic, regarded this earth with envious eyes'—an earth that is described as 'a morning star of hope' to the Martians on their dying planet, 'green with vegetation and grey with water, with a cloudy atmosphere eloquent of fertility'. Is this not the same earth that the envious Satan sees across the gulf of space in *Paradise Lost*, 'this pendant world, in brightness as a star', green, fertile, and vulnerable to his angelic intellect? The parallel should not surprise us. Milton's poem, as well as being the major transmitter of the Genesis myth in English, is also the first great work of science fiction, complete with War in the

---

connection is the 'Dawn of Man' prelude to Stanley Kubrick's *2001: A Space Odyssey*, a brilliant but ambivalent film with, it seems to me, unreconciled utopian and anti-utopian elements.

Air and interplanetary travel. The moral fable of *The War of the Worlds*
follows the pattern of *Paradise Lost* almost exactly. Man, foolish, vain
and over-confident, is routed by the intelligence of a ruthless and desperate extra-terrestrial power, but is saved providentially from complete destruction—in Milton by God's grace, in Wells by 'the humblest
things that God, in his wisdom, has put upon the earth' (bacteria, to
which the Martians are not immune). There is even a *felix culpa*
message at the end of *The War of the Worlds*:

> It may be that in the larger design of the universe this invasion
> from Mars is not without its ultimate benefit for man; it has robbed
> us of that serene confidence in the future which is the most fruitful
> source of decadence, the gifts to human science it has brought are
> enormous, and it has done much to promote the conception of the
> commonwealth of mankind.

The novel ends with these words:

> And strangest of all is it to hold my wife's hand again, and to think
> that I have counted her, and that she has counted me, among the
> dead.

Compare our last view of Adam and Eve (also, in a sense, reprieved
from death):

> Some natural tears they dropp'd, but wiped them soon;
> The world was all before them where to choose
> Their place of rest, and Providence their guide.
> They hand in hand with wand'ring steps and slow,
> Through Eden took their solitary way.

Milton is more wistful, but he surely furnished an archetypal gesture,
not only for Wells, but for all those *sci-fi* movies where, in the last reel,
the young man and woman who have escaped from a devastated earth
step out of their spaceship hand in hand to explore a virgin planet.
(Such optimistic post-catastrophe stories also get reinforcement from
the story of Noah and the Flood.) Beneath Milton's overt message of
regret for the Fall and trust in a Divine Redeemer, there is a strong
current of faith in human solidarity, which allows alternative interpretations of the poem and of the myth. One can either deny the tragic
irreversibility of the Fall (as optimistic utopists do), or defend the
solidarity of suffering (as most anti-utopists do). 'I don't want comfort,'
cries Aldous Huxley's John Savage to the World Controller,

'I want God, I want poetry, I want real danger, I want freedom, I want goodness, I want sin.'
'In fact', said Mustapha Mond, 'you're claiming the right to be unhappy.'

And Savage agrees. Most readers who reject the overt message of the Fourth Book of *Gulliver's Travels* claim the same right. The Utopia of the Houyhnhnms is intolerable: 'they may have all the reason, but the Yahoos have all the life'. Johnson's Prince Rasselas, cooped up in the Happy Valley, 'long[s] to see the miseries of the world, since the sight of them is necessary to happiness'. Voltaire's Candide voluntarily leaves Eldorado because it is boring; and besides, Cunegonde is not with him.

Cunegonde reminds us that Eros is invariably an anti-utopian force (though he is catered for in the specialized utopias of pornography— what Steven Marcus calls 'Pornotopia').[4] Wells is at his least happy in legislating for sexual morality in *A Modern Utopia*, and Huxley at his most effective in satirizing the bored, sterile promiscuities of *Brave New World*. In More's fairly liberal Utopia prospective marriage-partners are allowed to see each other naked before committing themselves, but fornication is punished severely 'because they realise that unless people were restrained from promiscuous relations, few would come together in conjugal love'. Reviewing a biography of William Morris recently, Lewis Mumford remarked that 'love is the one thing that still goes wrong in Morris' socialist utopia', *News From Nowhere*. The Houyhnhnms are singularly frigid, and it is a young female Yahoo (rather less repulsive than the rest of her tribe) who makes a pass at Gulliver. This takes us back once more to Genesis and Milton.

One of Milton's most daring additions to the Genesis myth was to make Adam participate in Eve's sin out of love for her, and we may see here a major source of that basic opposition between two lovers and a repressive regime which recurs so often in anti-utopian fictions. The pastoral and erotic idyll into which such lovers usually escape for a brief moment of happiness is a fairly obvious nostalgic image of a pre-lapsarian paradise; and William Empson has found it all too easy to identify Milton's God as 'Big Brother' and his Heaven as a totalitarian state.*

---

* In *Milton's God* (1965) Empson recalls a controversy about *1984* in the *Critical Quarterly*, to which he contributed. In the Spring issue of 1959, Richard Gerber wrote of Orwell's novel: 'On the surface it is doubtlessly a savage political satire in which the individual is opposed to the party collective. But there is more than this, for the individualistic, rational, liberal and humanist conception of man is

The rhetorical and mythical analysis of the utopian tradition must be supplemented by a historical analysis, by which I mean not merely a chronological ordering of the material, but some attempt to fit it into the history of ideas. As far as English is concerned, this would mean, for instance, studying the cultural debate described by Raymond Williams in *Culture and Society* (1958) and *The Long Revolution* (1961). The anti-scientific, or more precisely anti-technological attitudes characteristic of modern anti-utopias, can be traced directly to the running critique of industrialized mass society conducted by literary intellectuals in the nineteenth century. There is an obvious continuity between John Ruskin protesting that the Wye valley was being desecrated by a railway viaduct in order that a Buxton fool might find himself in Bakewell and a Bakewell fool in Buxton at the end of twelve minutes, or Arnold saying:

> Your middle class man thinks it the highest pitch of development and civilisation when his letters are carried twelve times a day from Islington to Camberwell, and from Camberwell to Islington, and if railway trains run between them every quarter of an hour; he thinks it nothing that the trains only carry him from an illiberal, dismal life at Islington to an illiberal, dismal life at Camberwell; and the letters only tell him that such is the life there. . . .

and Aldous Huxley saying in an essay in 1931:

> the more travelling there is, the more will culture and way of life tend everywhere to be standardised and therefore the less educative will travel become. There is still some point in going from Burslem to Udaipur. But when all the inhabitants of Burslem have been sufficiently often to Udaipur, and all the inhabitants of Udaipur have been sufficiently often to Burslem, there will be no point whatsoever in making the journey . . . the two towns will have become essentially indistinguishable.

---

opposed not only to party collectives, but also to the complete unconditional religious surrender to the transcendental, paradoxical nature of God. It almost seems as if Orwell . . . had filled his political satire with unconscious or half-conscious meanings of a different kind. . . . *1984* has the age-old symbolic structure, and even phraseology of resistant man's breakdown and conversion to some power which we generally call by the name of God.'

Empson agreed with the analysis, but indignantly denied that the underlying theme was either paradoxical or unconscious: Orwell *meant* to equate totalitarianism and Christianity.

Wells, in contrast, is entirely representative of the progressive utopist in rejoicing in the possibilities of fast and comfortable travel in his *Modern Utopia*, while taking its benefits more or less for granted. Studying this tradition of cultural criticism reinforces the mythical analysis sketched above, because most of the writers in it have believed either implicitly or explicitly in the idea of a Second Fall: some cultural shift or historical event—the Reformation, the Renaissance, Romanticism, the Industrial Revolution, Christianity itself—which fatally warped the development of mankind. To those who believe in the First Fall (e.g. T. E. Hulme) the Second was a blasphemous and doomed attempt to deny its effects. More commonly, the Second Fall is regarded as the more significant, or the only real one. But its consequences are deplored through the evocation of a largely mythical 'prelapsarian' past—the organic, agrarian, instinctual community, variously located in eighteenth-century England, the Middle Ages or primitive tribal life, but usually having overtones of the Biblical paradise. This perspective is not limited to pessimistic, conservative anti-utopians, because the optimistic utopist can suggest ways of exploiting developments in knowledge to restore the prelapsarian paradise. Hence William Morris's quaint fusion of Marxism and medievalism in *News from Nowhere*. Hence Claude Lévi-Strauss's confessedly 'utopian' vision of a world in which automation would free man to enjoy all the advantages of primitive life and none of its disadvantages:

> . . . the conversion of a type of civilisation which inaugurated historical development at the price of the transformation of men into machines into an ideal civilisation which would succeed in turning machines into men. Then, culture having entirely taken over the burden of manufacturing progress, society would be freed from the millennial curse which has compelled it to enslave men in order that there be progress. Henceforth, history would make itself by itself. Society, placed outside and above history would be able to exhibit once again that regular and, as it were, crystalline structure which the best-preserved of primitive societies teach us is not antagonistic to the human condition.[5]

It will be noted that this passage echoes, in its play on 'men' and 'machines' the passage quoted earlier from *The First Men in the Moon*, and offers a solution of the contradiction Wells got into. The utopianism of McLuhan has a similar appeal, carrying us forward and backward at the same time. The electronic age achieved by technological progress redeems us from the Second Fall of Gütenberg, and restores to us the oral-aural-tactile unified sensibility of primitive man by converting the world into a global village. In *Eros and Civilization* (1955) Herbert Marcuse likewise relied on technological progress to free mankind from the burden of the tragic paradox perceived by Freud: that the price of civilization is repression.

Finally (although this is far too big a subject to be more than glanced at here), the criticism of utopias must recognize that there have been two major, sustained attempts to create Utopia in modern history, and both have left their mark on literature. The first was America, and the second the Soviet Union.

In a large, quasi-metaphorical sense all significant American literature is utopian in spirit, and saturated in the myths of paradise lost or regained, either celebrating the potentialities of the American Adam, or brooding over where he went wrong. I don't know enough about Soviet literature to say whether there is any correspondence there, but it seems plausible. At any rate, modern utopias and anti-utopias tend to be modelled on, or projections of, either the United States or Soviet Russia. (*Brave New World* and *1984* are particularly pure examples.) Whether one takes an optimistic or pessimistic view of the future today, therefore, depends very much on whether one regards the American Dream and the Russian Revolution as experiments that have failed or experiments that are still in progress. In due course we may expect to see Mao's China appearing as the model for new utopias and anti-utopias.

13 Post-pill Paradise Lost: John Updike's *Couples*

Discussing some books about Utopia recently, I ventured the suggestion that 'Eros is traditionally an anti-utopian force, though he is catered for in the specialized utopias of pornography—what Steven Marcus has called "Pornotopia".'* I used the word 'traditionally' because we have seen in modern times the emergence of a school of thought that may properly be termed 'utopian', in that it is concerned to construct ideal models of the good life, but which inverts the values we normally associate with Utopia, recommending not the enhanced exercise of rationality but the liberation of instinct, not the perfecting of the mind, but 'the resurrection of the body'. The latter phrase is adopted by Norman O. Brown as a concluding slogan in *Life Against Death* (1959), a representative text of the new utopianism. It is not, of course, wholly new, and may be readily traced back to earlier sources— to Nietzsche, to Lawrence and, pre-eminently to Freud, on whom *Life Against Death* is a commentary.

Brown begins with the paradox propounded by Freud, that civilization or 'culture' (which is prized by traditional utopists, and which they wish to perfect) is based on the repression and sublimation of erotic energy. Freud himself was shifty about the proportionate loss and gain of this process, but Brown is quite certain and uncompromising: civilization is self-evidently neurotic, and the only solution is to end the tyranny of the reality-principle, to substitute 'conscious play' for alienated labour as the mainspring of society, and to restore to adult sexuality, narrowly fixated on genital and procreative functions, the 'polymorphous perverse' of infantile eroticism. This utopian adaptation of Freud both feeds and is fed by the sexual revolution in contemporary society, and the third interacting contribution comes from the arts. Thus, in this perspective, pornography is the product of a sexually repressed society and would disappear in the erotic utopia by a process of assimilation. Not surprisingly, therefore, we are witnessing today a determined effort by the arts to render pornography redundant by incorporating its characteristic materials into 'legitimate' art.

John Updike's *Couples* seems to me likely to be best understood and

* 'Utopia and Criticism', p. 233 above.

appreciated against this kind of background. It is concerned with the efforts of a number of couples in contemporary New England to create a clandestine, erotic utopia; and it is, notoriously, a serious novel which exploits extensively the matter and diction traditionally reserved for pornography. As this latter feature would suggest, the utopian enterprise is treated with a good deal of sympathy; and the novel is notable for its lyrical celebration of the sensual life, including the 'perverse' forms of love-making. But whereas Brown, at the outset of his book, asks the reader to make a 'willing suspension of common sense', Updike is, as a novelist, basically committed to realism (however much heightened by mythopoeic allusion) from which common sense— and the reality principle—cannot be excluded. Thus in *Couples* the note of celebration is checked by irony, the utopian enterprise fails on a communal level, and the struggle of life against death is ambiguously resolved.

Erotic utopianism is, of course, at odds with conventional Christian morality and with the Christian counsels of perfection through asceticism; yet at the same time it claims to be basically religious in its values, and to have in common with 'true' Christianity a virtuous indifference to worldly and materialistic standards of achievement and success. It thus draws on the Christian tradition of a pre-lapsarian paradise, which in turn has literary associations with the ideal world of pastoral. This matrix of ideas is kept constantly before us in *Couples*, sometimes lightly—as when the hero's first mistress stills his fears about conception with the gay greeting, 'Welcome to the post-pill paradise'— and sometimes gravely, as in the epigraph from Tillich:

> There is a tendency in the average citizen, even if he has a high
> standing in his profession, to consider the decisions relating to the
> life of the society to which he belongs as a matter of fate on which
> he has no influence—like the Roman subjects all over the world in
> the period of the Roman empire, a mood favourable for the
> resurgence of religion but unfavourable for the preservation of a
> living democracy.

The couples of Tarbox, a 'pastoral milltown', a 'bucolic paradise' as it is variously called, within commuting distance of Boston, re-enact or parody the situation of the early Christians. 'We're a subversive cell . . .' their 'high-priest' and 'gamesmaster', Freddy Thorne, the dentist, tells them. 'Like in the catacombs. Only they were trying to break out of hedonism. We're trying to break back into it. It's not easy.' It's not easy partly because the Christian religion still retains a vestigial hold over them. Of the Applebys and the Smiths, who first develop the protocol of wife-swapping, and earn the corporate title of the 'Applesmiths', Janet Appleby develops an 'inconvenient sense of evil' which the other three try patiently but unsuccessfully to assuage. The main characters, and most adventurous explorers of the erotic, Piet Hanema and Foxy Whitman, are also the most regular churchgoers of the group. Piet, indeed, is burdened with an inherited Calvinist conscience, much obsessed with death and damnation. This makes him the fitting culture-hero—and as it turns out, scapegoat—of the new cult; for in him the struggle of id against ego and super-ego is most intense and dramatic.

The sex-and-religion equation—sex as religion, sex versus religion, sex replacing religion—is insisted upon even in the topography of Tarbox, with its streets called Charity and Divinity leading to the landmark of the Congregational Church with its 'pricking steeple and flashing cock'. At the end of the story this church is destroyed by lightning in a furious thunderstorm that has overtones of Old Testament visitations upon sinners; but the damage reveals that the church has long been structurally unsound—in other words, the religious spirit has already passed into the intimate circle of the couples. 'He thinks we're a circle,' Piet's wife Angela says of Freddy Thorne, 'A magic circle of heads to keep the night out . . . He thinks we've made a church of each other.' The American couples, however, though they copy the early Christians' withdrawal from the public world in which secular history is made, lack their innocence and confidence. They are apt to feel that they are rejected rather than rejecting. 'God doesn't love us any more,' Piet asserts. Their magic circle is, in this light, not the seed of a brave new world but a temporary resource 'in one of those dark ages that visit mankind between millennia, between the death and rebirth of the gods, when there is nothing to steer by but sex and stoicism and the stars'.

This ambivalence is maintained by the two alternative notes that sound throughout the narrative: romantic-lyrical celebration, and realistic irony. The honorific description of the couples' attempt to 'improvise . . . a free way of life' in which 'duty and work yielded as ideals to truth and fun. Virtue was no longer sought in temple or market place but in the home—one's own home and the home of one's friends', is balanced by the more reductive comment, 'The men had stopped having careers and the women had stopped having children. Liquor and love were left.' Adultery opens the way to erotic delight which is far from being selfish or brutalizing, for in changing partners the ageing couples achieve an enhanced awareness of their own and other's beauty:

> Harold believed that beauty was what happened between people, was in a sense the trace of what had happened, so he in truth found her, though minutely creased and puckered and sagging, more beautiful than the unused girl whose ruins she thought of herself as inhabiting. Such generosity of perception returned upon himself; as he lay with Janet, lost in praise, Harold felt as if a glowing tumour of eternal life were consuming the cells of his mortality.

But adultery also imposes its own demeaning code of intrigue and stylized deception:

> 'Are you sleeping with Janet?'
> 'Why? Are you sleeping with Frank?'
> 'Of course not.'
> 'In that case, I'm not sleeping with Janet.'

The paradoxes and tensions of the theme are most dramatically enacted by Piet Hanema (partner in a Tarbox building firm) and Foxy Whitman (wife of a frigid biochemist who is still competing in the 'real' world, and hence hostile to the world of the couples). They dare, erotically, more than any of the other couples. Their affair is both the most romantically intense and the most sensual (their oral-genital lovemaking given an extra quality of polymorphous perversity by the circumstance that Foxy is heavily pregnant by her husband); but they also suffer most, both comically and tragically. Mastered by an over-whelming desire to suck the milk-filled breasts of his mistress at a party,* Piet locks himself in the bathroom with her, and escapes discovery by his wife only by leaping from the window, straight into the arms of another, sardonically teasing couple—hurting his leg into the bargain. Later in the story a stiffer and more traditional price is paid for sexual indulgence: Foxy, untypically in the post-pill paradise, fails to take contraceptive precautions in her first post-natal encounter with Piet, and becomes pregnant by him. An abortion, with all its attendant anxiety, misery and guilt, is arranged, but fails to conceal the affair. Piet and Foxy are banished by their respective spouses, and

---

* Brown quotes from Freud as follows: 'The state of being in love results from the fulfilment of infantile conditions of love ... whatever fulfils this condition of love becomes idealized.' 'The desire to suck includes within it the desire for the mother's breast, which is therefore the first object of sexual desire; I cannot convey to you any adequate idea of the importance of this first object in determining every later object adopted.'

cold-shouldered by the other couples, whose disregard for convention does not extend thus far, and who cannot forgive them for making the clandestine cult scandalously public. They go through a bad time; but when the wrath of God that Piet has always feared finally strikes, it does so harmlessly, merely symbolically, on the empty church. After their temporary purgatory of exile and separation, Piet and Foxy are allowed to marry, and settle happily enough in another town where, 'gradually, among people like themselves, they have been accepted, as another couple'.

Updike is, of course, neither the first nor the last American writer to take as his subject an attempt (usually unsuccessful) to found a new kind of human community, one based on values that run counter to those prevailing in society at large. The place of *Couples* in this tradition is not immediately apparent only because the utopian experiment it describes is interpersonal rather than social or economic, and thus, on the outside, scarcely distinguishable from the way of life it is rejecting. Utopian communities usually signal their intentions more openly: thus, the middle-aged radicals in Mary McCarthy's *A Source of Embarrassment* set off in covered station wagons to found an agricultural co-operative, and the hippies in the movie *Alice's Restaurant* set up their commune in a deconsecrated church. The tradition can be traced right back to *The Blithedale Romance* (1852), and it is interesting to place *Couples* beside that earlier account of 'an exploded scheme for beginning the life of Paradise anew' in New England.

Like Updike's couples, Hawthorne's characters have opted out of the competitive, acquisitive rat-race. The narrator, Coverdale, explains: 'We had left the rusty iron framework of society behind us; we had broken through many hindrances that are powerful enough to keep most people on the weary treadmill of the established system. . . .' In both novels the utopian experiment founders, eventually, on the reef of sex and sexual intrigue. In *The Blithedale Romance* Coverdale is in love with Priscilla who is in love with Hollingsworth who is in love with Zenobia who is secretly and unhappily married(?) to Westervelt who has a mesmeric hold on Priscilla. Coverdale might almost be describing Tarbox when he says:

> the footing on which we all associated at Blithedale was widely
> different from that of conventional society. While inclining us to
> the soft affections of the golden age, it seemed to authorise any
> individual, of either sex, to fall in love with any other, regardless
> of what would elsewhere be judged suitable and prudent (Chap. IX).

There are differences, obviously enough. Blithedale is, officially, dedicated to work rather than play, and its play never becomes overtly erotic. Nevertheless, *The Blithedale Romance* contains some of Hawthorne's sexiest writing. Coverdale, for instance, is naughtily given to imagining Zenobia in the nude:

> Assuredly, Zenobia could not have intended it—the fault must have been entirely in my imagination. But these last words, together with something in her manner, irresistibly brought up a picture of that fine, perfectly developed figure, in Eve's earliest garment. Her free, careless, generous modes of expression often had this effect of creating images which though pure, are hardly felt to be quite decorous when born of a thought that passes between man and woman. . . . One felt an influence breathing out of her such as we might suppose to come from Eve, when she was just made, and her creator brought her to Adam, saying, 'Behold! here is a woman!' Not that I would convey the idea of especial gentleness, grace, modesty and shyness, but of a certain warmth and rich characteristic, which seems, for the most part, to have been refined away out of the feminine system (Chap. III).

Coverdale thinks Zenobia should pose for sculptors, 'because the cold decorum of the marble would consist with the utmost scantiness of drapery, so that the eye might chastely be gladdened with her material perfection in its entireness'. Looking at 'the flesh-warmth over her round arms, and what was visible of her full bust' he sometimes has to close his eyes, 'as if it were not quite the privilege of modesty to gaze at her'. And he is sure that she is sexually experienced: 'Zenobia is a wife; Zenobia has lived and loved! There is no folded petal, no latent dew-drop, in this perfectly developed rose!' (Chap. VI).

There is no such carnal element in Coverdale's 'love' for Priscilla—who is, indeed, precisely the kind of de-sexualized Victorian maiden with whom Zenobia is contrasted in the first of these quotations. He apologizes for his suspicions about Zenobia: 'I acknowledged it as a masculine grossness—a sin of wicked interpretation, of which man is often guilty towards the other sex—thus to mistake the sweet, liberal, but womanly frankness of a noble and generous disposition.' But his suspicions prove well-founded, and Hawthorne evidently shared his narrator's mixture of guilty excitement and genteel *pudeur* when contemplating a fully sexual woman, since he is at pains to present Zenobia as a kind of witch, and sends her eventually to a sudden and sadistically relished death by drowning.

Updike, in contrast, is much more 'emancipated', much more tolerant and sympathetic towards the erotic, and lets his lawless lovers off lightly in the end. But there is something of the witch about Foxy, something sinister and depraved, Lamia-like, about the magnetism she holds for Piet, who is himself quite as much haunted by the God of Calvin as any Hawthorne hero. Indeed, the more one dwells on the comparison, the more plausible it becomes to see Hawthorne as Updike's literary ancestor among the classic American novelists. Both writers like to temper romance with realism, lyricism with irony; both tend to rely on ambivalent symbolism at crucial points in their narratives; both are highly literary, highly self-conscious stylists, fussing over every word to a degree that can be self-defeating; and both seem at their best in the short story, over-extended in the long narrative.

Updike's literary gifts, especially his remarkably precise, sensuous notation of the physical texture of ordinary experience, are well suited to the evocation of a suburban pastoral paradise with a snake in the grass. The descriptions of Tarbox, its couples and their way of life— the neglected beauty of the landscape, the comfortable elegance of the expensively remodelled homes, the casual entertaining, the ball games and parlour games, the plentiful food and drink, the intimate uninhibited conversations, as the children watch the blue flickerings of the TV bring meaningless messages of remote disasters and upheavals in the outer, public world (only the assassination of J. F. Kennedy, whose combination of personal stylishness and political weakness makes devious claims on their allegiance, disturbs the couples' calm assumption that 'news happened to other people')—all this is exquisitely rendered, so that we feel the charm, the allure of this way of life, and also its weakness, its fragility. The most eloquent passages in the novel are elegiac—for example:

> Foxy said, 'We must get back,' truly sad. She was to experience this sadness many times, this chronic sadness of late Sunday afternoon, when the couples had exhausted their game, basketball or beachgoing or tennis or touch football, and saw an evening weighing upon them, an evening without a game, an evening spent among flickering lamps and cranky children and leftover food and the nagging half-read newspaper with its weary portents and atrocities, an evening when marriages closed in upon themselves like flowers from which the sun is withdrawn, an evening giving like a smeared window on Monday and the long week when they must perform again their impersonations of working men, of stockbrokers and

dentists and engineers, of mothers and housekeepers, of adults who are not the world's guests but its hosts.

This passage illustrates very well how Updike has taken a large abstract theme about contemporary culture and embodied it in a densely-textured novel about a particular social milieu. On this level, and as long as he keeps our interest distributed fairly evenly over a considerable number of characters, *Couples* seemed to me remarkably successful. But in the latter half of the book the whole weight of the theme and structure is shifted on to the shoulders of Piet and Foxy, and they are not sufficiently realized to sustain it. Foxy is acceptable as a beautiful witch, but as an Eloise to Piet's Abelard, analysing her feelings in long, fey epistles, she becomes something of a bore. Piet is more solidly drawn, but his passiveness in the crisis of his marriage induces tedium; and Updike's incorrigible greed for stylistic effect makes nonsense of his attempt to portray his hero as a kind of primitive, a rough diamond who doesn't really belong among the college educated couples. Walking on the shore, for instance, Piet notices

> Wood flecks smoothed like creek pebbles, iron spikes mummified
> in the orange froth of oxidization, powerfully sunk horseshoe
> prints, the four-lined traces of racing dog paws, the shallow impress
> of human couples that had vanished (the female foot bare, with toe
> and a tender isthmus linking heel and forepad; the male
> mechanically shod in the waffle intaglio of sneaker soles and
> apparently dragging a stick), the wandering mollusk trails dim as
> the contours of a photograph over-developed in the pan of the
> tide [etc., etc.].

This is a poet's, not a builder's sensibility. The rather Shakespearian intrigue whereby Freddy Thorne arranges Foxy's abortion in return for a night with Piet's wife, Angela, who obliges without enquiring into the basis of the bargain, seems to violate the probabilities of the rest of the action. This is reminiscent of Hawthorne, and so is the device by which Updike displaces the catastrophe of his story from the human characters to the inanimate church—an effective set-piece, but too obviously stage-managed, a purely aesthetic climax where we have been led to expect a moral one.

For all that, *Couples* impressed me as an intelligent and skilfully composed novel on a significant theme, and most of the comment I have heard or read upon it seems to me to have done Updike less than justice.

Part VI

14 Crosscurrents in Modern English Criticism

There are many ways of categorizing and distinguishing literary critics, according to their methods and principles; theoretical and descriptive, historical and anti-historical, moral and formal, intentionalist and affective, impressionistic and analytical, Oxford and Cambridge, and so on. I shall have recourse to some of these terms in the course of this essay. But it may help to introduce some order into the extraordinarily complex and crowded scene of modern literary criticism to begin with a loosely sociological categorization—to begin by asking of any particular critic: in what context was he writing, for what audience, and to what implicit or explicit purpose?

I suggest that there are three main kinds of critic (and thus of criticism) in the period. The first is the academic, who is attached to a university or similar institution, who writes usually for an implied audience of fellow-academics and/or students, and for whom literature is in some sense a 'subject', a body of knowledge, and the study of it a 'discipline'. The second kind is the creative writer whose criticism is mainly a by-product of his creative work. He is less disinterested than the academic, more concerned to work out in the practice of criticism the aesthetic principles of his own art, and to create a climate of taste and opinion favourable to the reception of that art. He writes in the first place for fellow-artists, but as there are never very many of these he has to draw on a wider audience, either the academic one, or the 'general reader'. The latter is primarily served by the third kind of critic, for whom it is difficult to find a satisfactory name. After considering and rejecting 'professional', 'journalist', 'man of letters', I have decided to call him the 'freelance'. This kind of critic has usually had an academic training and often begins with ambitions to be a creative writer. He may achieve some minor distinction as the latter, but, whether by inclination or default, most of his energies go into the writing of criticism, characteristically in the form of magazine articles and reviews. Sometimes he becomes an editor or literary editor himself. He may borrow from the first kind of critic a sense of literature as a body of knowledge, and from the second kind a sense of the most creative possibilities in contemporary writing, both of which he is in a position to make available to a wider public. Or he may identify primarily with his audience, representing himself as their defender against the pedantries of academe and the subversions of the *avant-garde*. But his basic commitment is, perhaps, most often to the world of books as a way of life: to the pleasures of reading and to the inexhaustible fascination of the literary world—the rise and fall of reputations, the interweaving of trends and movements, the alliances and rivalries, feuds and conspiracies.

Examples of the first kind of critic are: George Saintsbury, I. A. Richards, F. R. Leavis, C. S. Lewis; of the second, Henry James, Robert Bridges, T. S. Eliot, D. H. Lawrence; of the third, Middleton Murry, Lytton Strachey, Cyril Connolly, John Lehmann. Obviously the compartments are not water-tight. It is not uncommon for one man to combine two of these roles. Both academics and creative writers use freelance media for their criticism on occasion, while creative writers and freelances are sometimes invited to address academic audiences. In the last ten years or so this fluidity has become very marked, and there are now quite a large number of critics who combine all three roles; that is, they are academics concerned with teaching and research who are also actively involved in creative writing and regular contributors to newspapers, magazines and broadcasting. In this way the academy has come to dominate criticism and to exercise an ever-increasing influence over the production of literature. Such a literary situation (which has in many ways gone further in America) is unprecedented and, in the eyes of many, sinister. It is certainly one of the most important consequences of the revolution in criticism that is the subject of this essay.

If the academic critic is the dominant type at the moment, he is also the most recent—he scarcely exists before this century. Most of the important English critics before this period were of the second type: Sydney, Dryden, Johnson, Wordsworth, Coleridge, Arnold. Arnold, to be sure, shifted in the course of his career from being a poet-critic to being a prototype academic critic, and modern academic criticism rightly reveres him as a father-figure. The third type, the freelance, emerged towards the end of the seventeenth century when social and economic changes, including the spread of literacy and the development of publishing and journalism, created an audience which required or accepted his services. In histories of criticism, which are naturally concerned with seminal ideas and authoritative *œuvres*, the freelance is inevitably neglected, for his work is bound to be ephemeral, if not derivative. In a survey as compressed as the present one this neglect can hardly be remedied, but it is as well to remember that the freelance can have a considerable day-to-day influence on the literary public, and thus on writers. That the freelances were failing in this respect was one of the most insistent refrains of academic and creative critics in the 'twenties and 'thirties. If one does not hear this complaint so often nowadays it may be because things have improved; or because academics and creative writers, having largely taken over literary journalism, have only themselves to blame for its inadequacies.

Of the many attempts to formulate the 'function of criticism' T. S. Eliot's 'the elucidation of works of art and the correction of taste' has perhaps the best chance of general acceptance, being flexible enough to admit a great many different approaches, but firm enough to give definition. As applied to English literature, criticism in this sense existed in a fairly fragmentary and casual form until the end of the nineteenth century, and occupied a relatively insignificant part of intellectual life. Since that time, the study of English literature has become a dominating element in the humanities, and the elucidation of works and the correction of taste have been carried out with unprecedented industry and rigour. The two developments which, more than any others, helped to bring about this revolution in criticism were the Modernist movement in literature and the rise of English studies in the universities.

In the first two decades of this century both English studies and Modernism were looking for a new poetic and a new sense of tradition. In the 'twenties they collaborated to find both these things, but since the collaboration was based on a partial misunderstanding, it did not survive for very long, and the academic and creative critics drew apart again. This divergence was accelerated by a complex of other factors. Modernism lost its impetus, got lost in politics, or emigrated. Academe was riven by internecine strife, which could be crudely described as a war between scholars and critics, between Oxford and Cambridge, between those who would interpret Eliot's definition broadly and those who interpreted it narrowly. Eventually the dust settled and a kind of truce was declared (the termination of *Scrutiny* in 1953 might be said to mark this point). But by this time the initiative had passed to America. That is how I see the outlines of the story, and I shall try to fill in the detail as best I can in the space available.

I begin with the rise of English studies. Looking around at the large and flourishing English departments in our universities today, and at the formidable industry of scholarship, criticism, and textbooks they maintain, it is difficult to believe that as an academic subject of any consequence English is scarcely older than the century. Oxford did not establish an Honours School of English until 1893, Cambridge until 1917. English literature was taught before this in Scotland, at the University of London and at the provincial universities founded throughout the nineteenth century. But given the almost total hegemony of Oxford and Cambridge, English could not become a respectable—or respected—subject of study until it was adopted by the ancient universities. They were not anxious to welcome it, and to this day there are colleges that discourage it. However, once the ancient universities admitted English they immediately became, by the nature of the social and educational system, its main custodians. Until very recently nearly all significant academic critics of English literature were educated at Oxford or Cambridge; and if by any chance a bright young man took his first degree at a provincial university, he was likely to be taught by graduates of Oxbridge, and to be sent there as a postgraduate. Only London managed to recruit from its own ranks on any considerable scale, and since London followed for the most part an austere version of the Oxford syllabus and approach, this had no significant effect on criticism. Only since the last war has the dominance of Oxford and Cambridge been seriously challenged, and then not by any identifiable rival School.

The main pressure from outside on Oxford and Cambridge to start an English Honours course was educational in its motives. Throughout the nineteenth century, and well into the twentieth, pupils at the best schools studied literature almost exclusively in Latin and Greek (with some excursions into the foreign vernaculars), as they had done in the eighteenth, seventeenth and sixteenth centuries. In that earlier point in time there had been the good reason that most books of information were written in Latin, but the practice survived the obsolescence of Latin as a learned tongue and acquired a new rationale as being providentially the best discipline for the youthful mind. As literacy and education developed, however, the narrowness and exclusiveness of this system became more and more apparent. Romantic and post-romantic critics of culture and society stressed the importance of literature as a reservoir of humanizing values with which to counteract the materialistic influences of the industrial revolution, the growth of science and the erosion of orthodox religion (Arnold being a representative figure here). The classics were not, as a rule, taught with this kind of emphasis, and in any case they were not available to the mass of the literate population. Hence the vernacular literature came to occupy a more and more important place on the lower levels of the educational system, as a kind of 'poor man's classics', but without any corresponding reinforcement on the higher levels. It was in the name of such reinforcement that Oxford was petitioned to initiate a School of English. But, as David Palmer has shown,[1] it was welcomed at Oxford, if it was welcomed at all, by a party who were primarily interested in early English as a specialized subject for linguistic research, increasing Oxford's stake in that expansion of historical philology which is such a striking feature of nineteenth-century European scholarship; while it was opposed by dons with a vested interest in more traditional disciplines as being a soft option (the smear still sticks) likely to encourage (particularly in its literary aspects) crammers and dilettantes. In consequence, when, after much intrigue and argument, the Honours School was finally established, it was saddled with a syllabus that had a forbiddingly large philological component and was heavily biased towards older literature. It did not nourish the educational possibilities of English nor promote the developmnet of English criticism. The result was that in its first few years the new School nearly died from lack of student enrolment and difficulties in recruiting staff. The credit for rescuing it and making it, within twenty-five years, the second most popular School in the university is generally accorded to Sir Walter Raleigh, Professor of English from 1904 to 1922, who succeeded in liberalizing the syllabus to allow students to take half their papers in literature from Shakespeare to 1830 (this terminal date has only recently been revised). The language *versus* literature controversy, however, continued to haunt English studies at Oxford and elsewhere, merging into the later war of Scholars and Critics, and its rumbles may still be heard occasionally. It had the unfortunate effect of discouraging a specifically critical interest in earlier literature; and of instilling in the 'literary' student a hostility to systematic language study which ultimately retarded the development of critical analysis.

The main argument of those who opposed the introduction of English as an Honours subject at Oxford, and fought to keep it, once admitted, in the thrall of philology, was that it was insufficiently factual to be either teachable or examinable. Since (it was assumed) no special skills were needed to read literature in the native modern vernacular, the study of such literature must inevitably degenerate into the having of opinions about it, and opinions of this kind could not, or should not, be taught as if they were facts, were not independently discoverable by immature minds, and could not in any case be satisfactorily displayed or tested within the conventions of a written examination. There is much cogency in all these arguments, and occasional cries of disillusionment are still heard from English academics as their force strikes belatedly home. It is in fact the premise on which they are based that is wrong, but it was some time before this was discovered, and documented by I. A. Richards. Their immediate effect was to throw the literary academics on to the defensive. One way of making the study of literature more factual was by stressing literary *history*, particularly the tracing of 'influences' and of the connections between an author's work and his life. In the absence of a critically informed sense of literary tradition, however, such literary history was easily trivialized. A more reliable defence manoeuvre was to take a leaf from the classicist's book (most of the early English dons had a classical education) and go in for editing. There were hundreds of English classics that no one had bothered to edit properly, and the new science of bibliography arose conveniently to give the English academic an impeccably 'objective' occupation and an excuse for postponing criticism.

Sometimes the best form of defence was thought to be attack—a display of bravado in enthusiastic celebration of the uplifting delights of literature, in elaborate flights of rhetorical fancy that lifted opinions beyond the range of rational enquiry, in disarming confessions of amateurism, manly acknowledgments that there were more important things in life than literature. In this way a kind of orthodoxy—an improvised poetic and literary tradition of diluted Romanticism—developed, which has been amusingly parodied by Cyril Connolly, recalling his schooldays at Eton just before the First World War:

> There is a natural tradition in English poetry . . . Chaucer begat
> Spenser, Spenser begat Shakespeare, Shakespeare begat Milton,
> Milton begat Keats, Coleridge, Shelley, Wordsworth, and they
> begat Tennyson who begat Longfellow, Stevenson, Kipling,
> Quiller-Couch and Sir Henry Newbolt. There were a few bad boys
> whom we do not talk about—Donne, Dryden, Pope, Blake, Byron,
> Browning, Fitzgerald who wrote *The Ruba'iyat of Omar Khayyam*
> and Oscar Wilde who was a criminal degenerate. Chaucer is
> medieval but coarse, Spenser is the poet's poet . . . a poem is good
> either because it is funny . . . or because it makes you want to cry.
> Some funny poems make you want to cry . . . that is because you are
> not a healthy little boy. You need more Character. The best poems
> have the most beautiful lines in them; these lines can be detached,
> they are purple passages and are Useful in Examinations. Gray's Elegy
> is almost all Purple Patch, and so is the *Ode to a Nightingale*, especially

Magic casements, opening on the foam
Of perilous seas, in faery lands forlorn.

When you come to a purple patch you can tell it by an alarm clock
going off, you feel a cold shiver, a lump in your throat, your eyes
fill with tears, and your hair stands on end.[2]

The actuality behind this parody may be sampled in the World's
Classics selection of *English Critical Essays* (First Series) edited by
Phyllis M. Jones. Many of the contributors had done useful work in
editing or literary history but, with the exception of W. P. Ker, their
criticism was characterized by, to quote E. M. W. Tillyard, 'gossiping,
often highly metaphorical description and unspecific praise'.[3] Here are
a few representative quotations:

Saintsbury on the Grand Style:

But the grandeur of its grandeur when it is grand!

Sir Edmund Chambers on Matthew Arnold:

I hope I speak to impenitent Victorians like myself who still find in
that bygone verse the cool refreshment which it breathed upon its
first readers, in days which seemed to Matthew Arnold feverish
enough, although they were far less feverish than ours. *Virgilium vidi
tantum.* I have a boyhood's image of an Olympian figure, moving
somewhat aloof on the outskirts of an Ambleside garden party;
and it was in the week in which I first came up as a freshman that
Arnold paid his last visit to Oxford, staying with Thomas Fowler
of genial memory, in my own college of Corpus, and took his last
walk in the happy coombes of Hinksey.

J. A. Chapman on Wordsworth and Literary Criticism:

'*Then music with her silver sound*—why "silver sound"? why
"music with her silver sound"?—What say you Simon Catling?'
(*Romeo and Juliet*)

That is 'chough's language, gabble enough'; but does not
professional criticism go about saying of poetry, why 'silver sound'?
Why 'music with her silver sound'? to the best of its ability,
when there is really no answer? There are things that a man can
know *enough*, and these are what Wordsworth will write of.

9*

This anthology, published in 1933, was a conservative selection. By this date the critical revolution was well under way, but it finds little representation here. In the defensive note of Chambers and Chapman we see the old guard's resistance to the new (their contributions are dated 1932 and 1931 respectively). 'Why "silver sound"? why "music with her silver sound"?' was indeed just the kind of question in which I. A. Richards and his disciples at Cambridge were interested (and Wordsworth too, incidentally).

At Cambridge, the introduction of an English Honours School had been even more bitterly resisted and longer postponed than at Oxford, but when it eventually came in 1917 the philological and antiquarian bias of the Oxford syllabus was avoided. The revised English Tripos of 1926 (which still obtains with some modifications) allowed the student to spend most of his time on English literature after 1350. This syllabus was a somewhat heterogeneous one, including papers on Life, Literature and Thought, Tragedy, The English Moralists, and Practical Criticism. The character of the degree as a whole, therefore, was likely to be determined by the imprint of the most influential teachers, and the most influential teacher of this period was I. A. Richards. He was largely responsible for making Cambridge the academic centre of the critical revolution that had already started in the world of contemporary letters.

I shall spend less time on Modernism than on the rise of English Studies, because the story is more familiar. It is generally agreed that the Modern movement in literature, characterized by formal experiment, logical discontinuity, anti-rationalism, subjectivism, symbolism, eclectic mythologizing, radical questioning of accepted values and passionate commitment to art as an autonomous activity, was the product of European Romanticism; that it was largely suppressed in Victorian England, but re-imported there towards the end of the nineteenth century from the continent of Europe as the English literary world became more cosmopolitan. In major artists like James, Conrad and Yeats, modernism was assimilated and domesticated to great advantage, but it was also taken up by inferior talents, and got confused with the life-styles of the Decadence and the doctrine of art-for-art's-sake. Consequently it fell into disrepute, a process that reached its climax in the traumatic scandal of Oscar Wilde's trial for homosexual offences in 1895. The result was a revulsion against aestheticism in the English literary public, a reversion to Victorian standards of moral health and direct relevance to 'life', which received reinforcement from the imperialistic patriotism of the time. Kipling and Newbolt were the most popular poets of the period, though serious lyric poetry was accorded respect if, like Bridges's, it observed the conventional post-romantic criteria of 'beauty' in poetic diction and subject matter. The Georgian poets provided an appearance of innovation without really disturbing the current orthodoxy. In the novel, Wells, Bennett and Galsworthy broke new ground in matter rather than form, while James and Conrad were neglected and Joyce could scarcely get his work published.[4]

This, very roughly, was the literary situation in England in the year immediately preceding the First World War, a situation which a number of *avant-garde* writers, notably Ezra Pound and T. S. Eliot, set about revolutionizing under Pound's banner 'Make it new'. Their first manœuvre was to establish media for their work and criticism sympathetic to it. Thus began a Golden Age of 'little magazines', which lasted well into the 'twenties: Ford Madox Hueffer's *English Review* and A. R. Orage's *The New Age* appeared in 1908; J. Middleton Murry's *Rhythm* in 1911; *The New Freewoman*, later called *The Egoist* in 1913; Wyndham Lewis's *Blast* in 1914; *The Signature* in 1915; *Form* in 1916; *Art and Letters* in 1917; a redesigned *Athenaeum* under Middleton Murry in 1919; *The Criterion* edited by Eliot in 1922; the *Adelphi*, again under Murry, in 1923; *The Calendar of Modern Letters* in 1925. These little magazines did not of course present a united front; they provided forums for different groups of writers, and often quarrelled between themselves, but between them they published the work, creative and critical, of most of the significant writers in the contemporary *avant-garde*: Eliot, Pound, Joyce, Lewis, Virginia Woolf, T. E. Hulme, D. H. Lawrence, Katherine Mansfield, Aldous Huxley, Robert Graves, the Sitwells, Herbert Read, E. M. Forster and many others. Of them all, the man who emerged as leader in the 'twenties was T. S. Eliot. He not only established himself as the most accomplished and revolutionary poet of the period; he also provided modern literature with a new poetic and a new concept of literary tradition.

Towards the end of his life, Eliot commented:

The best of my *literary* criticism—apart from a few notorious phrases which have had a truly embarrassing success in the world—consists of essays on poets and poetic dramatists who have influenced me. It is a by-product of my private poetry-workshop; or a prolongation of the thinking that went into the formation of my own verse.[5]

Eliot is, then, a typical example of the poet-critic who writes primarily
for fellow-poets. But as I suggested earlier, such critics will normally
try to enlarge their audience, by drawing in either the academics or the
general reader. The criticism of Yeats, also a quest for a new poetic
and a new tradition, never acquired the kind of currency Eliot's did,
partly because Yeats never captured an equivalent audience. Most
creative critics turn to face the general reader; but Eliot very definitely
inclined in the other direction. The subjects on which he wrote in his
early essays, characteristically Elizabethan and Jacobean dramatists
and poets, were usually too esoteric for the general reader, and assumed
a kind of interest and knowledge that was most likely to be found in
the expanding Schools of English. It was not surprising that he got a
hearing in these quarters, because, as I have suggested, there, too, the
need for a new poetic and a new tradition was keenly felt. The connection was made at Cambridge rather than Oxford because the infant
English School at the former was less entrenched in conservatism, and
in I. A. Richards it had a brilliant and influential teacher who was
sympathetic to Eliot's views. Tillyard has recalled that Eliot

> was the man really responsible for introducing into Cambridge a
> set of ideas that both shocked and satisfied. I cannot think of anyone
> else who counted in this way . . . Richards was Eliot's friend,
> helped substantially in getting his poetry and criticism recognized,
> and was no advocate of the less eminent exploiters of the poetic
> tradition against which Eliot had turned . . .[6]

By 1926, according to James Reeves, the freshman at Cambridge was
handed *Poems 1909–1925* and *The Sacred Wood* (1920) in much the
same spirit as 'the stranger who enters an Anglican Church at service
time is handed two books, *Hymns Ancient and Modern* and *The Book of
Common Prayer*'.[7] The analogy is perhaps more than superficially apt:
it has often been observed that, true to Arnold's prophecy, literature
has become the religion of the twentieth century, with criticism its
theology; and Cambridge has done much to bring this about. But I
anticipate.

T. S. Eliot's critical *œuvre* is a large and complex subject, and I shall
only try to indicate here the kind of influence he had on the general
development of criticism in the century. When one turns up the early
essays today, the alleged centrality of this influence is not immediately
apparent. They seem, especially in comparison with the modern

criticism which claims descent from him, somewhat slight, oblique, diffident, almost dilettante at times, and signally lacking in that 'analysis' which has become the hallmark of modern criticism. It seems that Eliot insinuated his revolutionary ideas under cover of a very skilful pastiche of the contemporary style of polite letters. This policy, in marked contrast to Ezra Pound's brashness, no doubt facilitated his access to 'Establishment' journals like the *Times Literary Supplement*. Pound is reputed to have said to him 'Let me throw the bricks through the front window. You go in at the back door and steal the swag.'

We must, therefore, be alert to pick up in Eliot's criticism the traces of ideas that were to be absorbed and explored and systematized by later critics. For instance, one of the main claims of modern criticism is to have established what may be called a 'cognitive' theory of literature; that is, a concept of the work of literature as an object of public knowledge, containing within itself the reasons why it is so and not otherwise, stating a meaning that is to be found in the work and not outside it, except insofar as it assumes a knowledge of the language in which it is written, and of the universe that language describes. As these qualifying clauses imply, it is a tricky concept, and one difficult to maintain in an absolute form; but it is a valuable ideal for the preservation of critical hygiene. Since the literary work is basically a linguistic utterance belonging to a communication process from author to reader, an examination of its meaning cannot eliminate an awareness of or speculations about its expressive source and must originate in a personal response. But when the critic bases his interpretation and evaluation *primarily* on either the origins of the work (e.g. the writer's life, expressed intentions, historical context, etc.) or alternatively on his own subjective responses to the work, he risks committing what two modern critics have called the intentionalist and affective fallacies.[8] Attacks on both these fallacies are to be found in two of Eliot's earliest essays.

'Tradition and the Individual Talent' (1919) attacks by implication most versions of the intentionalist fallacy. A narrow historicism is dismissed by pointing out that in literary matters tradition is not a fixed and immutable order, but 'an ideal order . . . which is modified by the introduction of the new (the really new) work of art'. The historical sense 'involves a perception, not only of the pastness of the past, but of its presence'. (Eliot is speaking of the poet, but critics were not slow to apply the dictum to criticism to justify concerning themselves with what a poem means *now*, rather than attempting to reconstruct what it meant *then*.) The romantic-expressive theory of poetry which encouraged biographical interpretations of literature is countered by a theory of the 'impersonality' of the poet:

> The progress of an artist is a continual self-sacrifice, a continual extinction of personality . . . the more perfect the artist, the more completely separate in him will be the man who suffers and the mind which creates. . . . The poet's mind is in fact a receptacle for storing up numberless feelings, phrases, images, which remain there until all the particles which can unite to form a new compound are present together . . . we must believe that 'emotion recollected in tranquillity' is an inexact formula. For it is neither emotion, nor recollection nor . . . tranquillity. It is a concentration, and a new thing resulting from the concentration of a very great number of experiences which to the practical person would not seem experiences at all; it is a concentration which does not happen consciously or of deliberation.

In 'The Function of Criticism' (1923) Eliot disposed of the affective fallacy, rather more polemically, for he clearly regarded it as the more pernicious:

> *fact* cannot corrupt taste; it can at worst gratify one taste—a taste for history, let us say, or antiquities, or biography—under the illusion that it is assisting another. The real corrupters are those who supply opinion or fancy.

Having defined the function of criticism in the words quoted earlier, Eliot declares that 'criticism, far from being a simple and orderly field of beneficent activity from which impostors can readily be ejected, is no better than a Sunday park of contending and contentious orators who have not even arrived at an articulation of their differences'. Criticism ought to be 'the common pursuit of true judgment'; it cannot be so as long as critics rely on their own subjective responses, the 'Inner Voice' (a phrase of Middleton Murry's) uncontrolled by any shared principles. 'Why have principles, when one has the Inner Voice? If I like a thing, that is all I want; and if enough of us, shouting all together, like it, that should be all that *you* (who don't like it) ought to want.'

The polemical strategy of this essay is based on an elaborate analogy in which Classicism, Catholicism, legitimate political authority and the common pursuit of true judgment are contrasted with Romanticism, Nonconformism, Whiggery and affective criticism, to the grave disadvantage of the latter set. When in 1928 Eliot made it clear that he held this analogy literally and in earnest, declaring himself 'a classicist in literature, royalist in politics and Anglo-Catholic in religion',[9] he dismayed many of his admirers in the literary and academic worlds, most of whom were, if not romantics, liberal or socialist in political sympathies and agnostic or heterodox in religious matters. But by that time he had, as well as indicating the lines along which a cognitive theory of literature might evolve, redefined the English poetic tradition; giving prominence to Elizabethan and Jacobean poetic drama, and to the Metaphysical poets, correcting bardolatry (see the essay on *Hamlet* (1919)), casting doubt upon the achievement of Milton, seriously undermining the reputation of the Romantic and post-romantic poets and justifying the character of modern poetry.

Of course this is a simplification and an overstatement. No man can carry out a critical revolution single-handed. To take one example, it would be absurd to say that Eliot 'discovered' Donne and the metaphysicals. A kind of 'underground' interest had been growing through the nineteenth century, and if anyone deserves credit for 'discovering' them it was Sir Herbert Grierson, who edited Donne in 1912, and whose anthology of *Metaphysical Lyrics and Poems of the Seventeenth Century* (1921) occasioned Eliot's famous essay 'The Metaphysical Poets'. But there seems little doubt that it was this short essay, in which the phrase 'dissociation of sensibility' was first used to define a degeneration in English poetry after the seventeenth century, that really excited the attention of poetry readers, and turned it in a significantly new direction—combined, of course, with the evidence of the lively possibilities of the metaphysical vein in Eliot's own verse. 'Dissociation of sensibility' was no doubt one of those phrases (another was 'objective correlative') whose success later embarrassed Eliot. But their success was not surprising. Criticism at this time stood in need not only of a new poetic and a new tradition, but also of a new vocabulary. This brings us back to academic criticism, to Cambridge, and to I. A. Richards.

As has been noted earlier, most of the first English dons were recruited from Classics, and the traces of this education are to be seen everywhere in their work. I. A. Richards was exceptional in having read Moral Sciences (in ordinary parlance, philosophy) at Cambridge. He brought to English studies an unusual aptitude for logical thought, and an interest in aesthetics, psychology and semantics. His first book was *The Foundation of Aesthetics* (1922) written in collaboration with C. K. Ogden and James Wood, and his second *The Meaning of Meaning* (1923) again with Ogden. His first book of specifically literary theory was *The Principles of Literary Criticism* (1924), a book of which, though its arguments have been largely discredited, and in many cases abandoned by Richards himself, it would be difficult to exaggerate the importance.

Richards begins in the spirit of Eliot's 'The Function of Criticism':

> A few conjectures, a supply of admonitions, many acute isolated observations, some brilliant guesses, much oratory and applied poetry, inexhaustible confusion, a sufficiency of dogma, no small stock of prejudices, whimsies and crotchets, a profusion of mysticism, a little genuine speculation, sundry stray inspirations, pregnant hints and random *aperçus*; of such as these . . . is extant critical theory composed.

This situation was particularly regrettable because 'the arts are our storehouses of recorded values. . . . The arts, if rightly approached, supply the best data for deciding what experiences are more valuable than others.' Criticism, to become a useful and intellectually respectable discipline must adopt the rigorous methods of scientific enquiry (though literature itself, as a mode of knowledge, is the antithesis of science). This is to be done by applying the new 'science' of psychology—psychology is invoked to provide an objective theory of value.

Experience is characterized by appetencies and aversions. Satisfying an appetency is 'good', and the more we can satisfy, the better. The main problem of life is how to satisfy one appetency without frustrating another: 'the best life is that in which as much as possible of our possible personality is engaged . . . without confusion.' Literature can educate us in this process, through its special way of using language.

> A statement may be used for the sake of the *reference*, true or false, which it causes. This is the *scientific* use of language. But it may also be used for the sake of the effects in emotion and attitude produced by the reference it occasions. This is the *emotive* use of language. . . . Poetry affords the clearest example of the subordination of reference to attitude. It is the supreme form of emotive language.

These are some of the salient points of *Principles*. It will be seen that they both contrast with and complement Eliot's views. Whereas Eliot was primarily concerned with the writing of poetry, Richards is primarily concerned with its reception. His motive is educational, as the phrase 'storehouse of recorded values' makes clear. The shadow of Matthew Arnold falls over both writers: just as we can trace Eliot back to the Arnold of the Preface to *Poems* (1853), so we can trace Richards back to the Arnold of 'The Study of Poetry' (1888), where he said:

> The future of poetry is immense, because in poetry, when it is worthy of its high destinies, our race, as time goes on, will find surer and surer stay. There is not a creed which is not shaken, not an accredited dogma which is not shown to be questionable, not a received tradition which does not threaten to dissolve. Our religion has materialised itself in the fact, in the supposed fact; it has attached its emotion to the fact, and now the fact is failing it. But for poetry the idea is everything.

This quotation stands as the epigraph to Richards's *Science and Poetry* (1926). It is worth remembering, as Tillyard does,[10] that as a philosophy student at Cambridge, Richards came under the influence of G. E. Moore, and thus of the modern anti-metaphysical, anti-idealist philosophical tradition which Moore to a large extent started. In this perspective, all non-verifiable statements, about God, the universe, the soul, etc., are what Richards calls 'pseudo-statements', and poetry is full of them.

> For centuries they have been believed; now they are gone, irrecoverably; and the knowledge which has killed them [i.e. *science*] is not of a kind on which an equally fine organization of the mind can be based. . . . The remedy . . . is to cut our pseudo-statements free from belief, and yet retain them, in their released state, as the main instruments by which we order our attitudes to one another and to the world.

It might seem that Richards, here, is risking the error that Eliot perceived in Arnold—'so conscious of what, for him, poetry was *for*, that he could not altogether see it for what it is'. But Richards also makes his point in a way which gives it a quite different emphasis: 'It is not what a poem says that matters, but what it *is*.' This seems much closer to the Symbolist doctrine of the aesthetic autonomy of the poem which Eliot inherited and developed, and which is epitomized in some often-quoted lines by Archibald McLeish:

A poem should not mean
But be.

And this is the central puzzle and paradox of Richards's criticism, that from it two quite different kinds of critical approach could be (and were) derived: (1) an essentially moral criticism which placed emphasis on the value of poems for the reader in organizing and evaluating experience for him, and (2) an essentially formal criticism which saw the nature and complexity of the organization as a value in itself.

Consider, for example, Richards's preference for a poetry of 'inclusion' rather than 'exclusion', i.e. a poetry which through its complex organization, and supremely thorough metaphor, brings into play and reconciles a wide variety of possible attitudes to experience, thus being invulnerable to 'ironic contemplation', because such irony has been anticipated and built into the structure and texture of the poem. We can see how this preference derives from the psychological theory of value, but it is possible to adopt the former without adopting the latter. This in fact is what William Empson and the American 'New Critics' did: thus terms like 'ambiguity', 'irony', 'paradox', 'tension', 'complexity', 'richness of texture' became the accepted words of approval in criticism that had little or nothing of Richards's affective theory of value in it.

Furthermore, one can see how Richards's theories fitted in with Eliot's precept and practice. Metaphysical poetry and the poetry Eliot was writing was manifestly a 'poetry of inclusion' ('When a poet's mind is perfectly equipped for its work, it is constantly amalgamating disparate experience' he wrote in 'The Metaphysical Poets'); just as the nineteenth-century poetry he disfavoured was a poetry of exclusion even at its best—'the ordered development of comparatively special and limited experience', as Richards put it. The impersonality of the poet was also common ground. Though Richards based his theories on psychology, he emphatically dissociated himself from the Freudian kind of psychoanalytical criticism that focuses attention on the personal sources of the poem: 'What concerns criticism is not the avowed or unavowed motives of the artist. . . . Whatever psychoanalysts may aver, the mental processes of the poet are not a very profitable field for investigation.' This is very much in accord with the anti-intentionalism of 'Tradition and the Individual Talent'.

Richards's theory of value was essentially affective, as we have seen, but he avoided the cruder kind of subjective impressionism castigated by Eliot in 'The Function of Criticism' by practising and preaching a kind of critical analysis which had some pretensions to objectivity— what came to be known as 'Practical Criticism'.

Richards's book of that title drew directly on his teaching experience at Cambridge in the 'twenties. Over several years he regularly distributed copies of various short unidentified poems, and invited his students to comment freely; then he would lecture on the poems and the responses they had evoked. The object of the exercise was to get students to give an honest and independent reading to poetry undistracted by prejudices and received ideas. What emerged, however, was that the majority of the students—not all students of English, but the most intelligent and articulate of their age group— when deprived of the usual props and directives, were largely incapable of either understanding or discriminating judiciously between what they read. The first half of *Practical Criticism* (1929) documents this experiment, and the second half suggests how the situation can be improved, proposing and defining a technical terminology for the analysis of poetry (e.g. the break down of Meaning into Sense, Feeling, Tone and Intention) and identifying characteristic obstacles to good reading (e.g. Irrelevant Associations and Stock Responses, Sentimentality and Inhibition).

The book had a very great influence. Practical Criticism as a way of teaching and testing students of literature, already well established at Cambridge by Richards himself, was gradually adopted by other universities, and by schools and training colleges, and it remains to this day in one form or another a staple of literary education. The terminology, style and criteria of Richards's own analysis passed into general currency. The book had a further influence on criticism which was in many ways unfortunate; it tended to encourage an anti-historicism in many ways as narrow and restrictive as the traditional 'Eng.Lit.' historicism with its apparatus of received opinions which it aimed to correct, leading to the extreme position that historical knowledge was completely irrelevant to the reading of literature. So there is some justice in George Watson's comment that no 'poetry was ever written for the purpose to which Richards applies it' in *Practical Criticism*, and that his experiment proved only that 'unhistorical reading is bad reading'.[11] However, it was Richards's disciples who abused the method rather than Richards himself. And the historical issue is perhaps not quite as simple as Watson suggests.

As regards the pedagogical aspect: experience suggests that had Richards's students been provided with dates and authors they would not have read the poems markedly better—their inadequacies would merely have been different in character. As regards the application to criticism: while it is true that we must read historically, we can never read *totally* historically: we can never totally recover the universe of discourse to which works of the past originally belonged, and the effort to do so can inhibit our sense of the 'presence of the past' and hence of the richness of meaning the poem can legitimately have for us. Hence a concentration on a poem's internal organization rather than its historical context can yield illuminating results. A case in point is William Empson, Richards's most brilliant pupil. Here is his commentary on Shakespeare's metaphor for leafless woods, 'Bare ruined choirs, where late the sweet birds sang':

> the comparison is sound because ruined monastery choirs are places in which to sing, because they involve sitting in a row, because they are made of wood, are carved into knots and so forth, because they used to be surrounded by a sheltering building crystallised out of the likeness of a forest, and coloured with stained glass and painting like flowers and leaves, because they are now abandoned by all but the grey walls coloured like the skies of winter, because the cold and Narcissistic charm suggested by choir-boys suits well with Shakespeare's feeling for the object of the Sonnets, and for various historical and sociological reasons ('for oh, the hobbyhorse is forgot' and the Puritans have cut down the Maypoles), which it would be difficult now to trace out in their proportions; . . .

It is obvious that Empson uses his historical sense to great advantage here, but does not allow it to dominate his reading. The *specifically* historical suggestion is held back until the end of the analysis, and is offered most tentatively. A more scholarly commentator might begin with this item, and regard it as the only hard fact in the analysis.

The story of the genesis of *Seven Types of Ambiguity* (1930) from which this quotation is taken, as related by I. A. Richards[12] is well-known, and a nice illustration of the fruitful interaction between the progressive creative writers and academics at this period. Empson began the work as an undergraduate under Richards's supervision, but his interest in the approach had first been excited by a little book by two young poets, Robert Graves and Laura Riding, called *A Survey of Modernist Poetry* (1927) in the course of which they analysed Shakespeare's sonnet, 'The expense of spirit in a waste of shame' revealing the very great number of 'interwoven meanings' it contained, and equating this density of meaning with value. Encouraged by Richards, Empson began exploring the possibilities of this approach, demonstrating through analysis that 'the machinations of ambiguity are among the very roots of poetry' (itself a somewhat ambiguous, or perhaps merely inelegant, formula).

Though Richards's self-deprecating account makes Graves and Riding appear Empson's main inspiration, his own influence is clear. Empson's 'ambiguity' is only a refinement of Richards's 'emotive'— an attempt to define the special character of literary language in a way which stresses the quality of 'inclusiveness'. Richards himself had observed in *Science and Poetry* that 'most words are ambiguous as regards their plain sense, especially in poetry'. The criterion of ambiguity also tended to support the revised poetic tradition of Eliot. Shakespeare and the Metaphysicals yielded choice examples of rich ambiguity, sustained in vivid metaphor and witty argument. The Romantic poets yielded ambiguities only of a vague and unsatisfactory kind. 'It is not clear what is *more deeply interfused* than what,' Empson irreverently remarked of a famous passage in *Tintern Abbey*.

Seven Types is a witty, intelligent and stimulating book, and its success was deserved. As its influence, and that of Richards, Eliot and, later, Leavis, permeated criticism more and more widely, however, a reaction set in, even among sympathizers, which asked, among other things, whether this kind of criticism was not too exclusive in its criteria, whether it did not revise the literary tradition simply by elevating poets who were amenable to its methods, and demoting those who were not. There is some truth in this objection, but two qualifications need to be made. Firstly, these critics did not trick the literary public into changing its right mind—they articulated a massive change of taste and sensibility which had all kinds of social, cultural and historical causes. Secondly, after all the just objections have been registered and concessions made, many of the basic principles and methods of these critics remain valid and useful. To cite one example; the most notorious victim of the critical revolution was Milton, but some of the most persuasive recent defences of Milton (e.g. Christopher Ricks's *Milton's Grand Style* (1964) and Stanley Fish's *Surprised by Sin* (1967)) have stressed his skilful exploitation of—of all things—ambiguity. With this mention of the Milton controversy, however, a consideration of F. R. Leavis can no longer be postponed.

Asked to name the greatest English literary critic of this century, most qualified observers would reply 'Leavis', even if some of them added '*hélas*'. It is, however, difficult, if not impossible to give an adequate account of his achievement in a survey such as this. It is not an achievement that can be reduced to a number of seminal ideas, because Leavis is not a deeply original thinker, and has, out of strong conviction, deliberately avoided the field of literary theory. For him, criticism is not discussible in the abstract, but only in the reader's engagement with an actual text. His own engagement with texts, however, cannot be adequately represented by a few quotations, because it assumes magnitude only when experienced in his total *œuvre*. There is, to be sure, a characteristic Leavisian style and tone—

> Here there appear to be possibilities; a situation is partly
> realized in an urgent and supple idiom, and there appears to be
> a reserve of meaning which might eventually make itself apparent.
> But as one reads on one discovers that the qualified success of
> this and later poems depends upon ambiguity—that when a
> point is reached at which a definite formulation of an attitude or
> an issue is made, one is confronted with a shallow common-
> place, something vaguely defined in terms of 'love', 'beauty'
> or 'good'—

or—

> It must be plain at once that such impressiveness as Johnson's
> poem has is conditioned by an absence of thought. This is poetry
> from the 'soul', that nineteenth-century region of specialized
> poetical experience where nothing has sharp definition and
> where effects of 'profundity' and 'intensity' depend upon a
> lulling of the mind. The large evocativeness begins in the third
> stanza, so that we needn't press the question whether 'clings' in
> the second . . . is the right word: we know that if we have lapsed
> properly into the kind of reading the poem claims such questions
> don't arise. . . .

—but this style and tone have proved fatally easy to imitate without maintaining the pressure of Leavis's kind of intelligence and sensibility. The first of the above quotations is in fact not from Leavis,[13] but I think that out of context it might easily be attributed to him. It is only in context that Leavis's distinction as a critic can be fully appreciated. All that can be done here is to indicate the way in which his work relates to the critical revolution already described, and the special character he gave to its continuation. And this will involve reference not only to F. R. Leavis himself, but also to his wife Q. D. Leavis, and the enormously influential journal *Scrutiny* which they helped to start in 1932, and which Leavis for the most part edited until its termination in 1953.

As we have seen, the principal leaders of the critical revolution were T. S. Eliot and I. A. Richards. According to R. C. Townsend, it was Leavis's destiny to consolidate the revolution by reconciling the ideas of its two progenitors. But Townsend acutely points to the difficulty of the undertaking:

> hoping that the study of English could enrich and discipline men's sensibility, Cambridge found in Eliot's criticism the means by which this might be accomplished; but in assimilating his criticism, they had to ignore the intentions behind it and ignore his scepticism about the teaching of literature.[14]

It is not surprising, therefore, that in the course of his career Leavis drew further and further apart from Eliot (and eventually from Richards too, though less painfully).

The initial attempt at reconciliation, however, is evident in Leavis's first book, *New Bearings in English Poetry* (1932). He describes it in his Prefatory Note as 'largely an acknowledgment, vicarious as well as personal, of indebtedness to a certain critic and poet' (i.e. Eliot) and deferential allusions to Richards are scattered through the text and footnotes. As the book's title suggests, it is essentially a defence, mainly conducted through detailed commentary, of modernist poetry, principally of Eliot, but also of Hopkins[15] and, with more qualifications, of Yeats and Pound. References to earlier poetry confirm the revised poetic tradition of Eliot:

> The mischievousness of the nineteenth-century conventions of the 'poetical' should by now be plain.

> If the poetic tradition of the nineteenth century had been less completely unlike the Metaphysical tradition, Mr. Yeats might have spent less of his powers outside poetry.

> There is no pressure in [Milton's] verse of any complex and varying current of feeling and sensation; the words have little substance or muscular quality: Milton is using only a small part of the resources of the English language.

Leavis also strikes an Arnoldian note more firmly than either Eliot or Richards in his insistence on the connection between the vitality of poetry, the degree of discriminating encouragement it gets, and the health of culture and society as a whole. Modernist poetry appeared on a literary scene 'in which there were no serious standards current, no live tradition of poetry, and no public capable of informed and serious interest'. It was inevitable, therefore, that poetry like *The Waste Land* was esoteric in its appeal:

> that the public for it is limited is one of the symptoms of the state of culture that produced the poem. Works expressing the finest consciousness of the age in which the word 'highbrow' has become current, are almost inevitably such as to appeal only to a tiny minority. It is still more serious that this minority should be more and more cut off from the world around it—should, indeed, be aware of a hostile and overwhelming environment.

This idea of representing an enlightened minority embattled by forces of cultural decadence inimical to the preservation of standards and the nourishment of creative achievement, was to become increasingly insistent in the criticism of Leavis and those associated with him.

Revaluation (1936) was designed as a complement to *New Bearings*, exploring the revised tradition that had served as a background to the earlier book, following 'The Line of Wit' through English seventeenth-century poetry as far as Pope, and concluding with a critical reappraisal of Wordsworth, Shelley and Keats. The hostile essay on 'Milton's Verse' in this volume acquired considerable notoriety. Coinciding with Eliot's 'A Note on the Verse of John Milton' of the same year, it provoked a Milton Controversy which continued well into the 'fifties, and is not entirely defunct today. Both Leavis and Eliot (who was to withdraw many of his criticisms in his British Academy Lecture of 1947) concentrated their attack on the artificiality and expressive limitations of Milton's language, contrasting it unfavourably with, for example, Shakespeare's. Later, in other hands, the focus shifted to Milton's failure to resolve the human and intellectual issues raised by his themes.[16] Those critics who rallied to the defence of Milton, such as C. S. Lewis and E. M. W. Tillyard, were for the most part, historical and scholarly in their orientation and justified Milton by an appeal to literary convention and religious tradition. Milton thus became a major battleground of the war between the Scholars and the Critics (there is of course a certain distortion in this nomenclature favourable to the latter party, who coined it). The result was a steady growth in Milton studies which was ultimately to the advantage of scholarship, criticism and Milton; but there were moments when Milton seemed only the pretext for personal and ideological conflicts.

Other battlegrounds included Shakespeare and Jane Austen. In Shakespeare studies, the mission of the new criticism was to wrest the Bard from the clutches of editors, annotators, historians of Elizabethan stage conventions, and pre-eminently from that nineteenth-century tradition, culminating impressively in A. C. Bradley's *Shakespeare's Tragedies* (1904), which discussed Shakespeare's characters as if they were characters in realistic fiction, if not real people. Empson had teased the annotators in *Seven Types*, finding delicate ambiguities where they saw only textual cruxes. A more representative figure in this field was L. C. Knights, one of the regular contributors to *Scrutiny*, and for a time a co-editor, the title of whose article 'How Many Children Had Lady Macbeth?'[17] acquired considerable currency as an example of the classically inappropriate question to ask of a work of imaginative literature. Against the Bradleyan approach, Knights and other *Scrutiny* critics recommended regarding Shakespeare's plays as dramatic poems, whose meaning was communicated through language, and especially iterative patterns of imagery. This approach had been independently and brilliantly initiated by Wilson Knight in books like *The Wheel of Fire* (1930) and *The Imperial Theme* (1931), and exploited critically the possibilities of a book of a much more 'scholarly' character, Caroline Spurgeon's *Shakespeare's Imagery and What It Tells Us* (1935). Out of this line of Shakespeare criticism was to develop later a fruitful criticism of prose fiction, playing down its narrative and mimetic qualities and concentrating attention on patterns of imagery and symbolism as keys to thematic meaning. In 1947 *Scrutiny* began a series of articles entitled 'The Novel as Dramatic Poem'.

Jane Austen had always been a favourite home of the gossiping, appreciative criticism of the 'pre-revolutionary' type, and *Scrutiny* set itself to dispel the myth of 'gentle Jane Austen', the 'instinctive and charming' (Henry James's curious misdescription) First Lady of English Letters. In a series of closely argued articles, Mrs Q. D. Leavis emphasized Jane Austen's painstaking, dedicated craftsmanship by speculating that the major novels went through several drafts before she was satisfied with them, a process that could be traced back to the early minor works.[18] Another characteristic *Scrutiny* article which achieved greater notoriety was D. W. Harding's 'Regulated Hatred:

an aspect of the art of Jane Austen'.[19] So far from being a gentle, consoling artist, comfortably endorsing the values of her own milieu, Jane Austen, Harding argued, was in many ways fiercely hostile to that milieu, and writing was her way of 'finding some mode of existence for her critical attitudes'.

Perhaps it is timely to observe here that the critical revolution I have been describing was not unresisted. Oxford was largely opposed to it, with exceptions like F. W. Bateson, whose *English Poetry and the English Language* (1934) was a useful extension of the new ideas. And it was far from being triumphant at Cambridge. 'Q'—Sir Arthur Quiller-Couch, whose critical approach was not unlike Raleigh's, was Professor of English Literature until 1944. E. M. W. Tillyard, who had been an ally of Richards in the early days, was not temperamentally at home in the critical revolution, and began to have doubts about its educational effects.[20] F. L. Lucas, Fellow of King's, made a contribution to *Cambridge University Studies* (1933), the occasion of a somewhat ungenerous attack on I. A. Richards and Mrs Leavis's *Fiction and the Reading Public*. The lines of battle were complicated, but may be studied in the pages of *Scrutiny*.[21]

As Richards and Empson left Cambridge for America and China respectively, and the critical revolution in England passed more and more into the custody of Leavis and *Scrutiny*, the alliance of the 'twenties between the academics and the literary *avant-garde* also began to break up. The *avant-garde* itself was fragmented between Bloomsbury, the increasingly conservative T. S. Eliot and his sympathizers, and the younger Marxist-orientated writers of the 'thirties (Auden, Isherwood, Stephen Spender, Day Lewis). With none of these groups could Leavis communicate. He never wavered in his regard for Eliot's early criticism, and his admiration for Eliot's verse was not diminished by its increasingly religious preoccupations. But a dogmatic Christianity was no more acceptable to him than a dogmatic Marxism, and he regarded Eliot's patronage of the Auden-Spender group in the *Criterion* as a cynical betrayal. *Scrutiny* described itself as 'liberal',[22] but it was a very different kind of liberalism from that of the Bloomsbury group, whose values, life-style and criticism (Strachey, Virginia Woolf and Forster tended to write a smarter, more sophisticated and satirical version of the old appreciative musing-in-the-library tradition) were antithetical to everything Leavis stood for.

What Leavis and *Scrutiny* stood for in the widest sense was the preservation through literature and the study of literature of certain life-enhancing values which were located in something called the 'organic community', that is, the agrarian socio-economic system that preceded the Industrial Revolution, and survived in a few isolated pockets till the end of the nineteenth century, to be totally submerged in the mechanized mass society of the twentieth century. In the organic community, so the theory ran, labour was not alienated but a fulfilling exercise of genuine craftsmanship, life and death were made meaningful by an instinctive connection with the soil and the rhythm of the seasons, and if most of its members were illiterate, they nevertheless had their own folk art and a richly expressive oral tradition which nourished the roots of higher culture. The connection made between these ideas and criticism is illustrated by Denys Thompson, writing in an early issue of *Scrutiny*:

> An understanding of this life will help to explain how
> Shakespeare's use of language differs from Milton's, in what way
> the idiom of the newspaper and best seller and advertising is
> destructive of fine language and of fine living, and why, since
> English traditional culture is dead, it is of the first importance
> that tradition should be sustained through literature.

Leavis himself does not draw the equations quite as baldly as that, but the assumptions are always there. In *Culture and Environment* (1933) he collaborated with Thompson to write a kind of textbook (intended primarily for schools) designed to inculcate the values of the organic society and to train discrimination and resistance in the face of contemporary civilization, particularly as expressed through popular literature, journalism and advertising. The authors draw freely for inspiration and documentation on Q. D. Leavis's *Fiction and the Reading Public* (1932), a pioneering but somewhat tendentious study, arguing that the homogeneous and vital literary culture of seventeenth- and eighteenth-century England was destroyed by the growth of literacy, and its commercial exploitation, culminating in a polarization of majority and minority tastes in the twentieth century, and a consequent collapse of standards. One of the (mostly leading) questions appended to *Culture and Environment* as exercises is:

> 'The best novel I've read this week is *Iron Man*.' What kind of
> standards are implied here? What would you judge to be the
> quality of the 'literature' he reads, and the reading he devotes
> to it?

Despite its naïvety and tendentiousness, most of the targets of *Culture and Environment* are well-selected (with the exception of jazz, of which the authors show a characteristically insular misunderstanding) and the book undoubtedly did more good than harm. But the underlying concept of the organic community is open to serious question. Though offered as history, it is nearer to myth. As Raymond Williams has observed, 'If there is one thing certain about the organic community, it is that it has always gone.' For Leavis and Thompson it was last seen in the late nineteenth century by George Bourne, from whose books *Change in the Village* and *The Wheelwright's Shop* they quote extensively. But Williams says he could reconstruct it from his own rural childhood in the 'thirties, while at the other end of the scale it had already passed for Goldsmith in *The Deserted Village*. It is, in fact, a variation on that nostalgia for a pastoral paradise which runs all through the history of culture, but acquires a special urgency and poignancy in post-industrial civilization (there are many versions of it in nineteenth-century literature); and while it has value as a myth, it does not, as Williams observes, encourage the constructive and beneficial transformation of our civilization.

This cultural aspect of Leavis's thought does much to explain the character of his literary criticism. It explains why, inheriting the mantle of Richards at Cambridge, he chose to display the moral and educational side of that reversible garment rather than the formalist side. His influence was most deeply felt by those whom he personally taught, on whom it was often charismatic, and he characteristically offered his criticism as the by-product of his teaching, not as the product of 'research'. He is deeply, and honourably, committed to the study of literature as a 'humane centre' in education, a self-sufficient discipline, yet one which trains discrimination in non-literary experience. His attacks on scholars and literary historians are motivated less by a belief that their approach is factually ill-founded, than by a conviction that it threatens to deprive literature of the only real life that it has—in the hands of living readers—by diverting them to the pursuit of a 'context' which is in any case best discovered from the literature itself.[23] The historical approach to literature tends inevitably towards relativity in judgment by proposing a special set of criteria for each work; and Leavis's opponents have argued that this is not only fairer to the literature than applying a single set of norms to a diversity of books, but educationally more valuable, since it encourages the student to enjoy as wide a range as possible of literary experience, and equips him with the knowledge that must precede a true judgment.[24]

But Leavis has always believed that 'some authors are better than others', and that establishing such preferences is the very life-blood of criticism.

He has, however, persistently refused to be drawn into an abstract statement and defence of his 'norms'. In a critical exchange in *Scrutiny*[25] provoked by *Revaluation*, René Wellek, a distinguished American literary theorist and critic more eclectic than either Leavis or his English adversaries, pointed out this evasion, and suggested that it weakened the force of Leavis's criticism. Leavis did not entirely disown the 'norms' which Wellek attributed to him (and they are as good a description as anyone has given), but he argued:

> Has any reader of my book been less aware of the essential
> criteria that emerge than he would have been if I had laid down
> such general propositions as: 'poetry must be in serious relation
> to actuality, it must have a firm grasp of the actual, of the
> object, it must be in relation to life, it must not be cut off
> from direct vulgar living, it should be normally human . . .'?
> If, as I did, I avoided such generalities, it was not out of timidity;
> it was because they seemed too clumsy to be of any use. I
> thought I had provided something better. My whole effort was
> to work in terms of concrete judgments and particular analyses:
> 'This—doesn't it?—bears such a relation to that; this kind of
> thing—don't you find it so?—wears better than that', etc.

Leavis has made the same point on many occasions. Judgment must be personal, but it aspires to be more than personal by drawing another reader into a dialogue in the form, 'This is so, is it not?' to which the constructive reply is 'Yes, but. . . .' It must be noted, however, that if the implied norms are not acceptable, or felt to be too narrow (this is the second part of Wellek's objection) the answer may have to be: 'No, not at all,' and the critical dialogue is abruptly terminated. The effectiveness of Leavis's critical method, therefore, depends on the analysis confirming the implied norms rather than the norms under-writing the analysis. The procedure requires a very delicate balance between criteria of formal excellence and of moral or spiritual excellence, for it is generally easier to reach agreement on the former than on the latter. It seems to me that in his later criticism Leavis often lost this balance, especially as his interest shifted from poetry to the novel, which lends itself more readily to moral criticism. Paradoxically, this shift of attention—which was reflected in the editorial policy of *Scrutiny*—was perhaps his most original contribution to the continuation of the critical revolution.

Since the novel has been the dominant literary form at all cultural levels for the last one hundred and fifty years, it seems odd, at first sight, that the critical revolution was so late in turning its attention to that form (nearly all the seminal early books were concerned with poetry or poetic drama). But on reflection several explanations suggest themselves. Eliot was a poet, and Richards's theories—both about literary value and about the special character of literary language—could be most conveniently illustrated from poetry, and short lyric poetry at that. Furthermore, if we trace their thinking back through Symbolism and Edgar Allan Poe to the English Romantics, we find a similar bias: Wordsworth, Coleridge and Shelley were poets, and the kind of claims they made for literature emphasized its transcendental qualities rather than the mimetic ones cultivated in the novel—art as a lamp rather than a mirror.

To Henry James the novel was, or ought to have been, both mirror and lamp. 'The only reason for the existence of a novel is that it does attempt to represent life'—but this representation could only be genuinely illuminating if controlled by an exacting concern for aesthetic form. Indeed, in 'The Art of Fiction' (1884) he described the formal organization of a novel with precisely that emphasis on the *organic* principle that is such a constant feature of Romantic poetics:

> A novel is a living thing, all one and continuous, like any other organism, and in proportion as it lives will it be found, I think, that in each of its parts there is something of each of the other parts.

In his criticism—in essays, reviews and the superb Prefaces to the New York edition of his novels—James defended and explored his high conception of the art of fiction with an intelligence and eloquence which make him indisputably the first major critic of prose fiction in English. But his wisdom fell largely on deaf ears. He was indeed *cher maître* to a number of younger novelists, but his quarrel with one of them, H. G. Wells, who was enjoying a much greater success both popular and literary, illustrates very vividly the resistance that the cosmopolitan 'art-novel', which James represented, met in England in the first decade of the century.[26]

One of James's main contributions to criticism of the novel was to make writers and critics more conscious of the aesthetic and moral significance of narrative method—the 'point of view' from which a story is told. His own preference was for experience reflected through the consciousness of one or more created characters, rendered in the flexible medium of third person narrative but observing the limitations of human knowledge in actuality—a method which he believed gained both in verisimilitude and aesthetic consistency over the omniscient method favoured by most of the nineteenth-century masters. Out of James's precept and practice, his friend and admirer Percy Lubbock constructed a theory of *The Craft of Fiction* (1921). 'The whole intricate question of method, in the craft of fiction, I take to be governed by the question of the point of view—the question of the relation in which the narrator stands to the story,' Lubbock wrote. He made great play with the terms 'picture' and 'drama'—the former covering all that in fiction has to be described by a narrator—for instance, scenery, physical appearance, events—and the latter covering the dialogue and confrontation of characters as they might appear on a stage. He concluded that the Jamesian method is the ideal one because it reconciles the two methods—it 'dramatises the picture by dramatising the narrator'.

The Craft of Fiction was a pioneering work which commanded considerable respect in the 'forties and 'fifties, especially in America, when the James revival was at its height, and it is always worth reading. Its deficiencies as a poetics of the novel are an excessive prejudice in favour of James's techniques, and an almost complete absence of quotation and analysis in critical discussion. In this last respect Vernon Lee's *The Handling of Words and Other Studies In Literary Psychology* (published 1923, but including work published much earlier) seems more deserving of the epithet 'pioneering'. In the course of this book Vernon Lee (her real name was Violet Paget, and she was another friend of James's) subjects a number of randomly-selected passages from novels to verbal analysis as 'close' and sensitive as anything that was to be found in novel criticism until very recently. Her interest in analysis and her general theory of literary communication seem to anticipate Richards in many ways, but his references to her are somewhat slighting, as are those of the Leavises. She seems to be one of the unacknowledged prophets of modern criticism.

It has often been remarked that E. M. Forster is the most traditional of 'modern' novelists, and something of the same ambivalence is perceptible in his critical book *Aspects of the Novel* (1927), originally delivered as the Clark Lectures at Cambridge. In his depreciation of the importance of narrative ('Oh dear, yes, the novel must tell a story') and his concept of 'rhythm' (that is, a pattern of reiterated symbols or motifs that enables an aesthetic and thematic ordering of fictional events) he showed himself to be in accord with the tendencies of modern fiction. But he is critical of James and Lubbock:

> for me the whole intricate question of method resolves itself not into formulae but into the power of the writer to bounce the reader into accepting what he says. . . . Logically *Bleak House* is all to pieces, but Dickens bounces us, so that we do not mind. . . . Critics are more apt to object than readers. . . .

The point is a fair one, and has been usefully explored since,[27] but the tone is not encouraging to critical investigation. Neither is the kind of emphasis Forster gives to the 'life' dimension of fiction—

> The intensely, stiflingly human quality of the novel is not to be avoided . . . if it is exorcised or even purified, the novel wilts, little is left but a bunch of words—

for the record shows that this kind of assertion is commonly made to deride formal experiment and formal analysis.

Exceptions to this rule occur when 'humanity' or 'life' are seen not as fixed absolutes but as changing phenomena with which form must keep pace. This was the burden of Virginia Woolf's famous modernist manifesto, 'Modern Fiction' (1919), in which she attacked Wells, Bennett and Galsworthy, seeing in the formal properties of their old-fashioned 'realism' an obsolete vision of reality. 'Is life like this? Must novels be like this?' she asked, and went on to answer her own question in terms very much in the spirit of Henry James:

> Look within and life, it seems, is very far from being 'like this' . . . the mind receives a myriad impressions—trivial, fantastic, evanescent, or engraved with the sharpness of steel. From all sides they come, an incessant shower of innumerable atoms . . . life is a luminous halo, a semi-transparent envelope surrounding us from the beginning of consciousness to the end.

This is obviously a programme for Virginia Woolf's own novels; but with certain rather prim reservations (later to become more emphatic) she also commends on these grounds the fiction of James Joyce, then appearing in the *Little Review*. When the completed *Ulysses* was finally published in 1922, Eliot saluted its elaborate use of myth (in which respect, indeed, it resembled *The Waste Land*) as a significant adjustment of form to life:

Instead of narrative method, we may now use the mythical method. It is, I seriously believe, a step towards making the modern world possible for art. . . .

Another writer belonging indisputably but awkwardly to the Modernist movement, holding utterly different views of 'life' from Virginia Woolf, and of myth from T. S. Eliot, but making considerable play with both terms, was D. H. Lawrence. Again, only a brief indication of how he fits into the general picture is possible here. In retrospect, he seems to have had almost as much influence on criticism of the novel as Eliot did in the field of poetry, though the two could scarcely have been more different in their conceptions of the critic's role. The opening paragraph of Lawrence's essay on Galsworthy is the antithesis of 'The Function of Criticism' (and its rapid acceleration from argument to polemic is entirely characteristic):

> Literary criticism can be no more than a reasoned account of
> the feeling produced upon the critic by the book he is criticising.
> Criticism can never be a science: it is, in the first place much too
> personal, and in the second, it is concerned with values which
> science ignores. The touchstone is emotion, not reason. We
> judge a work by its effect on our sincere and vital emotion, and
> nothing else. All the critical twiddle-twaddle about style and
> form, all this pseudo-scientific classifying and analysing of books
> in imitation-botanical fashion, is mere impertinence and
> usually dull jargon.

(A good way of determining any critic's principles, incidentally, is to get him to read this passage and to note when he stops nodding approval, or starts shaking his head.)

Affective critics are usually the most extreme anti-intentionalists, and so it is with Lawrence: 'Never trust the artist, trust the tale.' This slogan has been adopted by many critics who would perhaps hesitate to endorse the sentence which follows it: 'The proper function of the critic is to save the tale from the artist who created it.'[28] Lawrence is telling us to *distrust* the artist, to ignore not only the intentions expressed before or after writing the works, but also the intentions manifest in the work itself. While it has remote affinities to Platonic theories of artistic inspiration, such a critical position was scarcely possible prior to Freud, depending as it does on the assumption that our deepest and truest motives for behaviour, including artistic creation, are hidden from our own consciousness.

10

Little has been said so far about the influence of psychology on modern criticism, partly because, in England, this has been pervasive but rarely explicit or fully developed. It is rather surprising, for instance, to find Tillyard saying of his early Cambridge days, 'When it came to the type of practical criticism to which I tended, I expect I was influenced by the sort of Freudianism that was then in the air.' Yet the passage is a revealing one:

> As there is a mind below the surface mind, so, if you begin to dwell intently on the richer kind of poetry, something more than a surface meaning is likely to be revealed. And that other meaning was likely to be more important.[29]

Empson has acknowledged the influence of Freud on *Seven Types*, though he describes it as one that tended to lead him away from verbal analysis. There seems to be an interesting paradox here: Freudian psychoanalysis in one way tended to encourage 'practical criticism': one can draw an analogy between scepticism about a patient's avowed motives and anti-historicism in literary studies, between the depth-analysis of dream-symbolism and the probing of verbal ambiguities in poetry. In other words, both seem to be 'anti-intentionalist'. But taken further, the Freudian approach to literature tends towards a somewhat reductive theory of *un*conscious intention, derived from general theories about human behaviour, or from particular evidence about the writer's life and psyche. This kind of (often second-hand) Freudianism gave a new look to literary biography (e.g. Lytton Strachey), but was anathema to critics like I. A. Richards, as we have seen. As a systematic critical method it never really caught on in England. Ernest Jones's Oedipal interpretation of *Hamlet* (1910) is an exception, and that, significantly, was first published in America, where the literary mind has been more sympathetic to Freud's ideas. D. W. Harding, one of the regular contributors to *Scrutiny*, is an academic social psychologist, but his literary criticism (see for instance the essay on Jane Austen cited above) displays a thorough domestication of psychological insights to the orthodox manner of the new criticism, and in this he is, I think, representative.

The ideas of Jung have been a little more generously acknowledged, for a number of reasons. His attitude to imaginative writers was more respectful than Freud's, and the critical application of his ideas less reductive and deterministic. The notion of a collective unconscious expressing itself through archetypal themes and images tied in with the anthropological study of culture that took root in England more quickly than psychoanalysis, beginning with Sir James Frazer, and continuing with Gilbert Murray and a group of anthropologists at Cambridge led by F. M. Cornford who were well placed to influence literary criticism. The scholarly study of primitive myth and ritual also appealed deeply to the Modernist movement in literature, coming as it did at a time when Christianity, disinfected of its magical element by nineteenth-century rationalism, seemed inadequate as a source of poetic symbolism. The early work of Eliot is a case in point. The notes to *The Waste Land* acknowledge the influence of Frazer's *The Golden Bough* (1890–1915) and Jessie Weston's *From Ritual to Romance* (1920), an application of Frazer's ideas to medieval Grail legends. The title of *The Sacred Wood* is evidently taken from Frazer's introduction to his great work. In 1934 Maud Bodkin published *Archetypal Patterns in Poetry: Psychological Studies of Imagination*, in which she attempted to explain the enduring and mysterious power of certain literary works—*Hamlet*, *The Ancient Mariner*, *Kubla Khan* and the *Divine Comedy*, among others—by applying Jungian and anthropological insights to the affective responses evoked by such literature. This book has become something of a classic of modern criticism, but its initial impact was slight, according to Stanley Hyman,[30] especially in England. Perhaps the reason is that even in Miss Bodkin's sensitive hands, archetypal criticism does not lend itself to that kind of comparative evaluation of literary works which became the special interest of the critical revolution in England. Jung himself pointed out that it is not necessarily the 'best' books which exhibit the archetypes most strikingly.

A heterodox assimilation of psychological theories of all kinds is clearly visible in D. H. Lawrence, but this strain in his criticism was to have most influence in America, particularly as transmitted via *Studies in Classic American Literature* (1924). In England, his more immediate impact was in defining the moral element in literature, especially prose fiction:

> The business of art is to reveal the relation between man and
> his circumambient universe at the living moment. . . . And
> morality is that delicate, for ever trembling and changing balance
> between me and my circumambient universe, which precedes
> and accompanies a true relatedness. . . . The novel is the highest
> example of subtle inter-relatedness that man has discovered.
> Everything is true in its own time, place, circumstance, and

untrue outside of its own time, place, circumstance. . . . If a novel
reveals true and vivid relationships it is a moral work, no
matter what the relationships may consist in. . . . The novel is
the perfect medium for revealing to us the changing rainbow of
our living relationships. The novel can help us to live, as nothing
else can: no didactic Scripture, anyhow.

These quotations are taken from 'Morality and the Novel', an essay
first published in *The Calendar of Modern Letters*, a short-lived little
magazine that Leavis greatly admired, and which in a sense was the
model for *Scrutiny*. The appeal of Lawrence's ideas for Leavis is
obvious: they affirmed the moral value of literature, and hence of
literary study, without tying it down to a specific dogma or ethic—the
ideal solution for the secularized puritan conscience. Furthermore,
Lawrence's celebration, in essays and novels, of the primitive and
instinctual impulses in human nature, and his outraged criticism of
modern industrialized society, could, squinted at from a certain angle,
reinforce the idea of the 'organic community'. It is not surprising,
therefore, that in Leavis's later criticism Lawrence came to occupy
much the same position—both as a source of ideas and as a criterion of
literary achievement—that Eliot had held in his earlier criticism.

In *The Great Tradition* (published 1948, but largely a collection of
articles published in *Scrutiny* from 1937 onwards), Leavis 'revalued'
the English novel tradition even more drastically than he had the
poetic tradition. 'Jane Austen, George Eliot, Henry James, Conrad,
and D. H. Lawrence: the great tradition is there.' The influence of
Lawrence himself is evident in the criteria of election to this tradition:
'the major novelists not only change the possibilities of art for
practitioners and readers . . . they are significant in terms of that
human awareness they promote; awareness of the possibilities of life.'
In practice the latter point receives far more emphasis than the
former. The later phase of Henry James, for instance, in which he was
most obviously changing the possibilities of art, is seen as a regrettable
decline in his achievement. The novelists in the great tradition are 'all
very much concerned with "form", but their essential claim to
greatness is that they are all distinguished by a vital capacity for
experience, a kind of reverent openness before life, and a marked moral
intensity'. Leavis had travelled a long way from the declaration of
intent in the introduction to *New Bearings*: 'I have endeavoured to
confine myself as strictly as possible to literary criticism, and to
remember that poetry is made of words.' There is extensive quota-

tion in *The Great Tradition*, and intelligent commentary, but little analysis of the novelist's verbal art. In *D. H. Lawrence, Novelist* (1955) the quotations get longer, the commentary becomes more hectoring.

The Great Tradition intensified the polarization of English critics into admirers and opponents of Leavis, amounting sometimes to obsession on both sides. It was not so much the positive valuations he advanced that did this—the high estimates of Jane Austen, George Eliot, Henry James, Conrad and Lawrence met with general agreement, if not always on the same grounds—but the exclusiveness of *The Great Tradition*, the dismissal (in effect if not in intention) of the entire eighteenth-century novel, of Dickens (with the exception of *Hard Times*),[31] of Flaubert and of Joyce, not to mention 'the ruck of Gaskells and Trollopes and Merediths'. Taking a detached view, we can see that this exaggerated scale of value, with its dramatic peaks and abysses, is an integral part of Leavis's critical temper, an essential way, for him, of generating intellectual energy in himself and a quickened response in his audience. But he laid himself open, in this way, to the old objection against treating opinions as if they were facts; and the animus which he has provoked is in large part a tribute to the extent of his influence.

This, in fact, is a paradox which always confronts us in considering the work of Leavis and the critics closely associated with him. As one reads through the files of *Scrutiny*, and the various public utterances that have followed the demise of that journal, the note of isolation, of frustration and persecution grows more and more insistent, the idea of representing a disregarded minority becomes more and more personalized, the 'enemy' becomes more and more numerous and specific; the Auden-Spender 'gang', the academic establishment, the metropolitan literary 'racket', the BBC, the British Council, the *T.L.S.*, Mr Alan Pryce-Jones, Lord Snow. Yet over the same period the status and influence (the *real* status and influence, not the false kind they profess to despise) of Leavis and *Scrutiny* in the educational and literary communities has grown steadily. They have left an indelible mark on cultural life in Britain and the Commonwealth,[32] and if this was not always in exactly the way they intended, such is the usual fate of ideas and an inevitable part of growth. For example, though Leavis himself disapproves of *Lady Chatterley's Lover* and the BBC, no one can doubt that the acquittal of the former and the consolidation of the latter in the face of commercial broadcasting—two of the most significant events in recent British cultural life—owed a great deal to the work of Leavis.

In this last connection, two names immediately occur as examples of critics who are clearly indebted to Leavis, but who have significantly extended his kind of approach to literature and culture; Raymond Williams and Richard Hoggart. The finely written evocation of working-class life in the first part of Hoggart's *The Uses of Literacy* (1957) might be described as an attempt to locate and describe an 'organic community' as an observed actuality rather than as a literary or historical myth, and with a controlling awareness of the alternative dangers of sentimentality and condescension. In the second part of the book, a critical survey of 'mass art' (popular songs, magazines, cheap fiction, etc.) purveyed to the working class in conditions of post-war affluence, *Scrutiny*'s concern for 'standards' and moral objections to the commercialization of culture are obvious influences; but again Hoggart's critique is more open-minded and positive, as is implied in the second part of his general conclusion: that the working classes have tended to 'lose, culturally, much that was valuable and to gain less than their new situation should have allowed'. Since *The Uses of Literacy* Hoggart has advocated a still more tolerant and systematic application of literary-critical methods and principles to materials normally summoned to the bar of critical judgment for instant condemnation, on the assumption that the remedy for a fragmented culture is a common one, not an élitist one.

The same assumption, worked out much more explicitly and ideologically, informs the criticism of Raymond Williams. In the Foreword to *Culture and Society 1780–1950* (1958) Williams wrote: 'We live in an expanding culture, yet we spend much of our energy regretting the fact, rather than seeking to understand its nature and conditions.' The book is an attempt at such understanding through the investigation of the 'cultural debate' that literary intellectuals have generated and sustained since the end of the eighteenth century in response to the changes brought about by the Industrial Revolution, the growth of democracy and the development of the mass media. A skilful blend of cultural history, literary criticism and committed arguments, *Culture and Society* was followed by *The Long Revolution* (1961), a knottier, more fragmentary and speculative work, with more obvious political designs upon the reader.

Williams's insistence that all significant human activity, including art, is communal—'Reality in our terms is that which human beings make in common, by work or language'—is clearly Marxist in derivation; but his concern, both in judging literature, and in suggesting lines of social development for the future, is with the reconciliation of the claims of the individual and society, presenting them not as opposed absolutes, but as different aspects of the same entity. Thus in truly 'realistic' novels, 'Every aspect of the personal life is radically affected by the quality of the general life, yet the general life is seen at its most important in completely personal terms.' In this way Williams's thought incorporates the revolutionary dynamic of Marxism without appearing to endorse that brutal subordination of the individual to society that has been the least attractive feature of Marxism in political practice. He is probably the most influential British figure in the current revival of Marxism as a basis for political and literary thinking.

Like psychoanalysis, Marxism has rarely been applied in English literary criticism in any systematic way—or not, at least, to any great effect. Christopher Caudwell was the nearest thing to a Marxist critic England produced between the Wars, and he was killed in the Spanish Civil War before he had a chance to fulfil his promise, or to resolve the conflict between his basically symbolist aesthetics and his Marxist view of history.[33] A similar conflict, between Marxism and the orthodoxies of the new criticism, is discernible in the work of Arnold Kettle,[34] one of the few academic critics to have remained loyal to Marxism. The politically-conscious 'thirties threw up a great deal of Marxist-orientated criticism from creative and freelance critics, but little of it has survived. The Second World War, and disillusionment with Stalinism, quenched what spirit it had. Stephen Spender has become a chronicler and defender of the Modernism he once reacted against in the name of political engagement.[35] W. H. Auden has published in his expatriate period criticism of great wit, elegance and suggestiveness,[36] but it seems to exist in a curious vacuum of self-communing, undirected towards any identifiable audience, and thus only fortuitously contributing to the ongoing debate criticism must be. Of all this generation of English writers, George Orwell has the best record for keeping his head through the political storms of the 'thirties; and his influence—his identification with the under-privileged, his concern for the preservation of truth and decency in public life, his readiness to give serious attention to every kind of literature from Shakespeare and Dickens to Boys' Weeklies—is evident in the work of Raymond Williams and still more of Richard Hoggart.

The cultural criticism associated with Williams and Hoggart has perhaps been the only genuinely new trend to emerge in English criticism since the War capable of attracting a substantial following.[37] On the whole, the picture has been one of consolidation, the emergence of a sensible pluralism in critical method, but with undertones of disillusionment with the critical revolution and uncertainty about how to proceed. As I suggested at the outset, academe has strengthened its hold on the world of letters, and in the 'fifties initiated its own creative movement (called, very academically, 'The Movement') in which the shop-soiled remnants of modernism left over from before the War were dispatched, and the virtues of wit, common-sense, provinciality and dry-eyed moral decency cultivated. But the excitement was comparatively short-lived, and of late enquiring minds have been looking more and more towards America, whither both Modernism and modern criticism seem to have emigrated. In the late 'thirties, 'forties and 'fifties the seminal ideas of Richards, Eliot, Empson and the other critics of the 'revolution' in England, were adopted, explored and systematized, with rather more intellectual adventurousness than they were in England, under the banner of the 'New Criticism'. And the challenges that have been made to the New Criticism—Chicago neo-Aristotelianism, the varieties of myth criticism and psychoanalytical criticism, comparative literature, applied linguistics—as well as the best work along more traditional lines—literary history, history of ideas, literary biography—have appeared predominantly in America. Thus there has been a reversal of roles between English and American criticism since the last war: England, once the exporter of seminal ideas, has become, with good or ill grace, primarily an importer.

There is perhaps one respect in which English criticism continues to have the edge over American criticism: it is on the whole (we can all think of exceptions) generally better written in the sense of being more readable. The point is not a trivial one: it reveals a good deal about the development of English criticism in the twentieth century.

I have described this development in terms of a 'revolution' against a tradition of appreciative belletrism, but there is a sense in which the revolution could be described as a corrective continuation of that tradition. The continuity exists in what linguists would call the 'register' of criticism, that is, its characteristics as discourse, as determined by the assumed relationships between critic, text and reader. This, despite all the variations of personal style, has remained remarkably uniform throughout the century, and has been common to all of the three kinds of critics I began by distinguishing. It might be described as a register of persuasion or polite conversation rather than of exposition.

English criticism has traditionally been modelled on conversation. Much of it has been actually presented in the form of conversation or dialogue (Jonson's Conversations with Drummond, Dryden's *Essay of Dramatic Poesy*, Johnson in Boswell, Coleridge's Table Talk, Oscar Wilde's 'The Decay of Lying'); but the mode of the English 'essay' and the English lecture, which were the main vehicles of criticism through the eighteenth and nineteenth centuries, was also the mode of a heightened and one-sided conversation. The dangers inherent in this mode—dangers of self-indulgence, loose thinking, and irrelevant gossip —have been pointed out often enough. And the new criticism did much to correct these vices, substituting logical rigour, close attention to the text and exacting standards of relevance. But the extent to which the conversational model persisted may be seen by comparing the ways in which analysis developed in England and America respectively. For the further analysis is taken, the more difficult it becomes to maintain the register of conversation or persuasion: it becomes necessary at a certain point to use technical jargon, statistics, diagrams, numbered categories, all of which belong to the register of scientific exposition. In Richards's early work there was a tendency in this direction, but it was subsequently exploited in America. In England, Richards's approach was, if anything, tamed and domesticated to the native conversational mode. The often-remarked tortuousness of Leavis's prose style, for instance, is the result not of wilful obscurity or insensitivity, but of a tremendous effort to organize the maximum amount of data in a discourse that will not lose its personal and almost intimate character, using every device of imagery, syntactical inversion, elegant variation and parenthesis. It is an enormously difficult undertaking, and the strain of it shows in every line. Empson carried it off marvellously in *Seven Types*, but when in *The Structure of Complex Words* (1951) he attempted a more systematic and scientific kind of verbal analysis, it significantly collapsed under the eccentricity and incomprehensibility of its methodology. Eliot was never much interested in analysis, and made an Olympian version of the English conversational mode his own, with consummate skill.

This mode persists in English criticism through every possible variation of critical purpose and personal style: in, for instance, C. S. Lewis's urbane, good-humoured kind of common-sense historicism, in Raymond Williams's earnest, sometimes ponderous groping for vital connections between abstract concepts, in Richard Hoggart's characteristic blend of abstraction and racy idiom, in the epigrammatic brilliance of Frank Kermode's cosmopolitan eclecticism.

I think the quality of English criticism that I have tried to identify here is a more inclusive one than the 'amateurism' which is sometimes attributed to it, though there are no doubt connections between the two. There are certainly links to be made with the empirical tradition of English philosophy, inimical to grand theory, with the compactness of the English literary world, and with the traditional stress on undergraduate teaching in British universities. Taking all these factors together, it is not surprising that the extension of the critical revolution as a mode of *knowledge* has been carried on largely in America, where, for historical and ethnic reasons, quite different conditions obtain; or that critics in England, including Eliot himself, have expressed misgivings about that extension, and hence come to question the principles of the revolution itself.[38]

As with all such issues, the rights and wrongs of the matter are not easy to determine. Criticism differs from literature in that it can develop as well as change, and the possibilities for growth seem more promising in America than in England. On the other hand, criticism loses its *raison d'être* when it loses contact with an audience, and in its inherited grasp of this principle, English criticism has much to contribute in the increasingly cosmopolitan and collaborative enterprise of criticism.

Notes

1 The Novelist at the Crossroads

1 Quotations taken from *The Modern Tradition*, ed. Richard Ellmann and Charles Feidelson (1965), pp. 361 ff.
2 *Sunday Times*, 27 December 1953. Quoted by Rabinovitz, *op. cit.*, p. 98.
3 *Spectator*, 2 May 1958. Quoted by Rabinovitz, *op. cit.*, pp. 40–1.
4 'Reflections on Fiction', *New York Review of Books*, 13 February 1969, pp. 15–16. This article has a good deal of ground in common with the present essay, which was half-completed when the former appeared.
5 *Spectator*, 19 November 1954. Quoted by Rabinovitz, *op. cit.*, p. 40.
6 See Mario Praz's Introduction to the Penguin *Three Gothic Novels* (1968), p. 14.

3 Towards a Poetics of Fiction: An Approach through Language

1 From Edmond and Jules Goncourt, *Pages from the Goncourt Journal*, ed. and translated by Robert Baldick. Reprinted in *The Modern Tradition*, ed. Richard Ellmann and Charles Feidelson (1965), p. 126.
2 See Frank Kermode, *The Sense of an Ending* (1967), especially chapters 5 and 6.
3 Arnold Kettle, *An Introduction to the English Novel* (1951), Vol. I, chapter 1.

5 Graham Greene

1 Frank Kermode, 'Mr Greene's Eggs and Crosses', *Puzzles and Epiphanies* (1962), pp. 176–87.
2 John Atkins, *Graham Greene* (1957).
3 Philip Stratford, 'Unlocking the Potting Shed', *Kenyon Review*, XXIV (1962), pp. 129–43.
4 Richard Hoggart, 'The Force of Caricature: Aspects of the Art of Graham Greene', *Essays in Criticism*, III (1953), pp. 447–62.

6 The Uses and Abuses of Omniscience

1 Quoted by Rayner Heppenstall, *The Double Image* (London, 1947), p. 60.
2 Graham Greene, *Collected Essays* (London, 1969), pp. 116–17.
3 See Derek Stanford, *Muriel Spark* (London, 1963), p. 62.

4 This is not to say that she has entirely escaped the displeasure of liberal-humanist critics. See for instance, 'Fiery Particle: on Muriel Spark' by Richard Mayne, *Encounter*, XXV (1965), pp. 61–8, and Christopher Ricks, 'Extreme Instances', *New York Review*, 19 December 1968, pp. 31–2. 'Perhaps when man proposes, God disposes with as cool a disposition as Mrs. Spark's, though if He indeed looks upon His created world with the same eye with which she looks upon hers, then thank God I am an atheist,' says Mr Ricks.

5 *The Prime of Miss Jean Brodie*, Penguin edn (1969), pp. 80–1. Numerals in brackets subsequently are page references to this edition of the text, which runs from pp. 5–128.

6 *The Tablet*, 11 November 1961.

7 Just to complicate matters, the account of these schooldays is itself in large part an extended flashback from the point established in the opening scene, when the girls are aged sixteen.

8 Ricks, *op. cit.*—though in fact he specifically exempts *The Prime of Miss Jean Brodie* from his general criticism.

9 Frank Kermode, *The Sense of an Ending* (New York, 1967), pp. 39–40.

10 Graham Greene, *The Quiet American* (1955), p. 40.

11 Frank Kermode, *Continuities* (New York, 1969), p. 206.

7   *The Chesterbelloc and the Jews*

1 Robert Speaight, *The Life of Hilaire Belloc* (1957), p. 391.

2 *G. K. Chesterton; a selection from his non-fictional prose*. Selected by W. H. Auden (1970), p. 11.

3 *Life*, p. 184.

4 Norman Cohn, *Warrant for Genocide* (1967), p. 204.

5 *Life*, p. 457.

6 Maisie Ward, *Gilbert Keith Chesterton* (1944), pp. 227–8.

7 *Letters from Hilaire Belloc*, ed. Robert Speaight (1958), p. 122.

8 *Mr Clutterbuck's Election* (1908), Ch. X.

9 Maisie Ward, *Chesterton*, pp. 360–1.

10 *Life*, pp. 454–5.

11 Gertrude Himmelfarb, 'John Buchan; an untimely appreciation', *Encounter*, XV (1960), p. 50.

12 *Life*, p. 454.

13 James Joyce, *Ulysses*, Bodley Head edn (1954), p. 315.

10   *Hemingway's Clean, Well-lighted, Puzzling Place*

1 E.g. *The Essential Ernest Hemingway*, Penguin Books, 1969.

2 John V. Hagopian, 'Tidying Up Hemingway's "A Clean, Well-lighted Place" ', *Studies in Short Fiction*, I (1964), pp. 140–6.

3 F. P. Kroeger, 'The Dialogue in "A Clean, Well-lighted Place"';
William E. Colburn, 'Confusion in "A Clean, Well-lighted Place"',
College English, XX (1959), pp. 240–2.

4 Carlos Baker, *Hemingway: the writer as artist* (1963), p. 124.

5 Otto Reinert, 'Hemingway's Waiters Once More', *College English*, XX
(1959), pp. 417–18.

6 Edward Stone, 'Hemingway's Waiters Yet Once More', *American Speech*,
XXXVII (1962), pp. 239–40.

7 Hagopian, *op. cit.*

8 Joseph F. Gabriel, 'The Logic of Confusion in Hemingway's "A Clean,
Well-lighted Place"', *College English*, XXII (1961), pp. 539–46.

9 Philip Young, *Ernest Hemingway; A Reconsideration* (1952, revised 1966).

10 See, for example, Robert Penn Warren, 'Hemingway', *Kenyon Review*, IX
(1947), pp. 1–28; Harry Levin, 'Observations on the Style of Ernest
Hemingway' in *Contexts of Criticism* (1957); Baker, *op. cit.*; and Young,
op. cit.; Charles A. Fenton, *The Apprenticeship of Ernest Hemingway; the
early years* (1954).

11 In an otherwise rather simple-minded essay (which makes no reference to
the problem of line 69) William B. Bache comments perceptively that,
'From the older waiter to the old man lies a progression in despair, for the
three characters are actually part of an implied progression from youth
through middle age to old age.' 'Craftsmanship in "A Clean Well-lighted
Place"', *The Personalist*, XXXVII (1956), pp. 60–4.

11   *Assessing H. G. Wells*

1 Stephen Spender, *The Struggle of the Modern* (1963).

2 *Henry James and H. G. Wells: A Record of their Friendship, their Debate on the
Art of Fiction and their Quarrel* (1958).

3 For an account of Wells's reviewing at this period, see Gordon N. Ray,
'H. G. Wells Tries to be a Novelist', *Edwardians and Late Victorians*, ed.
Richard Ellmann (New York, 1960).

4 *Language of Fiction* (1966).

12   *Utopia and Criticism*

1 George Woodcock, 'Utopias in Negative', *Sewanee Review* (1956), p. 85.

2 *A Source of Embarrassment* (1950). As Professor Kateb observes: 'A spectre
has always haunted utopianism—the spectre of original sin.'

3 Walter J. Ong, *In The Human Grain: Further explorations of contemporary
culture* (1967).

4 Steven Marcus, *The Other Victorians* (1967).

5 *The Scope of Anthropology* (Cape edn, 1967).

14 *Crosscurrents in Modern English Criticism*

(Dates are of first publication in England, unless otherwise indicated)

1 David Palmer, *The Rise of English Studies* (1965). For a more lighthearted, but often acute account of the same subject, see Stephen Potter's *The Muse in Chains* (1937).
2 Cyril Connolly, *Enemies of Promise* (1938).
3 E. M. W. Tillyard, *The Muse Unchained* (1958).
4 An excellent account of this literary situation, particularly as it affected poetry, is to be found in C. K. Stead's *The New Poetic* (1964).
5 'The Frontiers of Criticism', *On Poets and Poetry* (1957).
6 Tillyard, *op. cit.*
7 Quoted by R. C. Townsend in 'The Idea of an English School: Cambridge English', *The Critical Survey* (Winter, 1967), a most lucid and informative study of the subject.
8 W. K. Wimsatt and Monroe C. Beardsley, *The Verbal Icon* (Lexington, Ky., 1954).
9 *For Lancelot Andrewes* (1928).
10 Tillyard, *op. cit.*
11 George Watson, *The English Critics* (1962).
12 In *Furioso* (Spring, 1940), quoted by Stanley Edgar Hyman, *The Armed Vision* (New York, 1948).
13 The first quotation is from R. G. Lienhardt, 'Auden's Inverted Development', and the second from F. R. Leavis, 'Thought and Emotional Quality', both in *Scrutiny*, XIII (1945).
14 R. C. Townsend, *op. cit.*
15 The poetry of Gerard Manley Hopkins, remarkably experimental for its time, was not generally known until Robert Bridges published his edition of 1918, and in the 1920s Hopkins became a modern poet by adoption.
16 See A. J. A. Waldock's *Paradise Lost and its Critics* (1947).
17 Reprinted in L. C. Knights's *Explorations* (1946).
18 Q. D. Leavis, 'A Critical Theory of Jane Austen's Writings', in four parts, *Scrutiny*, X (1941–2) and XII (1944).
19 *Scrutiny*, VIII (1940).
20 Tillyard, *op. cit.*
21 See especially the articles collected under the general headings, 'The Cambridge Tradition', 'Literary Culture', 'The Literary World' and 'Critics' in the very useful *A Selection from Scrutiny*, ed. F. R. Leavis (1968), and Dr Leavis's 'Retrospect' in Vol. XX of the 1963 reprint of *Scrutiny*.
22 F. R. Leavis, 'Retrospect of a Decade', *Scrutiny*, IX (1940).
23 The exchange between F. R. Leavis and F. W. Bateson, 'The Responsible Critic', *Scrutiny*, XIX (1953) is particularly revealing in this respect.
24 See, for example, Helen Gardner, *The Business of Criticism* (1959); C. S. Lewis, *An Experiment in Criticism* (1961); and Graham Hough, *The Dream and The Task: Literature and Morals in the Culture of Today* (1963).

25 'Literary Criticism and Philosophy', *Scrutiny*, V (1936–7) and VI (1937–8). Leavis's reply is reprinted in *The Common Pursuit* (1952).

26 See *Henry James and H. G. Wells: A Record of their Friendship, their Debate on the Art of Fiction, and their Quarrel*, ed. Leon Edel and Gordon N. Ray (1958).

27 Notably by Wayne Booth, *The Rhetoric of Fiction* (Chicago, 1961).

28 D. H. Lawrence, *Studies in Classic American Literature* (1924).

29 Tillyard, *op. cit.*

30 Hyman, *op. cit.*

31 Dr Leavis has subsequently revised this estimate, in Dickens's favour.

32 A missionary spirit was inherent in Leavis's approach to English Studies, and was carried into schools, training colleges and universities, as well as into criticism and literary journalism, by those whom he taught—either directly at Cambridge, or indirectly through his publications. It is noteworthy, however, that Leavis's influence in America has been very much smaller than that of Eliot, Richards or Empson, if one is to judge by the slight attention given to him in American surveys of modern criticism such as Hyman's *The Armed Vision* and W. K. Wimsatt's and Cleanth Brooks's *Literary Criticism: a Short History* (1957).

33 Caudwell's two critical books were *Illusion and Reality* (1937) and *Studies in a Dying Culture* (1938).

34 See Arnold Kettle, *An Introduction to the English Novel*, Vol. I (1951) and Vol. II (1953).

35 See Stephen Spender, *The Struggle of the Modern* (1963).

36 See W. H. Auden, *The Dyer's Hand* (1963).

37 It has been usefully described and contrasted with American trends in Martin Green's essay 'British Marxists and American Freudians', in *Innovations*, ed. Bernard Bergonzi (1968).

38 In 'The Frontiers of Criticism' (1956), Eliot said: 'These last thirty years have been, I think, a brilliant period in literary criticism, both in England and in America. It may come to seem, in retrospect, too brilliant.' See also Graham Hough, *The Dream and the Task*; John Holloway, 'The Critical Intimidation' in *The Charted Mirror* (1960); and George Steiner, 'To Educate Our Gentlemen' in *Literature and Silence* (1967).

Index